MILLER'S

John Bly's
ANTIQUES
MASTERCLASS

John Bly's

ANTIQUES
MASTERCLASS

Dating and Identifying your Period Pieces

For my wonderful family, present and past

John Bly's Antiques Masterclass

First published in Great Britain in 2005 by Miller's,
a division of Mitchell Beazley,
imprints of Octopus Publishing Group Ltd,
2–4 Heron Quays, London E14 4JP
Miller's is a registered trademark of Octopus Publishing Ltd

ISBN 1 84000 917 9

A CIP record for this book is available from the British Library

Set in Bliss, Minion, Palace Script, Trajan, and Trifont

Colour reproduction by Sang Choy, Singapore
Printed and bound in China by Toppan

Senior Executive Editor Anna Sanderson
Executive Art Editor Rhonda Summerbell
Senior Editor Emily Anderson
Editor Claire Musters
Design John Round Design
Illustrator Tim Brown
Production Jane Rogers
Picture Research Emma O'Neill

Front cover illustrations (clockwise from top left): Detail of scene in
a bedchamber by unknown artist, English, 18th century; Detail of *Portrait
of Captain Coram* by William Hogarth; Detail of *The Graham Children*
by William Hogarth, 1742; Detail of *Sir Bourchier Wrey in a Ship's
Cabin* by George Knapton, 1744
Back cover illustrations (left to right): Detail of *Interior with a Lady at
the Virginal* by Emanuel de Witte, c.1665–70; Detail of *Sir Henry Gough
and his Family* by William Verelst, 1741; Renaissance-inspired wares by
French maker Froment-Meurice for the Great Exhibition of 1851
Page 1: Silver and inlaid ivory jar and cover, Japanese, c.1875–1900
Page 2: *La Souper*, an engraving after Jean-Baptiste Huet
Page 3: Hard-paste porcelain plate, Bavaria, c.1915
Page 5: *Lady at her Toilet*, Dutch, c.1650–80

CONTENTS

INTRODUCTION

There is immense pleasure to be had from looking at an antique piece of furniture, porcelain, silver, or glass and deducing its age and origin by means of various clues and signs. Taking just one single view of the item denies the bigger picture; we must also consider its place in history, its relevance in society, and its affect on how we live today. It may be a piece of furniture or a racing car, a porcelain figure or a telephone – anything that at one time or another has been invented, improved, and served to either delight our eye or make life more agreeable.

It is not necessary to undergo years of concentrated study in order to enjoy this pleasure; there are just a few guidelines to follow on what to look for and where to look, and the importance of having a totally open mind. There is no justification for the air of mystique that surrounds knowledge of our heirlooms, for everything around us is an heirloom of one sort or another – it is simply that we are not taught to look at them in the right way. Take any item in a living room or on a bus, a street, or in a shop, and consider when it was made, who invented it, what it is made of, and any number of similar questions, and the answers will be an insight into social history, however ancient or recent that may be. Take the case of Shakespeare's typewriter, for example: we all laugh at such a nonsense idea because he didn't have one. But why not? Well, neither the technology nor the materials were available. Surprising really when you consider that every educated person in Shakespeare's time was multi-lingual, could read, write, draw, play a musical instrument, understand astronomy (as far as the heavens were known) and geography (as far as the earth was known), and create complex poetry with captivating story lines.

Today we all have a natural ability to comprehend those things that intrigue us, we are just not encouraged to use it. I'm sure that most people looking at the picture on page 7 will instinctively know that it is a 17th-century scene. Fewer people will know why they know: it depicts the time of the cavaliers and roundheads, and that's about it. However, there is so much more to see in this picture without having to understand the artistic merits of the painting. It shows *Dirck Wilre in the Castle of Elmina*, painted by Pieter de Wit *c.*1669. Wilre is looking at a picture of an estuary scene, sufficiently prized as to have a curtain protecting it, which is held back by his negro servant. And what about the servant, poor chap, half-naked in a cold, northern climate. The two upholstered chairs tell us that the picture must date after the 1650s, and the style of the inkpot and globe frame on the carpet-covered table support this. The man's clothes, his stance, the chained monkey, and the other little objects dotted around the room all give the impression of a wealthy person observant of the height of fashion at this period.

Not quite so many people would immediately recognize the period of the picture on page 8. Georgian might spring to mind, or early-Victorian, or perhaps Regency. The first era would suffice, but Georgian covers a long time, from 1714 to 1830. Regency is the better option because, in design terms, it narrows the field to between 1784 and 1830. However, with a little practice, and, hopefully, when you have read this book, it will be easy

to date this picture quite accurately in the same way as before: from the style of the furniture and the costumes it has to be between 1810 and 1825. This is in fact the *Empress' Bedroom with the Duchesse de Montebello and Jean-Nicolas Corvisart*, painted by Marie-Louise de Hapsburg-Lorraine in 1813.

As we have now delved into the world of interior paintings for some groundwork, I think most people would opt for Victorian when they look at the picture on page 9. But why? Is it just the less accurately detailed style of the painting? Well, that can contribute but on its own it is not conclusive. Again, it will be the objects, the clothes, and the overall style of the room that give the clues. Certainly the young woman could be considered to have a relatively historical look, with her early-Tudor hairstyle and Guinevere-type dress. From that aspect alone the picture could be either 16th-century or 19th-century-revival. There is a grandfather clock that precludes a date before 1660, and neither the hairstyle or clothes would fit that period. The fire screen must be post-1700, the brass fender is of a type not known until the early 1800s, and the big, splashy flowers in the picture behind the girl have the look of the late 19th century. But the important clues are the Japanese fans on the mantel and the Japanese sunshade in the fireplace, which date it firmly to after the 1860s. Once you have found the latest-date clue, that then sets the benchmark that the item cannot pre-date. So it can be deduced that this is a painting of a young girl

very much caught up in the Aesthetic movement of the 1880s. It is, in fact, a detail from a painting by Albert Ludovici (1820–94), which was published as a greetings card c.1880.

The aim of this book, then, is to show how easy it is to enjoy simply looking at and learning about the everyday things around us, as well as the great works of art, and recognizing how so many ordinary things have become grand, and how many grand things we now use and take for granted. Hopefully, this knowledge will give an added pleasure to every room you visit, in paintings or in reality, old and new, and will prove invaluable when buying antiques to collect.

EMERGING DESIGNS

1550–1660

In the peaceful landscape of Elizabethan England fewer people inhabited the entire country than now live in London. The houses of the newly emerging middle classes were sparsely furnished by modern standards but, even so, they had a certain sophistication. At this time, the development of society led to the evolution of everyday domestic items.

◄ 1 **The Great Chamber at Chastleton House, England.** As it was completed only 12 years into the 17th century, it is not surprising that this largely unaltered house shows important Elizabethan decorative elements, such as the complex geometric panelling and the pendanted strapwork plaster ceiling. There is more of this strapwork in the Great Hall, and the Gallery ceiling is barrel-vaulted

*A*ided by the lessening threat of warring barons, better travel facilities, and thus improved communication, artisans and professionals in even the furthest reaches of the country became less remote in their knowledge of cultural developments in the major cities. Improvements in navigation meant the import of novelties and rarities from Muscovy, the East, and the New World: coconuts and ostrich eggs, tobacco, porcelain, lacquer, silk, spices, and a printed cotton called "chint".

Historical accounts record Her Majesty Queen Elizabeth I as tall, talented, an intellectual linguist, calligrapher, accomplished dancer, and keen walker. In the highest and most polite society hers was an age of intelligent subtlety, innuendo, sophisticated foolery, and the "device". This could be a simple mannerism, a glance, a simply held posy, or an item of adornment. A fine example is the pearl, a symbol of chastity, which can clearly be seen enriching the Queen's dress in her every portrait.

The lace border around her neck, as seen in plate 2, created the effect of an aura, and was repeated in other items of clothing of the day, such as a pair of gloves (*see* Pl. 4), or architecturally, and much more dramatically, in the parapet outlines of such great Elizabethan houses as Hardwick Hall and Burghley House (*see* Pl. 3). The German-made Canning Jewel, a baroque pearl brilliantly fashioned to represent a human torso, similarly shows an exuberant outline embellishment, making it unmistakably 16th-century in appearance and illustrating the international popularity of this style. Thus there emerges a series of design shapes that define the Elizabethan period in the civilized areas of the Western world; there is most definitely an Elizabethan "look".

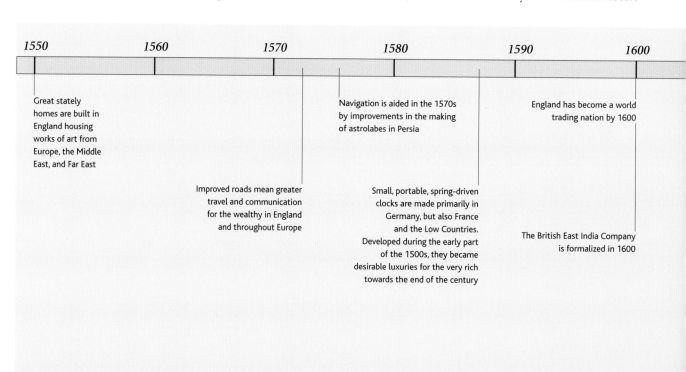

| 1550 | 1560 | 1570 | 1580 | 1590 | 1600 |

Great stately homes are built in England housing works of art from Europe, the Middle East, and Far East

Improved roads mean greater travel and communication for the wealthy in England and throughout Europe

Navigation is aided in the 1570s by improvements in the making of astrolabes in Persia

Small, portable, spring-driven clocks are made primarily in Germany, but also France and the Low Countries. Developed during the early part of the 1500s, they became desirable luxuries for the very rich towards the end of the century

England has become a world trading nation by 1600

The British East India Company is formalized in 1600

WORLD EVENTS & THE DECORATIVE ARTS 1550–1660

On domestic articles the most obvious example of a common design is the "Cup and Cover". As its name implies, it stems from the shape of the ceremonial covered cups, such as the Howard Grace Cup (Pl. 6), but it is also reflected in the legs of tables and chairs, the puffed and slashed sleeves and pantaloons of fashionable clothing, and, of course, the impressive posts of the Elizabethan bed.

Throughout Europe the bed was still among the most prestigious pieces of furniture in the house, and remained so well into the 18th century. From the earliest times births, marriages, and deaths, as well as the reception of guests and other social gatherings, were all events in which the bed played an integral part. So from the Tudor, Elizabethan, and Jacobean periods it is one of the best-documented items of furniture, and contemporary records of its construction, form, and decoration give us detailed insight into the advances in those fields (*see* p.26).

▶ **2 Portrait of Queen Elizabeth I,** *c.*1574, **by Nicholas Hilliard,** showing the mixture of severe propriety and excessive adornment that was clearly visible in Elizabethan architecture and *objets d'art,* as well as costume (*see* Pl. 4). The decorations were all emblematic, and grand houses and great artifacts were built and fashioned to follow the same patterns (*see* Pl. 3).

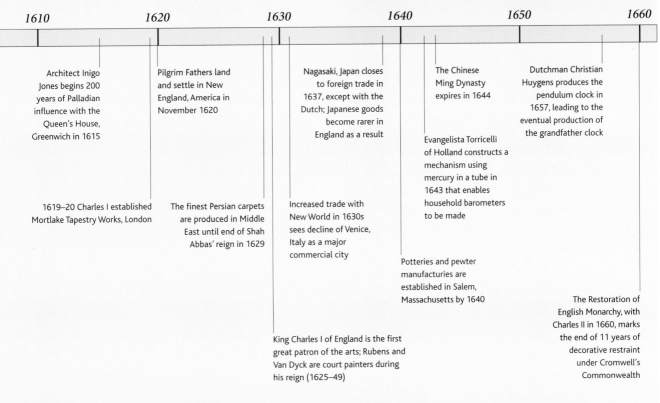

1610	1620	1630	1640	1650	1660

Architect Inigo Jones begins 200 years of Palladian influence with the Queen's House, Greenwich in 1615

Pilgrim Fathers land and settle in New England, America in November 1620

Nagasaki, Japan closes to foreign trade in 1637, except with the Dutch; Japanese goods become rarer in England as a result

The Chinese Ming Dynasty expires in 1644

Dutchman Christian Huygens produces the pendulum clock in 1657, leading to the eventual production of the grandfather clock

Evangelista Torricelli of Holland constructs a mechanism using mercury in a tube in 1643 that enables household barometers to be made

1619–20 Charles I established Mortlake Tapestry Works, London

The finest Persian carpets are produced in Middle East until end of Shah Abbas' reign in 1629

Increased trade with New World in 1630s sees decline of Venice, Italy as a major commercial city

Potteries and pewter manufactures are established in Salem, Massachusetts by 1640

The Restoration of English Monarchy, with Charles II in 1660, marks the end of 11 years of decorative restraint under Cromwell's Commonwealth

King Charles I of England is the first great patron of the arts; Rubens and Van Dyck are court painters during his reign (1625–49)

In contrast to the ordered asymmetry of costume and skyline decoration, a totally balanced geometric appliqué pattern was equally popular. On page 18 the moulded plaster ceiling at Aston Hall and the chiselled stone hallway at Burghley House show a close relationship with the Knot Garden at Moseley Old Hall, and the vertical bands of chased decoration on the silver-gilt tankard. On silverware this was a most popular motif for both sacred and secular pieces. It lasted well into the 17th century before receding from high-style fashion by the 1630s. It remained as an acceptable feature on some types of case furniture, particularly the coffer, until the 1680s (*see* p.33).

Sometimes referred to as "strapwork" (*see* p.18), the earliest idea of repeating patterns of interlaced bands appears to be based on the symbol for infinity – "oo" –

and was popularized for garden layouts in an Italian book of diagrams related to carpets, or *tapeti*, called *Hypnerotomachia Poliphili* by Francesco Collona, which was published in 1499.

Traditions and protocols

Much attention was paid to the correct manner of preparing and serving food and its ceremonial consumption, and to the arrangement of sleeping facilities. The protocol of both had been established by the aristocracy generations before. It is important to bear in mind that, despite a female monarch, this was still a male-dominated society. For example, the Earl of Derby's household staff, which in the 1580s numbered around 120, contained no more than 6 women, while the Northumberland household of 160 retained no more than 9 women. Such great establishments utilized the Feudal hierarchical system of Gentlemen, Yeomen, and Grooms, with all housework, cooking, serving, clearing, and cleaning done by them. The only work that was done by women was the laundry.

▼ **3 Burghley House, Stamford, England**, completed after 32 years in 1587 for William Cecil, Lord Burghley (1520–98). The ornate tracery of the majestic but complex skyline clearly repeats the effects created on fashionable costume and jewellery of the Elizabethan period (*see* Pls. 2, 4, and 5).

▲ **4 Pair of leather gloves, English, early 17th-century**, with silver and metal work on the gauntlets that slightly pre-empted the Elizabethan taste for borders of tracery and filigree effects, and remained in fashion for the rest of the century

▶ **5 The Canning Jewel, Italian, *c*.1570**. A pendant with a baroque pearl mounted as the torso of a merman, and enriched with enamelled gold, set with rubies, diamonds, and pearls. The whole effect is one of distinctly Elizabethan intricate outline.

Placement at mealtimes was of the utmost importance. Among the elite, the salt cellar was still considered the most significant item on the table (as it had been since Medieval times). It was placed in front of the head of the household and covered – a tradition that stemmed from when the fire, placed in the middle of the great hall, produced soot that would steadily fall like snow. The most worthy male guest was seated at the immediate right hand of the master, while members of the household sat in order of seniority to the left of his lady. This is the origin of the sayings "right hand man" and a person being "worth his salt". Knives and spoons were used at this time but forks were not in general use until after the Restoration of the Monarchy under Charles II in 1660. Mustard was used but it was always a dry powder, pepper was adored, and nutmeg was a luxury cure-all.

During the Elizabethan period in particular (but less so into the 17th century), the dining hall was emptied after the evening meal to make way for dancing and entertainment. The interval during which servants emptied the hall was known as "the void", and while they did this guests took their sticky puddings and sweet wine and walked the leads of the house (the areas of lead between the sloping roofs and the parapets) or the gallery – according to the weather.

The servants carried trays, formerly called "voyders". When the language was updated to modern French the "void" was replaced with "desert", hence our "dessert" on today's menu. When time came for bed, tradition still ruled in most families and several slept together in the same room. The great bed was high off the ground, which meant there was room enough for one or two smaller beds to be placed underneath. These small beds were called "truckle"

CUP AND COVER

One of the most distinctive shapes pertaining to any one particular period is the bold, broad "cup and its cover" from the age of Elizabeth I. It is to be seen on bedposts, table and chair legs, buffet columns, and, of course, on cups and their covers. It is also evident in the puffed sleeves of men's and women's costumes, and on the pantaloons that were fashionable for men at that time. The pantaloons' outer material was slashed through to reveal bright silk linings, and this was often replicated in stylized form in the carved decoration on furniture. Creating such a shape was costly in terms of material usage, and so not all customers could afford the extreme versions. Slimmer lines followed the general outline as best they could, and within a few years of the Queen's death in 1603 the heavy "cup and cover" had gone out of fashion, to be replaced by a modified version of the pattern, as seen on the stool pictured below.

6 The Howard Grace Cup, English, 1525–6. A turned ivory cup mounted in silver gilt and showing two distinctive features that were to become mainstays of design throughout the Elizabethan period: the overall cup-and-cover shape and the filigree borders.

7 Wassail bowl, English, 1600s, turned from *lignum vitae* (the hardest known wood, imported from America and the West Indies) using just a pole lathe. Wassail is an ancient Elizabethan celebration, usually connected with Twelfth Night or blessing the apple crops. The wassail bowl is one of the few cup-and-cover shapes to not go out of fashion.

8 Oak stool, England, 1640s, with a less pronounced cup-and-cover shape on its turned legs. The proportions during this period were often retained by creating a mock cover approximately one third of the way down the body using an incised band, as featured on this little country-made stool.

7

8

6

or "trundle" beds and were affixed with four small wooden wheels – the earliest type of castor – that enabled them to be pulled out for use. In 1662 Samuel Pepys noted that his man, Will, slept in his bedchamber "in the truckle bed"; indeed most records suggest that such beds were intended for children or servants. This practice continued well into the 18th century.

Elizabethan doctors recommended daily exercise for good health, and covered walkways, later adjoined to the house and known as galleries, facilitated walking in bad weather. Galleries open to one side were ideal for warm but wet weather in summer, while enclosed galleries were better for the winter. In a closed gallery the exterior walls had as many windows as possible and it became the practice to hang portraits on the interior walls facing them. This is presumably why today one generally finds paintings in a gallery.

Industry

The development of glassmaking in England during the 17th century meant more than just the availability of better drinking glasses. Larger mirror plates were now possible, and clearer window glass was available in greater quantity. Later the manufacture of clear glass tubing was to enable the production of weather-forecasting barometers to become an industry. But glassmaking's earliest and most significant influence was in the construction of great buildings. Suddenly windows were, by comparison to earlier decades, huge and of casement or hinge-opening type. Hardwick Hall is an extreme example, but Burghley House and Longleat also illustrate well the change made to windows during this time.

The cabinet

Aside from the bed, a prestigious and, in England, rare piece of furniture was the cabinet. The term can be used correctly to describe a small room that was set aside either for writing, for the display to close acquaintances of rare and precious objects, or for select and confidential meetings. It also describes an arrangement of small drawers and compartments in a case that is enclosed by doors hinged at the sides, or a single panel opening forward and down to create a writing surface. The former

▶ **9 Miniature Portrait of Sir Christopher Hatton by Nicolas Hilliard, English, 1588–91**, with Sir Christopher's formal dress reflecting the Elizabethan adoption of the cup-and-cover form in many aspects of life, including the sleeves and pantaloons of men's costume.

EAST INDIA COMPANY

Britain's earliest dealings with the riches of the East were not of the noblest order. It had taken the Portuguese the best part of a century to establish trade with China and Japan, eventually renting the town and port of Macao. But their patience had paid off and the profits were of such magnitude that Lisbon became one of the leading cities of Europe. It was not long before other nations saw the potential, and piracy on the high seas became as much a hazard as the weather.

To begin with, Elizabeth I granted licence to privateers to plunder Spanish and Portuguese ships and to bring the spoils back home, but, profitable as this was, in 1600 the Queen wisely granted a charter to a new joint-stock company for a monopoly in trading in India and the Far East – The East India Company. Not only was it to make vast fortunes for the shareholders, it was to change the perceptions and aspirations of educated Westerners forever. Clothing, décor, drinking, and eating habits were all affected. An awareness of new artistic forms in material, shape, and decoration, and a culture that we still do not fully understand, was the result.

STRAPWORK

The term "strapwork" occurs twice in the world of the decorative arts and has two distinctly different meanings. When used in the context of silverware it describes the method of decoration wherein an additional layer of silver was applied and fixed to the outer surface of an item. Strapwork saw two periods of popularity – the 1690s to c.1740, and the early 1800s to the 1840s. Much earlier, in the time of Elizabeth I, fine silverware had been decorated with the other type of strapwork, a geometric pattern, usually chased onto the surface, showing a strong kinship with the formality of the "pleasance" and "knot" gardens popular in the 16th and 17th centuries.

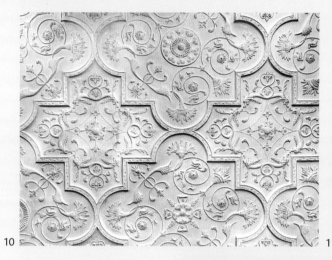

10

11

10 Long Gallery ceiling, Aston Hall, England, c.1625, illustrating that the strapwork pattern was used as decoration on ceilings in many Elizabethan and Stuart houses.

11 Burghley House staircase, England, c.1580, showing the same pattern as was used on archways and walls, proving that strapwork provides a style guide to this period.

12 Knot Garden at Moseley Old Hall, near Wolverhampton, England, based on an early-17th-century design. The gravel, pebbles, and trimmed miniature box hedges form the geometric strapwork patterns so popular from the Elizabethan to James I periods.

12

13

13 Parcel-gilt silver tankard, England, 1587, with the maker's mark, "CB". The tapering sides are decorated with vertical panels of chased geometric strapwork, a motif echoed in the architectural decoration of fashionable interiors (*see* Pl. 11), as well as Elizabethan knot gardens (*see* Pl. 12).

◀ 14 Panelled interior from
Sizergh Castle, England, late
16th century, the geometric
designs repeating those of the
knot gardens, plaster and stone
ceilings, and walls of the period.
The panels include sections of
geometric inlays in contrasting
coloured timbers – a recent
innovation that lasted well
into the 17th century.

version with doors became a display item during the
early 18th century with the development of glazed doors
enclosing open shelves, and the latter developed into the
bureau and, later, the secretaire. However, here we must
concentrate on the Elizabethan cabinet, which is believed
to have originated in its European form in Italy. Highly
decorated with the application of patterns or pictures
created from various materials on each door and interior
drawer front, the basic cabinet (on a separate open-frame
stand) soon became a status symbol on the Continent.
On some the outer doors were left off to allow immediate
sight of the intricacies and colourful impact produced by
semi-precious stones, marbles, dyed ivories, tortoiseshell,
and gilded metals burnished to lustre.

From Italy the cabinet travelled to France, where it caught
the attention of the English and the Dutch. In Holland it
became popular to paint cabinets with scenes on the
various drawer and door fronts, but English versions were
plainer and more functional – usually covered with Italian
cloth fixed with metal mounts. It is fair to say that the
European high-style furniture makers were well ahead of
their British counterparts and would remain so until the
18th century. However, it is important to remember that
the British were already making sets of drawers within a
carcase during the 16th century, one hundred years before
the craft of "cabinet-making" became established in England.

A charming record in Sir William More of Loseley's
Account Book for 1556 notes a "little coffyen of boxes" as

▲ **15 Carved oak court cupboard, English, *c*.1590**. A "cup board" in the earliest sense as it displays the wholehearted effect of the cup-and-cover design in Elizabethan furniture, as well as the appearance of geometric inlay.

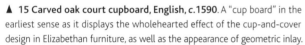

▶ **16 Oak and inlaid armchair, *c*.1650**, showing a change from geometric to foliate inlay designs. Most striking is the high cresting rail that looks like a gentleman's hat, or the high-piled hair that was high-fashion at that time.

costing two shillings, but had he wished to impress his friends he would have had to import something from Italy or France and pay many thousand times that.

Early importation

Elizabeth's father, Henry VIII, had decreed that it was of the utmost importance to maintain "young men of promising hopes in foreign countries for the more complete polishing of their Parts and Studies". So the benefits of travel overseas had been recognized long before Britain set up the East India Company in 1600. However, the company made the exercise easier, and it became commercial; through trade beyond the Straights of Magellan or the Cape of Good Hope Britain's horizons in the appreciation of the decorative and fine arts from other countries were expanded greatly.

Among the many and wondrous items that began to filter through from abroad during Elizabeth's reign was Chinese hard-paste porcelain. The bulk of this was decorated with cobalt blue and is known as "blue and

white". Its clear, hard glaze reflected daylight and candle light and protected the finely drawn decoration beneath, captivating eyes that had seen nothing like it before. It was so highly prized that wealthy collectors would have pieces mounted in gold or silver-gilt (*see* Pl. 19).

Part of the intrigue of porcelain from the Orient was that British manufacturers couldn't make it. There was British-made pottery – a term that describes anything made of clay, such as earthenware and stoneware – but none of the wonderful, white, translucent, non-porous, heat-resistant material that is now called porcelain. The Chinese had developed its manufacture from the 8th century but it was not until the 18th century that commercial production began in Europe.

The Japanese, too, could have benefited from the Western demand for their goods but by 1640 Japan had closed its doors to Western incursion and allowed only the Chinese and the Dutch to trade through an island in Nagasaki harbour. They remained commercially isolated in this way until the 1850s.

Items in the home

The materials available for the manufacture of household items were limited in Britain, but sufficient for an able craftsman to still work wonders and create masterpieces. Iron, bronze, brass, copper, and pewter were used to make domestic metalwares. The average household would have contained no glassware, as production in the UK was still limited and the Italian imports were far too costly. Thus day-to-day utensils were made of local wood, leather, and horn. Local timbers were used to make the common furniture, while some English oak was used for the better pieces in rural areas. Imported Baltic oak was the material of choice for fine furniture, while imported and local walnut was the luxury timber. Cheaper woods were often painted with bright and primary colours or in such a way that simulated a superior grain. These paints can sometimes be seen on surviving pieces, faded but still defiant as they peer through layers of aged patina.

Iron is the fourth-most abundant element in the crust of the earth. It is obtained from its ores by heat – smelting in a blast furnace – to create pig-iron, which can then be converted into cast iron, wrought iron, and steel. Iron was typically used for the log supports (also known as andirons or fire-dogs) in fireplaces (*see* Pl. 22), and for the large cast plates that are called firebacks. Although Shakespeare mentions in his play *Henry IV*: "sitting … by a sea cole fire", wood was the principal heating fuel and remained so for some time, so andirons were important in the fireplace. Cobirons, which were like andirons but had taller uprights at the front with hooks that supported cooking spits, were an integral part of the kitchen. Iron was also necessary to make many of the fitments that were by this time being attached to furniture – hinges, hasps, latches, and locks with keys of steel.

Bronze is an alloy of copper and tin and could be cast to form skillets (three-legged saucepans that sat in the embers), mortars and pestles for grinding food, and other cooking vessels. Brass is an alloy of copper and zinc that, until the early 18th century, was used within wealthier houses mainly for small and decorative items, accessories, and candlesticks.

Copper is a metal obtained from its ores by heat – smelting in a reverberatory furnace – and, rather like

brass, was not much used domestically until the early 18th century. At that time it was made safe for cooking by coating the inner surface with tin. It could, alternatively, be made to look very grand by plating it with gold.

Pewter is an alloy of copper, lead, tin, and, more rarely, bismuth. The higher the tin content the better the pewter. In the 16th and 17th centuries pewter stood alone in the field of non-precious metalware. As early as 1348 the London Guild of Pewterers announced its ordinances for the control of the craft. This was followed by 18 similar Pewterers' Guilds being set up in major cities throughout the British Isles over the next 300 years. Each was established to provide apprenticeships, freedoms (given to apprentices when they had become proficient in their trade), and a series of marks to be stamped on their wares to identify the maker and the place of origin.

The earliest specimens of pewter known to date are spoons, but by the 1650s basins, beakers, bowls, candlesticks, chargers, dishes, flagons, measures, mugs, plates, and salt cellars – in fact all known household items – were made of pewter. Later would come sugar and spice casters, inkstands, shoe-buckles, and snuff-boxes, but brass, copper, and tin wares would prove to be strong competition.

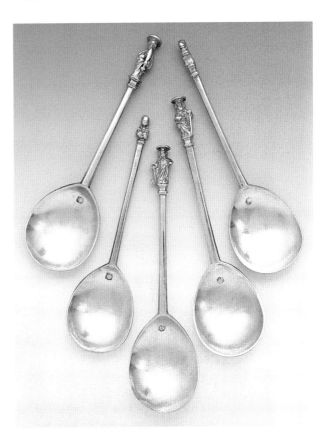

► **17 Elizabethan and James I seal top and apostle top spoons, English, c.1580–1620,** for which the early name of "spone" gave rise to the word "sponsor", as they were popularly given to a child by its godfather. Spoons of this period bear a maker's mark inside the bowl, near the handle (*see* hallmarks pp.111–12).

CHINOISERIE

From the 1630s to the 1920s England enjoyed four main periods of Orientalism; the first three are known as Chinoiserie and the last as Japonaiserie. Each was distinctly different. In the 17th century Chinese taste was exemplified by items imported from the East, such as porcelain, printed calicoes from India (known as *chint* – from the Hindu word meaning variegated), silk (which revolutionized the clothing industry), lacquer work, and, of course, tea (*see* p.50).

In the second period, *c.* 1720–1770, typically European items were made "Oriental" by their ornamentation, and architecture was a direct copy of the original. The four-poster bed from Badminton on page 76 is a fine example of the former, and the pagoda tower at Stowe epitomizes the latter.

The third period, which began in identifiable form at the turn of the 18th to 19th century, can best be summed up in the interior fitments and contents at Brighton Pavillion. Here, Chinese designs were extended into fantasy over walls and ceilings, and the furniture and *objets* were both genuine imports of bamboo, lacquer, and porcelain, as well as sheer fabrications from French and English imaginations. The availability of cheap, mass-produced goods prolonged this taste and set the scene for a national fervour to own something that pertained to the mystic East for the rest of the Victorian period. This was particularly the case after the 1860s, when Japan once again began open trading with the West. This had wide-reaching effects, from imports of the finest lacquer, ivory carvings, and Imari porcelains, to hairstyles, sunshades, and the writing of the operetta *The Mikado*.

▲ **18 Glass goblet, English, c.1685.** This has mould-blown ribbing, pinched trailing, and little buttons on the stem called "prunts", all in the manner of George Ravenscroft who, by the 1670s, had made such advances in the manufacture of glass that he was granted patents.

▶ **19 Porcelain bowl, Chinese, c.1580–1600.** A rare piece of blue-and-white from the Wanli dynasty. To the Elizabethans Chinese porcelain was wondrous, as it was attributed with magical powers. The mounting of silver-gilt straps, rim, and foot, quadrupled its value. This bowl, from Burghley House, was reputedly presented by Elizabeth I to her godson, Thomas Walsingham.

▲ **20 Brass chandelier, Flemish,** with a cup-and-cover-shaped base but a more moderate upper part that places it nearer to 1620. One made *c.*1560 would have had a central stem comprising a series of spheres.

◄ **21 Cast-iron andirons, English, early 1600s,** with modified cup-and-cover finials showing an Elizabethan influence. The architectural, double-scroll base may be seen replicated on gravestones from 1620 to 1670.

Early furniture-making

Until well into the 17th century furniture in rural areas was still made out of simple board, or a plank construction, and was slotted to fit together and then fixed with nails. However, the more sophisticated method of "joining" was becoming more widespread. This entailed thin-cut panels of timber contained within a framework, which enabled the creation of large but lightweight furniture. At its most basic, joining was a derivation of the Dutch method of making wagons larger without making them heavier. To increase the carrying capacity of a wagon the sides were made bigger by adding planks of wood. But too many planks made the wagon too heavy to move, so an open framework was devised. Looking at the front of a coffer chest or wainscot panelling is like looking at an old Dutch wagon side. In fact, the word wainscot is a corruption of *wagonschot*, presumably meaning "wagon's cut".

A joined frame was fastened together by means of a slot cut in the end of one piece of wood and a tongue formed at the end of another to create a mortice and tenon joint. The slot or mortice ("mortess" originally) was made to receive the tongue or tenon ("tenant" originally), and the two pieces were drawn together tightly by the insertion of two split-willow pegs. These were driven into two holes through the joint, which had been previously drilled slightly off-centre. Split, rather than cut, willow was used because it has a long and fibrous grain.

For carcase furniture (i.e., anything that had a body, or carcase), the inside edges of the frame were grooved to allow the outer edges of the panel to slot in and form the solid surface. For open-frame pieces, such as tables and stools, the upright pieces were often turned and carved (*see* below).

Turning and treen

Turning created the great bulbous shapes that formed the uprights and legs for all the abovementioned pieces and their variants, such as dressers and court-cupboards. The dresser gets its name from the board on which food was

▲ **22 Parlour room setting, Geffrye Museum, England,** showing items in fashionable use from the 1580s to 1640s. In front of the linen-fold carved panelling hangs a portrait of a woman in the latest plain formal dress, with noticeable Dutch influence. The tapestry, inlaid and carved court cupboard, pewter plates, tigerware jug, and bell-base candlestick indicate some wealth.

dressed, particularly, and ceremoniously, last thing at night in readiness for the head of the household or anyone else who might suffer "night-starvation". So raiding the fridge in the early hours is not a new phenomenon.

The cupboard gets its name from the board on which the "cuppes" were displayed. These cuppes showed the wealth of the family through their number, size, and, of course, material. Gold, silver, and, at this time still rarely, the occasional piece of Oriental porcelain were the most venerated. Over time enclosed compartments were added to the top of the cupboard.

Turning also created the wonderful mazer cups and wassail bowls so sought after today by collectors of early treen (*see* Pl. 7). The word treen is used to describe any items made of wood that are not furniture. "Mazer" is said to be derived from the German *maizer*, meaning measles. Such vessels were usually made using the densest part of a tree, the knot, and when exposed by turning it had a tendency to look "spotty".

When you see the fineness of the turning achieved by a skilled hand it is difficult to comprehend that, prior to the latter part of the 17th century, such work was done on a pole lathe. This involved fixing a rope attached to a cord to the top of a springy young tree, and tying the cord to a treadle; operating the treadle would then make the tree pull back and forth. The piece of wood to be turned was secured into a lathe frame directly in line with the cord. After releasing the end from the treadle, the cord was wound several times around the piece of wood before re-fixing it to the treadle. Pushing down on the treadle therefore made the piece of wood spin one way, while taking pressure off the treadle allowed it to spin back. Careful and experienced choice of close-grained timber and very sharp tools were needed to allow the turner's ability to show, and the creation of large vessels in the hardest of all woods – *lignum vitae* – by means of a pole lathe is a great feat (*see* Pl. 7).

Turned parts of furniture, such as legs, bed supports, and stretcher rails, could further be decorated with

▼ **23 Engraving of an interior by Abraham Bosse, French, *c*.1665**, called *The Sense of Touch*, one of a set named *The Five Senses*. Interest lies in the furniture and fitments: the upholstered farthingale chairs, and the tapestry-covered walls.

▶ **24 Farthingale chair, English, *c*.1610**, made of oak, and reputedly so-named to accommodate the fashionable hooped skirts of the period; it shows an early use of Turkeywork upholstery. The back is tilted, but not yet the back legs.

carving. This decoration was regular and symmetrical throughout the period covered in this chapter, and was of foliate or geometric design. Vertical flat surfaces, particularly panels in chairs, chests, walls, and bed boards, were also carved but it was more popular either to apply mouldings in geometric patterns or inlay with contrasting coloured woods, both of which methods can be seen in Pl. 25. Inlay in this context should not be confused with marquetry or parquetry, although the appearance is similar. Inlay means exactly what it says: it is the placing of any material into a surface by first gouging out the required pattern from the original surface in order to receive the new substance. (Marquetry and parquetry are described on page 56.)

The bed

The bed of this time was almost a room within a room, with its own curtained walls and overhead cover, or "tester". For several centuries the textile hangings rather than their simple frame had been the indication of the bed's, and therefore the family's, status. These fabrics were often the most highly prized inheritance and were passed on for several generations until they rotted away. By the Elizabethan period the tester was a solid wood framed-and-panelled structure just like a ceiling, supported by

▲ **25 Chest-of-drawers, English, *c*.1650**, with the typical disguised drawer near the top, deep drawer below, and three lower drawers enclosed by doors, of this period. The applied mouldings and inlays of imported and native materials display several foreign influences, and indicate a quality piece.

DOVETAILING

There is much to learn from the simple act of opening a drawer: the main lessons come in establishing the age and quality of the piece of furniture. By the late 17th century the best-made drawers were supported by a "runner", fixed inside the body or carcase of the chest, and fitting into a rebate cut into the sides of the drawer. Despite its superior efficiency, this method had already gone out of fashion by the 1720s and did not reappear until the 20th century. At the same time that the side runner was used the drawers were joined with two dovetails, the top one larger than the lower and traditionally fixed with one hand-made nail (Fig. I, below). Between 1700 and 1725 the dovetails became equal in size and the nail was no longer used. The drawer ran on a strip of wood at the bottom edge of each side; sometimes the drawer side was extended and reinforced so the strip did not show (Fig. 2). By the middle of the 18th century three or four dovetails were used, and by 1800 refinements in manufacturing meant that many more, and finer, joints could be made (Figs. 3 and 4). Generally speaking, the best drawer linings for the sides and bottom were made of oak until the last quarter of the 18th century, after which mahogany and cedar were commonly used.

▲ **26 Mortlake tapestry, English, c.1620–22**, from the Vulcan and Venus series, depicting Neptune and Cupid pleading for the lovers. The border shows the Italianate Renaissance influence, which became popular in England during the early 16th century, with small and delicate figures between cartouches of paper-scroll form (*see* pp.236–7).

▼ **27 Part-silk needlework carpet, French, first half 17th century**, clearly showing the widespread popularity of strapwork decoration in its all-over design. This style of decoration was to affect English interiors, gardens, and domestic items for the next hundred years.

four columns – the front two turned and carved in a bulbous cup-and-cover form. The headboard was of carved wood and inlaid panels. The craftsmen who formed the panelled linings to the walls of great rooms, decorated the ceilings, and made the beds themselves were known as "ceilers and joiners".

By the end of the 17th century a type of bed with a shorter canopy over the head of the bed, supported by brackets or chains to the ceiling of the room, had been introduced. This was known as a "half-tester" and, although out of fashion during much of the 18th century, it became popular again during the late Georgian and Victorian periods of the 19th century.

Tapestry

Tapestry had long been connected with pomp and ceremony in England, the earliest examples being imported from the Continent to be hung in the streets on great occasions, and on the walls of the nobility's houses the rest of the time. Notably huge collections were formed by Henry VIII and Cardinal Wolsey. By the middle of the 1500s immigrant weavers enabled the establishment of a major manufactory in Warwickshire, which was started by William Sheldon (who gave the enterprise his name). And by the 1620s the

famous tapestry works at Mortlake had been established at the instigation of Charles, Prince of Wales, who was later to become King Charles I.

The Queen is dead, God save the King

In comparison to the personal influence Elizabeth exerted over changes in the life and styles of her time, James I had relatively little. James IV of Scotland, son of Mary Queen of Scots, acceded to the throne as James I of England in 1603 (which marked the beginning of the Stuart period). The political and religious arenas were troubled during his reign but, almost as if unnoticed by the monarch (who was preoccupied with his love of hunting and wine), fantastic developments in architecture occurred within the first 30 years of the 17th century. The man largely responsible for this was Inigo Jones.

Born in 1573, Jones trained as a joiner and for a while worked at the Danish Court, later becoming chief architect to the English Crown. He travelled to Italy and returned to England with Andrea Palladio's *Four Books of Architecture*, which inspired him to build houses for the nobility in the Classical style of ancient Rome. The "Queen's House" in Greenwich was the first in this rectangular form, which replaced all former established plans and elevations and remained an inspiration and basis of design for architects for the next 200 years.

In Italy and France at this time the wealthy were becoming less itinerant in habit, and their palaces showed their inclination to reside on a more permanent basis, and to entertain and display their collections of fine and decorative art. This ideal reached England and the layout of the Palladian house suited the mood admirably. Rooms running off a central area, rather than joined in a line by a passage running through from one to the next, allowed greater privacy and encouraged the

NAVIGATION

Towards the end of the 15th century a simplified version of the astrolabe was developed in Portugal for navigational purposes. Known as the mariner's astrolabe, it was relied upon until the latter part of the 17th century, when more specialized and accurate instruments replaced it.

The original astrolabe was a highly sophisticated, manually operated astronomical computer, which was in use before AD 400. A series of plates engraved with a map of the stars, scales of degrees, and other tables could be adjusted to give (at its simplest) a complete picture of the sky, the time of day or night, the time of sunrise or sunset, and a reference to celestial positions. By AD 800 astrolabes were highly developed in Islam, and came to Europe by 1200. During the 16th century they were made in various European countries, particularly in Germany, who became the leading makers. They were expensive to make and to buy, so were the exclusive property of royalty and the very rich. A fine example of a mid-17th-century astrolabe, by the Indian master-maker Muhammad Muquin, is pictured right.

In the 19th century there was a revival of interest, and Arabic astrolabes were made in large numbers. However, in order to make them affordable to the masses these were for show only, as they had no workings inside.

Brass astrolabe, Indian, c.1650, with a solar quadrant, shadow square, lunar mansions, and Zodiacal signs. It is signed on the back by Muhammad Muquin, who was one of the most prolific astrolabists in 17th-century India, and descended from the Royal Astrolabist of Lahore.

▲ **28 Commonwealth-period silver tankard, English, 1654**. Silver from this period is rare, but the general shape of tankards remained much the same for the rest of the 1600s, with a flat lid, raised thumb piece, and thick hollow handle. Only the base changed – it was narrower after the 1660s.

also when the potter Philip Drinker arrived in Charlestown and potters William Vincent and John Pride reached Salem, hopefully in time to witness Richard Graves opening his, and the town's, first pewterer's shop.

During this period in America the design of household goods followed those established by the origins of the migrant families who arrived after the pilgrims in 1620. British, Dutch, Swedish, Spanish, and French mannerisms, which were at first proudly separated, were soon to become blended into styles that, by the beginning of the 18th century, can be seen as uniquely American.

Meanwhile the union of England and Scotland gave the British their first Union Jack flag, although strictly speaking it is the "Great Union", being a "Jack" only when flying from the jackstaff of a ship of war.

In style the cup-and-cover shapes quite quickly disappeared, as did the formalized strapwork decoration. In protocol the subtlety of the "device" was lost. But by the end of the early Stuart period the first collections of decorative as well as fine arts were being formed, and for a while the years of religious and dynastic conflict gave way to an environment that encouraged the manufacture of domestic articles.

This enthusiasm was furthered by the accession to the throne of Charles I in 1625. He was the only surviving son of James I and was also the first great connoisseur, patron, and collector of art. Under his direction Rubens and Van Dyck were painting at court, a tapestry works was established at Mortlake, and Dutch craftsmen skilled in the art of applying veneers, marquetry, and parquetry were employed in England to bolster the making of fine furniture.

Charles was fond of, and advocated, reading, which boosted the printing trade and the production of shelf and case furniture in Britain. His marriage to Henrietta Maria, daughter of Henry IV of France, also further increased the general Continental influence on etiquette, fashion, and design within the country.

In the 1620s the first lantern clocks (*see* Pl. 32) were introduced into English society. Since the 1450s household wall clocks, as distinct from public clocks, had been made in Germany, Switzerland, and Holland, and the British version was a development of such designs. Among its distinguishing features are its four turned columns that create the frame to contain the movement – known as a posted frame – and a large bell on the top. Later models are also known as Cromwellian clocks.

feeling of a "home". This arrangement was also well suited to the more modest houses of the rapidly expanding upper and wealthy middle classes. Their buildings had traditionally been constructed of timber and plaster but plaster was soon to be replaced by brick. And as timber became scarce and brickmaking more widespread, these houses began to be built of brick alone.

Building with bricks of baked clay is something we know to have been done at least since the earliest records of civilized man. However, in its more sophisticated form it began in strength throughout Europe in the Medieval period and was given impetus in England in the 15th century. This was when the English knights, who had captured and occupied brick-built castles in France, returned home to recreate similar buildings for themselves. Hurstmonceux Castle in Sussex, *c*.1446, is one of several awe-inspiring extant examples. During the first half of the 16th century Cardinal Wolsey and Henry VIII spared no expense in creating the largest house in England – Hampton Court – using brick.

Shortly before the arrival of *The Mayflower* in New Plymouth, Massachusetts in November 1620, brickmaking in America was recorded, in 1612 in Virginia, and later in Salem and Boston in 1629 and 1635. The year 1635 was

◄ **29 The Blue Silk Dressing Room at Burghley House, Stamford, England**, the interior of which was completed in the late 17th/early 18th century, and shows a fine example of a corner chimney with receding shelves above in the manner of Daniel Marot (*see* p.64). This is an early example of a "conversion", as this and the ensuing four rooms occupy a space that was originally one long gallery (the Elizabethan pendanted ceiling may still exist above the new ones).

Instruments for time and weather

During the Civil War, which began in 1642, and the Commonwealth (1649–60) early developments were being made in the fields of accurate recording of time and the forecasting of weather, which were to have a visible effect in every well-to-do household by the end of the century. In 1643 Evangelista Torricelli, an Italian physicist, was working on a theory by Galileo – whom he succeeded as professor of mathematics at Florence University – when he discovered that atmosphere exerts pressure. He demonstrated this by placing a measured amount of mercury, which does not evaporate, into a tube and then sealing it. The empty part, or vacuum, in the tube expands or contracts, thus causing the mercury to rise or fall in response to the external atmosphere or barometric pressure. This was the technique used to provide the first-ever scientifically accurate weather forecast.

▲ **30 Monstrance, German, 1560s**, with decorative elements of the European Renaissance that influenced England in the late 16th century. The silver ornamentation is reflected in costume and architecture of the period.

◄ **31 Tigerware jug, German, c.1570**, with English silver mounts. These earthenware pots were imported from the Rhineland, mounted, and used as drinking vessels from the 1550s. They remained popular into the 1600s.

Another Galileo theory was adopted by the Dutchman Christian Huygens who, in 1657, recorded the importance of the applied pendulum in creating a reliable clock. By giving the pendulum momentum from a weight suspended on a chain or specially woven rope placed over a toothed wheel, and controlling the power by a mechanical escapement, it was possible to correct the arc of the pendulum's swing and give a regulated power source to the clock.

The Commonwealth

The execution of Charles I in 1649 saw the end of an era of great advances in the creation and appreciation of art and objects. By its very nature the Puritanism inherent in the Commonwealth period determined a lessening of decoration and adornment in all walks of life, a contrast best and most simply illustrated in the popular names of the opposing sides in the Civil War – Roundheads and Cavaliers. From clothes to chattels, plainer and more austere lines were sought and created, and a definite Cromwellian "look" emerged. The ruffs, frills, and curls so favoured by the previous Carolean court (1625–49) were not to be seen, and the flamboyant application of multicoloured veneers and split-turned attachments on furniture (*see* Pl. 25), heavily embossed silver and gold, and the most sumptuous of imported fabrics for hangings and covers were also out, to be replaced by designs that relied on simplicity and balance for their visual impact. The Puritans' life was well ordered, with work, rest, and play apportioned in a manner more similar to the 20th century than the 1600s, with Cromwell advocating that the main meal of the day (dinner) be taken at 1pm. "Lunch" was yet to be formalized and given a name.

However, this repression of progress and control of the spirit in a time of expansion in foreign trade and international exchange of ideas and ideals simply could not last. This period was the lull before the storm. The death of Oliver Cromwell in 1658 and his son Richard's abdication the following year resulted in the fall of the Protectorate, and the reinstatement of the monarchy through the Restoration, with the return of King Charles II from exile in Europe.

◄ **32 Brass lantern clock, English, mid-17th century**, signed "Thomas Knifton en Lothbury" (in the city of London). Knifton was a prolific maker of fine clocks between 1640 and 1667. Early clocks were upgraded as the industry advanced at a rapid pace during the next hundred years. Beware of late-19th-century fakes, which were produced in large numbers.

INNOVATION & INVENTION

1660–1740

On 29 May 1660 Charles II landed at Dover and within a few months England had as much a French Court as an English one. In contrast to Puritan disciplines, the new exuberance set the scene for the next 80 years. During this time the western world enjoyed a period of unparalleled development in the decorative arts.

◄ 1 **View through the State Apartments at Chatsworth House, Derbyshire, England.** One of the greatest houses in Britain, Chatsworth illustrates the evolution of interior decoration from the 16th to the 18th century. The traditional Elizabethan corridor of rooms displays panelled, carved, and painted walls, mantels, overdoors, and ceilings created by the leading craftsmen and artists of successive generations, culled from all parts of Europe.

*J*ust before the Civil War Inigo Jones had planned London's first square – Covent Garden. Shortly after, fanatical Puritans like Richard "Blue Dick" Culmer were wrecking churches – it was he who smashed the stained-glass windows at Canterbury Cathedral. But when work began in the 1660s on replacing ecclesiastical heritage, there was a surge in creative output. This required a revitalized apprenticeship system in fine woodwork, metalware, jewellery, textiles, architecture, masonry, and building.

The return to the throne of Charles II ensured that not all of these energies went only into the Church. There was nothing that the King declared a passion for that did not filter through to society at large. His love of theatre-going, horseracing, animals (particularly his dogs and ducks), his exotic dress, humour, gambling, mistresses, and children, and his inherited appreciation of the arts all created employment in one form or another for keepers, gardeners, courtiers, bookkeepers, actors, teachers, trainers, households full of staff at different levels (now more equally distributed between the sexes), and dozens more disparate occupations.

In addition to the repair and rebuilding of desecrated churches and a flamboyant new court, the Great Plague of 1665 and the Great Fire of London in 1666 created even more work for artisans and craftsmen. Approximately 100,000 people died from the Plague, and the Fire engulfed the city for four days, razing to the ground 13,200 houses and 87 churches over 437 acres.

The timbered houses of London were rebuilt in brick and stone and all manner of household items of furniture were needed to furnish them. But there had to be an

▶ **2 The Tea-Party**, **Dutch, c.1700**. An interior scene painted on a fan-leaf that tells us much about the people and the period. High-bonneted ladies are taking tea from blue-and-white Chinese porcelain bowls and seated at a folding table, illustrating fashion, customs, and the early use of occasional furniture.

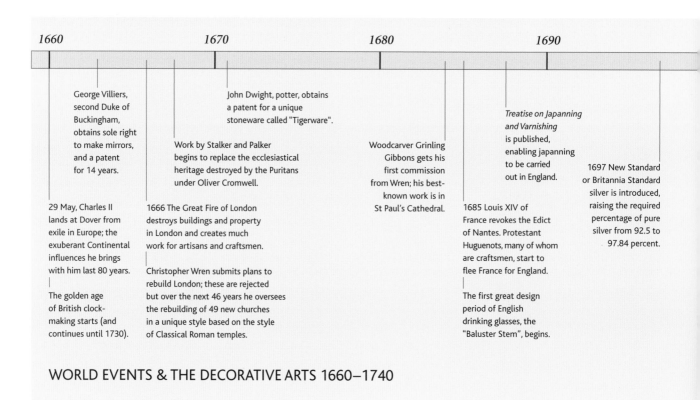

1660	1670	1680	1690

George Villiers, second Duke of Buckingham, obtains sole right to make mirrors, and a patent for 14 years.

John Dwight, potter, obtains a patent for a unique stoneware called "Tigerware".

Work by Stalker and Palker begins to replace the ecclesiastical heritage destroyed by the Puritans under Oliver Cromwell.

Woodcarver Grinling Gibbons gets his first commission from Wren; his best-known work is in St Paul's Cathedral.

Treatise on Japanning and Varnishing is published, enabling japanning to be carried out in England.

1697 New Standard or Britannia Standard silver is introduced, raising the required percentage of pure silver from 92.5 to 97.84 percent.

29 May, Charles II lands at Dover from exile in Europe; the exuberant Continental influences he brings with him last 80 years.

1666 The Great Fire of London destroys buildings and property in London and creates much work for artisans and craftsmen.

1685 Louis XIV of France revokes the Edict of Nantes. Protestant Huguenots, many of whom are craftsmen, start to flee France for England.

The golden age of British clock-making starts (and continues until 1730).

Christopher Wren submits plans to rebuild London; these are rejected but over the next 46 years he oversees the rebuilding of 49 new churches in a unique style based on the style of Classical Roman temples.

The first great design period of English drinking glasses, the "Baluster Stem", begins.

WORLD EVENTS & THE DECORATIVE ARTS 1660–1740

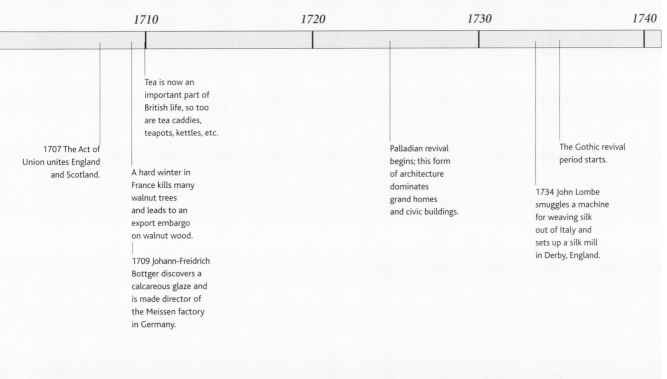

1710　　　**1720**　　　**1730**　　　**1740**

Tea is now an
important part of
British life, so too
are tea caddies,
teapots, kettles, etc.

1707 The Act of
Union unites England
and Scotland.

A hard winter in
France kills many
walnut trees
and leads to an
export embargo
on walnut wood.

1709 Johann-Freidrich
Bottger discovers a
calcareous glaze and
is made director of
the Meissen factory
in Germany.

Palladian revival
begins; this form
of architecture
dominates
grand homes
and civic buildings.

The Gothic revival
period starts.

1734 John Lombe
smuggles a machine
for weaving silk
out of Italy and
sets up a silk mill
in Derby, England.

overall vision for the new, rebuilt city, and the first to submit such a plan was Sir Christopher Wren. It was rejected on the grounds of excessive cost, but his ingenuity at fitting new buildings into established irregular sites ensured that he built 49 of the new churches, 36 of the great halls, and gave the City its most famous landmark – St Paul's Cathedral.

The Palladian designs of Inigo Jones (1573–1652) are singular and restrained when compared to the work of Christopher Wren. For the rest of the 17th century there was a move toward infinite variety and diversification in architectural decoration: formal pediments supported by Classical columns with bases, capitals and entablatures, frame paintings, armorial bearings, and windows as well as doorways that incorporated mouldings of egg and dart, vitruvian scrolls, stylized acanthus leaves, swags of fruit and flowers, and the heads or even whole bodies of cherubs. All such decoration found its way onto fashionable furniture and metalware too, sometimes more appropriately than others – particularly when incorporating the unbridled lines of the dominant European Baroque style (*see* Pl. 36).

Whigs and Tories, Roundheads and Cavaliers

The Restoration really meant the restoration to power of the Cavaliers, or "Tories", with their principles of loyalty to

▲ **3 Cabinet on stand, English, *c*.1680–1700**, showing a Continental flavour in its six-legged base (seen on Italian, French, and Dutch cabinets), its angularity, and the colourful floral marquetry – a decorative technique imported from Holland. On the top is a mass of blue-and-white Chinese porcelain, reflecting an obsession with this material throughout the 1600s.

▲ **4 Black-and-gilt lacquer cabinet on silvered, carved wood stand, *c*.1685**. The popularity of this kind of Oriental decoration caused it to be replicated extensively in Europe. Irrespective of origin, it was mixed with totally European fitments such as stands and pediments, as seen here, whose elaborate baroque form had gone out of fashion by 1710.

▲ **5 William-and-Mary escritoire on chest, c.1700**, in the standard form that predated the sloping-front bureau with drawers below of c.1710. The front is hinged at the bottom, opening to create a writing surface and expose drawers and compartments. Country squires or doctors had plain oak models; one with seaweed marquetry, such as this, would be for wealthy merchants.

▲ **6 Detail of Boulle marquetry, French, c.1685**, from a chest in Burghley House. This clearly illustrates the dramatic effect created by the contrasting materials of tortoiseshell and brass. Named after its leading exponent, A.C. Boulle, the technique avoided wastage by using the remaining patterns in reverse, known as *contre-boulle*.

the Church of England and the Crown, insularity, and the avoidance of foreign wars. The name Tory is said to come from *Toiridhe*, the word used to describe Irish supporters of the House of Stuart. Although ousted, the Roundheads, or "Whigs" remained a powerful force in opposition, with their loyalties to Parliament and the Free Church, as well as the expansion of foreign trade and the Empire, even at the risk of war. Whig is said to come from *Whiggamore*, the derisory nickname given to Scots Presbyterians. There was no class difference between the two; both were aristocracy-led and were also instrumental in maintaining the demand and supply of improvements in the standard of living.

The Huguenots

In 1685 Louis XIV of France revoked the Edict of Nantes, a law that had, for the best part of 100 years, given his Protestant subjects religious freedom and full civil rights. Now outlawed, the Huguenot refugees sought safe haven in other European countries. Many arrived in England, as the newly restored King was well accustomed to their qualities as citizens and, above all, fine craftsmen.

Several thousand settled within a few years, particularly in London and Norwich, and quickly became integrated, imparting their skills and education. Many became tutors, keenly accepted by the Whigs for their beliefs and aristocratic French, while others instructed on gardening techniques (in Spitalfields they formed the first gardening societies). But it was for their expertise in weaving tapestries and silk, cabinet-making, and silversmithing that Britain was to be most grateful. Huguenots from the Low Countries had introduced marquetry cutting prior to the Civil War, but after 1685 they were to influence the whole of the furniture- and cabinet-making industries with veneering techniques, japanning, and gesso. At home in France they had worked for royalty and the wealthiest aristocracy so they were used to the highest-grade timbers and top-quality, thick-gauge silver and gold. The names of Huguenot silversmiths were to appear in inventories of the finest collections for generations to come, with pieces by the most famous of them all, Paul de Lamerie (1712–*c.*1750), commanding a higher price than work by his contemporaries. They used cut-card or strapwork, embossing, casting and chasing, and superlative engraving to decorate items of exquisite proportions that even when left plain are outstanding. It was also the Huguenots who brought the soup tureen to England.

Tea

Britain had imported tea from China since the early part of the 17th century, but it was not until the Restoration that it was drunk, experimentally, in society. In 1660 Pepys mentioned in his famous diary that he "did send for a cup

THE FIRST MILLED COINS

Until the Restoration English silver coins were stamped with a die and trimmed by hand. It had become a common practice to snip off a little bit of the edge of a coin before passing it on – once enough fragments were collected they were melted into an ingot and sold to a silversmith. Such a crime was punishable by death or branding but the rewards were great, as one "clipper" could fetch up to £6,000 ($9,000). To curb clipping, a machine was devised to stamp and trim the coins to a circle, giving them a legend around the rim, which later became serrated or "milled". As a result old clipped coins became worth half their face value; with both these and the new coins in circulation it meant the monetary exchange was in a mess. Various measures to alleviate the problem were tried but the most meaningful was in 1697, when the required standard of wrought plate – items made of silver – was raised from 92.5 percent pure silver to alloy up to 97.84 percent. The new standard, known as New Sterling or Britannia Standard, was denoted by two new hallmarks – the figure of Britannia and the Lion's Head Erased (*see* p.154). The Britannia Standard was the only legal quality of silver to be used from 1697 until 1720.

▲ **7 Cushion-frame mirror, English, *c.*1690**. An example of the new and beautiful furniture being made at the time. Veneers of laburnum wood cut at an angle to create "oysters" remained popular until the early 1700s.

◄ **8 Embroidered mirror frame, English, *c.*1660**, in a form popular for a short while after the Restoration. Depending on the fabric's date, the royal figures might be Charles II and Catharine of Braganza, or William and Mary.

of tee (a China drink) of which I never had drank before", and later notes that it was good for a hangover and his wife's "defluxions". By the end of the century it had become so popular that it impacted on furniture and silver manufacture. In 1706 a pound of tea cost the equivalent of a skilled craftsman's weekly wage, which made it prohibitively expensive. Nevertheless an idea of just how many people were drinking it is given by the fact that between 1696 and 1700 Britain imported over 6,500 lacquered tea tables from the Far East, in addition to those made at home.

The tea was shipped in chests containing small boxes called katis, each holding about a pound (*avoirdupois*) in weight. These boxes were usually made of tin and decorated with lacquer or light Chinese-style engraving and so, being attractive objects, became prized in their own right. The name soon became corrupted to "caddy", and from the early 18th century the tea caddy gained an important place in the English home, particularly when fitted with a lock and key to keep the valuable leaves safe from the hands of servants. Part of the magic of tea and its service was the fine Chinese porcelain or dense red pottery used to dispense it, neither of which British manufacturers could yet make, and the fastidious etiquette that the affected wealthy applied to its "taking".

It was the silversmith who benefited most of all from the new fashion of tea drinking. In 1660 the general line of merchandise included ewers, jugs, and other hollow vessels of every kind, plates and platters, chargers and basins, patens and tazzas, the odd inkstand or "standish", candlesticks, and ornaments. However, from 1710 the line was extended to tea urns, teapots, kettles, cream jugs, teaspoons and spoon trays, sugar bowls and covers, tongs, and tea caddies.

Industry

Until the early 18th century most things were handmade, without the benefit of machinery in production, and the divide between manufacturer and consumer was by no means as clearcut as it is today. The very term workshop gives an indication that the customer went to the place of production to view and buy, or commission, a purchase. The retail trade as we know it had yet to become established. Businesses simply grew from the master craftsman creating, with the help of assistants and apprentices, his wares in whatever field – be it wood, metal, cloth, stone, or glass.

In rural areas most craftsmen had to be multi-talented, and their inadequacies in certain aspects such as turning, carving, or finishing give us an immediate indication of

OAK COFFERS

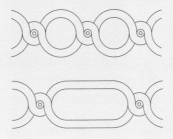

9 Examples of guilloche design (interwoven bands), taken from Greek and Roman architectural decoration and intermittently popular on furniture of the Elizabethan period, through to the late 19th century, particularly on 17th-century oak chests.

The interlaced design for carved decoration shown above is called Guilloche and has many variations. It was used on the 17th-century panelled chests (*see* Pl. 11), rather than on the earlier simple board construction, which had been made since Medieval times. These continued to be made, usually plain, in rural areas long after the panelled chests had gone out of fashion, but by the 1700s the corner joints were often coarsely dovetailed rather than nailed.

10

11

10 Oak chest, *c*.1580–1660. One of two basic types of coffer, it is of six-board construction: one at each end, a front, back, base, and lid. The originality of its carving is dubious, as it is a type popular in the late 1400s.

11 Oak chest, *c*.1660, with a traditional three-panel front and top; sometimes the tops are solid planks. The carved decoration indicates some status when new. By this time joined furniture had spread into the domestic market.

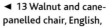

◄ 13 Walnut and cane-panelled chair, English, c.1670, with scrolling front legs (a precursor of the cabriole leg of the ealy 1700s) joined with a deeply curved stretcher known as a Dutch Bow. The arms and turned columns to the back are delicate in comparison to the extraordinary cresting rail, which has the appearance of the head of King Charles II himself in his elaborate curly wig.

▼ 14 Walnut-frame daybed, English, c.1670, with cane seat and panel to the back. The very stance of this bed makes it unmistakeably of the late Carolean period; the Dutch-inspired scroll legs and elaborately carved and pierced back with its top rail look like a coiffured courtesan. Within ten years the weaving of the cane, which came from the Far East, would become much finer.

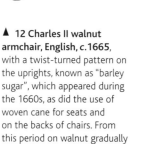

▲ 12 Charles II walnut armchair, English, c.1665, with a twist-turned pattern on the uprights, known as "barley sugar", which appeared during the 1660s, as did the use of woven cane for seats and on the backs of chairs. From this period on walnut gradually replaced oak as the primary timber.

► 15 Mirror, 1730s. The frame, with its exaggerated scrolling "swan-neck" cornice flanking a cartouche, was inspired by the current architectural taste. The severe straight lines at the top are countered by a curvilinear base, while the sides are decorated with foliate carving in the manner of Grinling Gibbons (*see* pp.60–1). This type of mirror was made in large numbers and a wide variety of patterns and quality; this is a fine example, made with Virginia walnut and parcel gilding.

a provincial background. In major cities, skills were more specialized and outworkers were employed to make accessories such as handles, finials, and other adornments for leading companies. These can give us equally definitive clues as to provenance, as the exact same features are seen on various items attributable or traceable to a specific leading maker. Quite quickly the outworkers themselves grew into sizeable specialist producers, particularly in the hardware and cutlery industries of Birmingham and Sheffield, and then later in the potteries of Staffordshire.

Wool and cotton cloths were mostly produced in sheds adjoining farms; leather goods, hosiery, and lace were also produced locally according to the availability of raw materials. The factory was yet to be established – this happened in 1734 with the introduction of machinery to make fine-quality silk.

The potter

The fine, white, hard-paste porcelain from China that so delighted the aristocracy of the Western world towards the end of the 16th century remained a mystery in its manufacture for more than another hundred years, but by 1700 great advances in the making of pottery had been achieved. Porcelain and pottery both come under the heading of "ceramics" – a term derived from the Greek word *keramos*, meaning clay.

▲ **16 Porcelain tea bowl, China, c.1725**, from the Yongzheng Period (1723–35), decorated *en grisaille* and showing a European woman drinking tea. Sometimes referred to as "Jesuit China", such European subjects painted in this way were highly sought-after in the West. The high hair and billowing dress confirm the date as earlier rather than later in the period.

The basic craft of forming a vessel from wet clay and baking or "firing" it in an oven or kiln goes back thousands of years. As a result of this process the clay takes on a permanent shape, but the body remains porous. At first the successful production of this earthenware depended on the local availability of suitable raw material, so potteries grew up where the clay was fine. The colour of the clay varied from region to region, with iron-rich soil giving a rusty red body, and white Devon clay used to create creamware. However, it was not long before large-scale production in areas such as Staffordshire meant the importation of clays from other parts of the country, and so trying to determine origins from body colour alone is inconclusive.

By the 17th century there were two types of pottery: earthenware and stoneware. The latter is a more sophisticated version, being, as its name suggests, harder through consisting of finer clay that is fired at a higher temperature. Nevertheless both are porous until covered with a glaze. There are many types of glaze but they all have one essential purpose – to seal the clay.

Comprising a silica, a flux, and an alumina, glazes can be glossy or matt, textured or plain, hard or soft, transparent or dense, and clear or coloured. The glaze is applied either before or after firing, when the silica becomes glass-like or vitreous, the flux reduces its melting

▲ **17 Detail from *The Tea Party*, Dutch, c.1700**, an oil painting by N. Verkolje (1673–1746) that illustrates a distinctive fashion note in the man's high wig – an outline that can be seen repeated in furniture of the period. Also noteworthy is an early record of the delicate ladder-back chair.

point, and the alumina acts as a fixative for the glaze to the body of the piece being fired.

The most common type is a tin glaze made by the addition of tin oxide to a lead glaze. This was first produced in Mesopatamia around 1000BC. It was used there to decorate painted pottery in the 9th century and from there, via the southern shores of the Mediterranean and through the hands of Islamic potters, it reached Spain, Italy, and France. It also eventually reached Holland,

England, and the New World. Much of the Spanish ware (*Hispano-Moresque*) reached Italy through Majorca, from where it is presumed the name for the Italian version, *maiolica*, comes. The French name for painted pottery is *faience* and the Dutch is *Delft*, after the town of its principal production. English tin-glazed earthenware is known as delftware, with a small "d", and was first made at Southwark and Lambeth in London and then Bristol, Liverpool, and Dublin.

Stoneware appeared in Britain from Germany towards the end of the 17th century. Its hard, fine, but still granular body was a dull grey colour and this pottery was popularly used for drinking vessels. In 1671 John Dwight of Fukham, a pioneering potter, obtained a patent for his own unique stoneware, known as saltglaze stoneware, production of which was quickly taken up by the potters of Staffordshire. A coat of iron oxide turned the surface colour to brown, and salt thrown into the kiln during firing produced a mottled surface.

In America there was a greater demand for homemade bricks than pottery. Although potters were slowly becoming established, it is important to bear in mind that by 1690 there were still fewer than a quarter of a million colonists and only 18,500 of them lived in the five major towns, so there was no great customer base. Until well into the middle of the 18th century most luxury goods were imported into America – mainly from Britain.

Lacquer

The import of Oriental lacquer to the West in the 17th century amazed and delighted Europeans in their quest for novelty and sensation. Lacquer was originally created by the application of thin layers of cured resin made from the sap of the lac tree onto a base of wood, but substitute materials were quickly found to supply the demand. In 1688 *A Treatise on Japanning and Varnishing* was published by Messrs Stalker and Parker, and this enabled imitation "japan" to be manufactured in England.

There were two main types of Oriental lacquer, both of which first appeared in the form of large panelled screens or trunks (originally called "tronks"). One was incised and known as *coromandel* (or bantam lacquer); the other had the decoration applied to stand proud of the surface, as on the bureau bookcase shown in Plate 4. To begin with the screens were often cut to be made into parts for more useful pieces of furniture, such as doors for

▲ **20 Tin-glaze plate, Italian,** *c.***1540**, with a portrait within a geometric border, which has replaced the central panel of script shown in the plate below (Pl. 22). From now on there was a turn in the direction of recreating scenes that had been made popular in tapestries by skilful painting onto earthenware such as this.

▲ **21 Tin-glaze plate, Italian,** *c.***1620**, depicting an all-over scene of a shepherd playing a flute, with trees and buildings beyond. This plate shows a burgeoning mastery of the technique of realistic painting in this medium, as the colours were inclined to run. Single-colour decoration is called monochrome; multi-coloured, such as this, is known as polychrome.

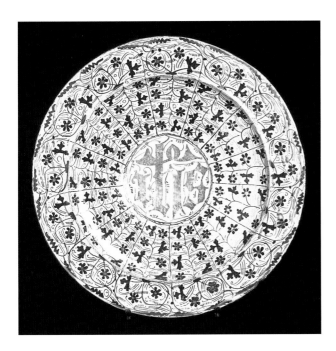

▲ **22 Tin-glaze plate, Spanish,** *c.***1480**. An example of a style of wares, known as *Hispano-Moresque*, that were the forerunners of the Italian *majolica*. The lustre decoration was introduced in the 13th century, and within a hundred years an element of portraiture appeared on these grand plates that were intended for display rather than use.

▲ **23 Tin-glaze plate, French,** *c.***1660**. The replication of a scene adapted from two prints by Antonio Tempesta shows complete mastery of the technique. The popularity of this type of earthenware had spread across Europe by the 17th century, with each country having its own peculiarities in the production and decoration.

▼ **24 Delft pottery tulip vase, Dutch, late 17th century**, with a multi-spouted vase in Oriental style and the base and lower part of the body in deeply lobed form. Tulips were brought to the Netherlands from Turkey in the early 1600s, and in the late 1630s the European fascination with them turned into an obsession. Towards the end of the century decorative tulip vases were being made in large numbers.

► **25 Porcelain tulip vase, Chinese, late 17th century, sometimes known as a "tulipiere".** The pagoda form of this one reflects the ever present influence of the East during the last quarter of the 17th century. It is difficult to comprehend that when this luxurious item was new the flowers it held would have cost more than the vase itself.

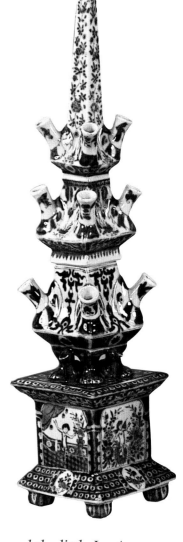

cabinets, but it was not long before every known item was subject to the lacquer treatment, some made in the West to be shipped East for decoration, some made and decorated in the East, and some produced solely in Europe.

Despite the extraordinary volume of this two-way traffic it is still difficult to say precisely where these wonderful objects came from. Inventories of the time often include references to India Ware, and the term japanning indicates uncertainty of origin, but one thing is certain – from the Restoration of the English Monarchy in 1660 through to the early 1740s all forms of lacquer provided some of the most glorious furniture of all time.

Climate and the little Ice Age

The importance of gleaning even a surface understanding of every aspect of social history cannot be overstressed in recognizing and enjoying antiques. The weather is one such aspect. There was a cooling in temperature throughout Europe from the mid-12th until the mid-14th century and thereafter, particularly from the 1560s until the mid-Victorian period. During these years there was a very cold climate with one or two freak hot spells. This meant poorer harvests, and therefore poorer diet. Malnutrition inevitably resulted in less resistance to disease, and this was a contributory factor in the outbreaks of bubonic plague, especially the last Great Plague of London, which caused such an alarmingly high death rate.

There are five types of indigenous mosquito capable of carrying malaria in England; all favour brackish water, such as the "unwholesome fens" mentioned by Shakespeare, which stank of sulphur. The word malaria is derived from the Italian *mala aria* or "bad air". Otherwise known as the ague, it was this that killed Oliver Cromwell in 1658.

But for bad weather, the Restoration therefore may never have happened. As the climate worsened, English wine production dwindled into insignificance, having been, during the reign of Henry VIII, healthy economic competition to that of France. Between the 15th and 18th centuries German wine production was at times only 20 percent of its pre-1300 amount, so there was less need all round for wine casks, stoneware jugs, and other drinking accessories. In 1709 France suffered an exceptionally hard winter, which resulted in famine and a high human death toll. It also killed great swathes of woodland, including France's all-important walnut trees that supplied the English cabinet-makers with their prize raw material. In 1720 an embargo was placed on its export from France, no doubt hastening the advent of the "Age of Mahogany" and the cessation of fanciful veneering for 50 years.

Allowing for the strictures of fashion, civilian clothing has always reflected the climate – just think of those thick tweed three-piece suits worn by men in the 1930s and early post-World War II years compared to the normal two-piece lightweight cloths we wear today. The same

▼ **26 Travelling knife and fork set**, **Irish**, **1690s**, with tapering cylindrical handles covered with tortoiseshell and mounted with silver; the working ends are steel and the case is covered with shagreen (leather). Until the early 1700s people travelled with their own cutlery in cases such as this, including a large knife with a scimitar blade, a small cutting knife, and a fork with three tines (a fourth tine was added in the late 18th century).

COFFEE HOUSES

The first coffee house was opened in Oxford in 1650 and was known as Jacob's (the name of the proprietor). Two years later he moved to Holborn, London, where his concept was so immediately popular that by 1663 there were 81 other coffee houses in the city (and by the end of the century 500 were registered under their owners' names). They offered coffee (as well as tea and chocolate), pamphlets and newsletters, and basic accommodation where customers could sit and enjoy conversation. They quickly became places where like-minded people met, and were the foundations of the gentlemen's clubs of the next generation.

On Tuesday 4 January 1698 John Castaing, a broker, published the first "Course of the Exchange, and Other Things", basically the first stock-market report, "at his office at Jonathans Coffee-house"; those whose interests lay in insurance frequented Mr Lloyd's. One problem was that coffee houses were so crowded that it was often difficult to get served. Rather than having customers waving money in the air it became the custom to fix a moneybox on the counter or a post with the words "To Insure Prompt Service". This was the "TIPS" box and the origin of our word for service today.

Due to its immense popularity, the coffee house created yet further demand for pots, cups, mugs, and other paraphernalia from the pewterers, silversmiths, and potters.

▶ **27 Walnut-case stick barometer, English, c.1720.** The basic shape of these remained the same well into the 1800s, with only minor changes to detailed decoration and case material. During most of the 1700s the section containing the register plate was enclosed by a glass door and followed an architectural style with a pedimented top. Stick barometers originally were made for ships, but the style was so popular that many were made for men who would never go to sea.

▲ **28 Mahogany-cased signpost barometer by Charles Orme of Ashby-de-la-Zouche, England, 1734.** The angle of the arm allows the mercury to travel further under the same pressure, thereby giving a more accurate reading. Signpost barometers were, and are, highly prized, and Orme was a leading specialist maker.

phenomena occurred in the 18th century, when men's heavy frocked coats and thick breeches and women's multi-layered skirts over hooped frames gave way to lighter-weight silks for the former, and simple, thin Empire-line dresses for the latter, indicating some warm hiccups in the cold weather pattern during the 1780s and '90s.

Marquetry

Craftsmen from the Low Countries introduced the marquetry that superseded the inlay work of the Elizabethan period during the 1640s, but the Civil War and the Protectorate hindered its development. It sprang back to life in the Restoration of the 1660s, and retained, for most of this period, a distinctly Dutch look.

The technique of marquetry is simpler to explain than to practise. Thin sheets of contrasting coloured woods are fixed together with a water-soluble glue to form a multi-coloured laminate. A design is drawn onto one outer surface and the lines followed and cut through. The glue that holds the laminate together is melted so that it falls apart, and a picture is formed from the pieces using appropriate colours: red for a flower head, green for a leaf, and so on. This picture is then pasted onto a piece of paper and the whole is placed onto the piece of furniture to be decorated (its surface will have been coated with wet glue first). Pressure is applied until the glue has seeped though to the upper surface of the picture, making it literally part of the piece.

The process was made possible by the development of veneer cutting, which is slicing timber across its grain to show its medullar rays, or the "fan". Thus it was known as "faneer" cutting but this was soon corrupted and became known as "veneer" cutting instead.

▲ **29 Table clock, English, c.1695**, made by Simon De Charmes. This is an example of the very best and most modern table (later known as bracket) clocks of this period, and in general appearance they changed little for the next 75 years, simply becoming less decorated and made with walnut and then mahogany cases.

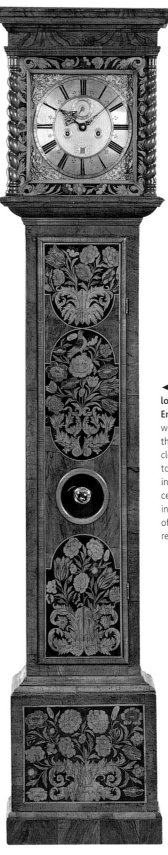

◄ **30 Walnut and marquetry longcase clock by Henry Aske, English, c.1695**. Such cases were introduced to protect the pendulum of weight-driven clocks. Great developments took place in the clock-making industry from the mid-17th century, and longcases, decorated in harmony with other pieces of furniture, added to the items requested of cabinet-makers.

There are several types of marquetry, some using no more than two woods and delicate scrolling designs, known as "Seaweed". Another type uses a variety of woods and ivory to create foliate panels with birds and butterflies, and is known as "Foliate" or "Arabesque", while yet another, using brass and tortoiseshell, is named "Boulle" or "Buhl" after its chief exponent, Andre Charles Boulle (*see* Pl. 6).

Another use for veneer during this early period was the application of separate small regular-sized pieces laid one against another to form a geometric pattern. The wood most used for this was laburnum, a branch of which could be cut at right angles to form a circle or at 45 degrees to form an oval. The latter was called an "oyster" and such decoration was, and still is, known as oyster wood veneer (*see* Pl. 7). The process employed to create this is parquetry.

Mirrors and glassmaking

Shakespeare's *Richard II* has the King dash a mirror to the ground, making it "crack'd in a hundred shivers", so we know that the Elizabethans had glass mirrors. But records of them are scant and it is not until the latter part of the 17th century that their manufacture in England became established on a commercial basis.

Nevertheless a type of glass had been made in Chiddingfold in Surrey since the 14th century and in 1618 Sir Robert Mansell took over the works and introduced "expert strangers from foreign parts to teach the natives of this kingdom in the making of looking glass plates". He obtained patents and by 1623 was employing 500 people. Once again the Protectorate under Cromwell hindered progress in what was considered luxury trade and little more was heard of glass or mirrors until the Restoration.

In 1663 George Villiers, second Duke of Buckingham and son of the great Royalist, who had been tinkering with the manufacture of drinking glasses for some time, obtained the sole right to make mirrors and got a patent for 14 years. Despite being referred to by Dryden as a "chymist, fiddler, statesman and buffoon", Villiers established

---

17th-CENTURY CHINOISERIE

From the 1520s considerable amounts of Ming porcelain were shipped into England. The designs on these items – from costumed figures to pagodas, plants, and animals – were all Europeans knew of Oriental life and so when they tried to imitate the style they copied the image rather than the reality. This practice worked reasonably well on pottery, and became an amateur as well as professional activity in the *faux-lacquer* decoration of furniture. But in silver it had a short and limited production, hence its current rarity. English 17th-century silver in the Chinoiserie taste is in one style only and is typified in the Monteith shown below. The decoration is created by chasing, i.e. the design is visible on the reverse without altering the profile. The popularity of cloth from India and China continued to grow and by the early 1660s European dignitaries were sending their own patterns to be printed or woven into the material. The obsession for Chinoiserie waned around 1700, apart from tea drinking, and it was only lacquer, or japan, that spanned the gap between the first Chinoserie period and the next, which began in the 1720s. Despite a lack of authentic materials lacquer was the one medium that Europeans were able to imitate – in England thanks to the publication of *A Treatise on Japanning and Varnishing* by John Stalker and George Parker in 1688 (*see* p.44).

▲ **31 Silver montieth, English, 1684.** This exemplifies the lightly chased Chinoiserie decoration that appeared for about ten years after 1678. The scenes are simplistically drawn and show a close resemblance to those on Chinese porcelain imported at the time. The shaped rim was to hold the stems of wine glasses while cooling or rinsing the bowls.

▶ **32 Porcelain jar mounted as a tankard, Chinese and English, early 1600s.** At this period Chinese porcelain was so highly valued that enriching it with silver or gilt mounts was money well spent. However, the thin-cast handle with bead edge and the scalloped borders to collar and foot are distinctly English and relate back to Elizabethan style.

▲ **33 Walnut lowboy (dressing table), Dutch, c.1720**. The open base with cabriole legs and no stretchers was a form that appeared during the early 18th century and, with minor regional differences, remained popular throughout Europe and America until the 1770s. The cabriole here is more exaggerated than it would be on an English example.

◄ **34 Burr walnut and tiger-maple veneered chest-on-stand (highboy), American, c.1700–25**, from Boston or North Shore, Massachusetts. The essential form is that of an English piece made prior to 1700, but the cornice over the concealed top drawer is moderated, and the two tiers of drawers to the base are not traditionally English.

his glassworks at Vauxhall, London and so started the most prestigious mirror production, any genuine example of which has remained highly prized ever since.

Plate glass for mirrors was first made by blowing molten glass into a bubble, extending it, and cutting off each end to form a tube. This was sliced lengthways, opened up, and rolled flat. Even with immense skill in the blowing and painstaking effort in grinding and polishing, it was extremely difficult to achieve a flat and regular surface. Towards the end of the 17th century French glassmakers developed a means of pouring molten glass onto a framed metal slab, allowing greater evenness. Curiously the English never really took to this "casting" of glass until late in 1773 when the British Cast Plate-Glass Company was formed.

There is no doubt that the greatest innovation in mirror-making came during the last 20 years of the 17th century, when the new techniques employed by the French permitted the construction of the Galerie des Glaces at Versailles, completed by Le Brun for Louis XIV in 1682.

The term "silvering" is a misnomer when describing mirrors made before the 1840s, for until then the reflective surface was created by applying an amalgam of tin and mercury. Approaching the middle of the 19th century the German chemist J. von Liebig discovered a way of applying a layer of silver to glass with the aid of chemicals, but the ravages of time and atmosphere have proved the superiority of the former method. It is certainly not advisable to restore an 18th-century or earlier mirror plate that may have some discoloration – it is costly and will diminish its value; far better to buy a modern, lightweight replacement and carefully store the original for future generations.

Cutlery
Another change in lifestyle came in the 1660s with the introduction of a full set of eating implements laid out on the table prior to the meal. Until then only spoons and knives were commonly used and these belonged to the individual rather than the household, hence the

popularity and often luxurious decoration of sets of travelling utensils (*see* Pl. 26).

At first two-pronged forks were used, but by the beginning of the 18th century a third prong, or tine, was introduced, and the fourth prong was established by 1800. While knives and forks led to the supremacy of the Sheffield cutlery industry, the spoon now holds most interest for the collector. From its earliest natural form of scallop, or other shell, to carved and whittled wood, and from pewter stirrer to gilded presentation piece, the spoon's shape and material give us access to its history and mirror once again the developing society.

As any item becomes desirable to a collector, so fakes and copies are produced, but usually with a giveaway that is obvious to someone who studies their subject. While tea and silver were around in 1700 there was no caddy spoon. The faker making a "Queen Anne Caddy Spoon" is thus foiled because finely chopped tea was not served until the 1740s, the time of George II. Prior to that the tea was of larger leaf form – Lady Walpole is depicted in a family

▲ **35 Beech open armchair (*fauteuil à la reine*), French,** by Jean Boucault (1705–86). An example of the Louis XV furniture with original curvilinear lines that so influenced the English and their cabinet-makers from the 1720s to the 1770s. It was also the basis for much Victorian furniture, so beware, although sadly the later versions did not adopt these huge cushions.

▶ **36 Interior of Queluz National Palace, Portugal, first half 1700s.** This is the Queen's dressing room, decorated in the Baroque style that rejected the disciplines of ancient Classicism. For the first time, sculptors, furniture-makers, goldsmiths, and ceramicists joined forces to create an illusionistic environment that was an unabashed display of wealth.

▲ **37 The four major French leg shapes used in furniture in the 18th century.** From left to right they are: Louis XIV (1660–1710); Regence (1710–30); Louis XV (1730–74); and Louis XVI (1774–92), including *Directoire* through the 1790s.

▲ **38 Carved and gilt wood side table, English, c.1716.** French influence is apparent in the legs; the general architectural form was the foundation of the Palladian revival to come. The crest and cipher are all-important as they tell us the table was made for Baron Cobham before he was a Viscount by the number of pearls on the coronet – four for a baron, five for an earl.

▲ **39 Drawing showing interior of Samuel Pepys' Library, London, c.1693**. The glazed-door bookcases on the right and left are among 12 that Pepys had made between 1666 and 1703. They follow the style of the period with wide overhanging cornices and were among the first such cabinets to be glazed.

FURNITURE AND FASHION

From the 1650s to the 1850s fashion was closely related to furniture styles, particularly chairs. Take, for example, the "farthingale" chair of the 1670s (*see* Pl. 24, ch.1), or the caned-back daybed with high cresting rail (*see* Pl. 14), which closely follow the men's high wigs of the time. These show a strong Dutch influence. Now look at the stout, wide-seat, cabriole-leg, and broad-back 1740s model (*see* Pl. 53), where the curvilinear form shows a French influence. Here is a chair on which a man could spread himself and his several coats, looking every inch the early Georgian gentleman. Compare this with the elegant, delicate ,and very upright chair of the 1780s on which one perched rather than relaxed (*see* p.96). Here every element of the new Classical designs can be seen: the vase-shape back, the square taper legs, and the painted decoration. This clearly reflects the necessary fine composure of the sitter and the less bulky clothes. For most of the 18th century, relaxed or not, the gentry strove never to be seen in company less than elegant in posture, and part of every upper-class education was to take dancing lessons – for men as much as for women.

portrait during the 1720s as transferring the tea to the pot by means of the cover from the sugar bowl. The handle shapes of spoons can give definite evidence of a "not-before" date, as can their decoration (*see* spoon handles analysis, pp.224–5).

In Tudor and Elizabethan times it was popular for the wealthy godfather of a child to present one or more silver spoons, the most lavish having the end of the handle cast to represent one of the Apostles. Primarily made in sets of 12 or 13, these Apostle spoons have always been sought-after and were much copied in the late 19th and early 20th centuries, but unless you are looking at a deliberate and illegal fake the hallmarks will identify this late manufacture. As the early word for spoon was "spone", the godfather was referred to as the "sponesor", hence the term "sponsor".

An international flavour
From the 1680s an international theme was seen in British architecture and furnishings, identifiable by regional differences as being German, French, or another European

origin, complicated by Middle and Far Eastern motifs. After the Palladian style came Baroque, instantly recognizable but also the most complicated and difficult to define, for the term seems to describe so many things: a style, a period, a musical genre, a type of art. Baroque is one of those concepts that one must sit quietly and slowly dissect into areas in a way that suits you. In the context of this book it is not necessary to grasp the whole subject, but rather to understand its importance in the same way that your times tables put the rest of the mathematical picture into perspective, making further study easier and more enjoyable. The word Baroque is said to derive from the Spanish *barrucco*, meaning a misshapen pearl. This is more indicative of the style's embellishment of the established Classical orders of earlier disciplines than a description of asymmetry.

The Baroque style began in 17th-century Italy, where the Roman Catholic Church began to elaborate on inherited architectural and decorative tenets, breaking new ground with interrupted verticals and horizontals interspersed with countless scrolls, curves, and foliate sprays, and applying the work of the sculptor on walls, ceilings, and furniture. These human-, bird-, and animal-form mounts can be seen to represent the cherubic and emblematic figures depicted in abundance throughout the religious art of Caravaggio and Rubens, and whether in marble for fireplaces, plaster composition for walls, or ormolu (gilded bronze) for furniture, they continued to decorate the most lavish European houses for the first 50 years of the 18th century. While Italy and Germany remained divided by either secular or religious rulers, France, Spain, and England were controlled by great monarchies, and there

◄ **40 "Armorial" porcelain coffee pot, Chinese, c.1740**, with a cartouche of balanced drapes, swags, and festoons and a Rococo coat-of-arms that is typically asymmetrical. The straight taper was an alternative shape for pots during the first half of the 18th century. Usually cylindrical, hexagonal, and octagonal forms were used in metal and pottery.

▲ **41 Silver coffee pot by Simon Pantin, English, 1723.** This displays the close relationship between the Chinese potter (*see* Pl. 40) and the European silversmith, despite their very disparate origins. This straight, tapering shape was the exception to the overriding curvilinear style of the period, but it had waned by the mid-1740s.

BALUSTER

There was one basic shape that affected domestic items for most of the 18th century: the baluster. The double-curved outline of jugs, mugs, and chair backs (in the centre panel as well as outer frame, and in stems for tables and drinking glasses) started to appear during the later years of Queen Anne's reign, and by 1720 was well established. It lasted until the 1780s, when it was replaced by the Classical vase shape (*see* p.96). Among the many reasons for its popularity was that it was a perfect and pleasing shape that would take any amount of surface embellishment, whether carved in wood or stone, embossed in silver, or modelled in ceramics, but could be equally attractive plain.

43

42 Chiswick House, England. The origins of the baluster shape are in the architectural forms of the balustrade. Indeed with a little imagination it is possible to look at the outside of Chiswick House – or many a Palladian mansion, and see a row of Georgian coffee pots.

43 Walnut chairback settee, English, c.1720. The outline of the baluster is clearly visible in the two back panels, or "splats". As it is walnut-veneered and solid, the settee will be earlier than if made of mahogany and cut with pierced decoration. The dividing line between the styles is c.1735.

44 Trumpet-bowl drinking glass, English, c.1745. The baluster shape that formed the basis for so many domestic items in the first 75 years of the 18th century is here upside down, or "inverted", in the stem.

42

44

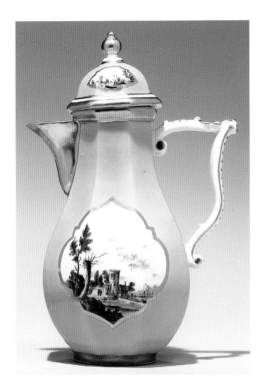

▲ **47 Watercolour painting, Dutch, c.1750**, of Venetian noblemen in a café by Jan van Grevenbroeck (1731–1807). We know the waiter is preparing chocolate because the pot he tends has an aperture in the lid for the stirring stick. The baluster shape of the pot conforms to the "look" of the early 1700s, and the fashionable flat shape of the men's hair and wigs.

is no doubt that it was the unqualified approbation of the French King, Louis XIV, that led to the international secular appeal of the Baroque movement.

Part of the magnificence of Baroque decoration was the realism of the carving, and one of its greatest exponents was Grinling Gibbons (1648–1721). Born in Holland, Gibbons was found practising his craft in a humble cottage in Deptford, England, by the eminent diarist John Evelyn, early in January 1671. Struck by the outstanding quality of Gibbons' work, Evelyn was inclined and able to introduce him to the King and other leading members of society, and through this he was drawn to the attention of the great architect Sir Christopher Wren.

In 1684 Gibbons received his first commission from Wren to contribute to the decoration of St James' Church in Piccadilly, and his further work at Windsor Castle, Hampton Court, and Kensington Palace won him royal approbation to the extent that he was made "Wood Carver to the Crown", a post he held until the reign of George I in 1714. His best-known and most-seen masterpieces are in St Paul's Cathedral, but, superlative as these are, we should not forget he was one among several brilliant contemporaries and his particular importance is his part in establishing a genre. Carved decoration in wood, stone, and marble was to remain as a statement of wealth and education right through until the 1780s.

▲ **48 Bureau cabinet, English, c.1700**, decorated throughout with red lacquer in the Chinoiserie manner. The shape of the lower part is, in effect, a baluster form – on case furniture sometimes called a "kettle" or "bombe" base. It conforms to the curvilinear fashion of the first half of the 18th century. The three rather than four drawers below an applied moulding, just beneath the angled front, are features of purely English design at this period. In contrast are the curvilinear corners, which show a Continental influence, and the feet, which represent the Chinese dragon's claw holding the sacred pearl of wisdom, are in tune with the Chinoiserie decoration.

The birth of new furniture

By the beginning of the 18th century there were many newly developed types of furniture. Some were permanently placed, others were "occasional", like the folding table, to be moved according to the time of day and the activity in progress. In the evening, card and games tables with hinged double tops, which might be placed against the wall when not in use, were brought into the room, opened, and set up for play. Informal family meals were taken without pomp or ceremony using dining or supping tables that had their tops divided into three sections; the two larger outer "leaves" were attached with hinges to fold down when not in use, and supported, when open, on swing-out frames or "gates". From the 1660s gate-leg tables of all sizes became increasingly popular. The first, naturally, were made of oak, then walnut, and, by the 1740s, mahogany, by which time the framed "gate" was replaced by a single leg that swung out from a deep and finely cut hinge. Variations on this format developed throughout Europe and Scandinavia and all continue to be made up to the present day. As reading and writing became more widespread and no longer restricted to the clergy and the wealthy, small writing desks evolved from the *scritoire* into

▲ **49 Pole screen, c.1730**, with tripod base. The legs sweeping down from a three-sided central platform, as opposed to a centre column (as in the tea table, Pl. 50) helps to date this screen. Such small tripods often had the baluster inverted, as here, and it is elongated and very finely drawn. The needlework banner, or screen, is often later or earlier than the tripod base.

► **50 Tripod tea table, USA, c.1760**. Acknowledged as one of the best examples of its type, it was made in Philadelphia by an anonymous craftsman known as the "Garvan Carver". There could scarcely be a better illustration of the features that date this table, from the bold and well-formed legs and feet to the baluster in the stem, and the top's fluid carved pie-crust border.

the bureau. The former was like a luxurious school desk, the upper part with a sloping top hinged at the front that opened forwards to provide a writing surface for the sitter, with room for the knees underneath. The supports were principled on the same framed gate as the table mentioned previously. By 1710 this valuable space was taken up by a carcase containing three or four drawers. The bureau was born at this time and remained a staple piece of household furniture thereafter. The first versions were made in two parts, the desk section being slightly smaller than the base, but by 1720 the most up-to-date examples were made as one solid piece of furniture. On the Continent the angled sloping front was less popular than what is called a "cylinder fall" – a front made of a quarter-circle lid that slides up and back into the body of the piece, giving access to the writing surface – which can be slid forward towards the sitter. On more sophisticated

► 51 The Reredos, carved by Grinling Gibbons for the Chapel of Trinity College, Oxford, c.1693. Acknowledged as one of Gibbons' finest works this is a masterpiece of English Baroque, displaying French-influenced Italian origins. His work was to affect both sacred and secular interiors for 50 years spanning the late 17th and early 18th centuries.

Famille verte included yellow, black, blue, and aubergine, while *famille rose*, which replaced it in the 1720s, was lighter – with wonderful translucent pinks and reds as well as yellows, blues, and greens.

A calmer style

From *c.*1700 to the 1730s a calmer look affected most household items in England. Chair backs were lower, and stretchers disappeared as turned legs became curved and shaped with knees and ankles, terminating in pad or claw-and-ball feet (*see* p.62). Faultless proportion rather than elaborate decoration created the impression of quality, and well-selected veneers of walnut replaced excessive carving. This was the period of the much-loved Queen Anne bureau bookcase, bachelor's chest, and cabriole-leg chair and table. It can be seen as a fashion that appealed in cost and style to the more reticent upper middle class, as well as an inevitable swing away from the excesses of the previous 30 years. But it was not to last, and by the 1730s the introduction of mahogany and newfound wealth saw the beginning of another period of exuberance.

▲ **52 Life-size wood carving, *c.*1690s,** of a gentleman's cravat in Venetian needlepoint. This masterpiece by Grinling Gibbons showed his ability outside his architectural achievements to such a degree that many believed it to be a real cravat. It represents the best of neckwear of the late 1600s but proved to be timeless, for later in the 18th century Horace Walpole wore this style.

models the rising lid activates the forward motion of the writing surface. From the 1680s rapid improvements in the manufacture of glass and cabinet-making enabled the introduction of an upper part to the bureau. This was a shallow cupboard, the two doors of which were framed and panelled with either panes of glass, solid wood (known as "blind doors"), or mirrors. Those with blind or mirror doors are known as bureau cabinets, while those with glass doors are called bureau bookcases, although they were, and still are, also popular for displaying collections of porcelain and other precious items. Until the 1740s most glazed doors had the retaining bars in a rectangular pattern.

So it is within the period covered by this chapter that most, but by no means all, of the furniture and household artifacts now taken so much for granted were brought into people's daily lives. It also covers the periods of Chinese porcelain of the K'ang-shi and Yung-cheng periods, 1662–1722 and 1723–35, during which time the palettes of predominant enamel colours we now refer to as *famille verte* and *famille rose* so enchanted the Western world.

A LITTLE ROYAL INFLUENCE

James II, William and Mary, and Queen Anne had less personal influence on invention and design than their Carolean predecessors. We refer to items as being "Queen Anne", but it was not until the 1780s, under George III, that a member of the English royal family exercised such control over taste and fashion.

However, William of Orange can be credited for popularizing the drink of hot punch, which led to the plethora of delft or porcelain punch bowls and ladles, lemon strainers, and nutmeg graters. Punch bowls are highly collectable and, as the drink has remained popular ever since, have changed little. But the ladle saw improvements that give us distinct clues to its date. The bowl is traditionally made of silver and the earliest prototypes had a silver handle. As silver conducts heat this was impractical, but it was not until the 1720s that a turned wood handle was introduced. This too had its disadvantages, for silver and wood expand and contract at different rates and wood reacts poorly to hot alcoholic liquid. The perfect answer took another 30 or so years, when it was discovered that whalebone was impervious to heat and liquid. The shape of the bowl followed fashion and this too can aid the dating process. The early form is plain and egg-shaped, but by the 1730s the rim had a wavy Rococo cut.

The names that changed design

William Chambers, who laid out Kew Gardens and designed Somerset House and was to become one of King George III's appointed architects and furniture designers, travelled to China when he was only 16 years old. He served as supercargo officer aboard an East Indiaman, unlike many young men, who took the Grand Tour. They were from all educated classes – students, teachers, artists, architects, and historians, as well as aristocrats and nobility – and were often accompanied by older tutors, or "bear-leaders" as they were called. The less well-off but talented young men were supported by groups of mentors at home, who were expecting to retrieve their outlay in the practice of the work experience gained by their protégé on his return. One man who more than satisfied this criterion was William Kent.

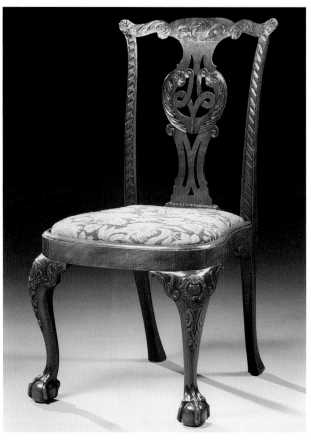

▶ **53 Mahogany side chair, English, c.1745**, with a pattern of pierced back that is often associated with Ireland at around this date. Interestingly the curved seat, legs, and feet have a distinctly 1730s feel to them. This was a chair made specifically to be part-latest fashion, part-traditional.

▼ **54 Walnut-veneered card table, English, c.1735–40**, with rounded ends ("turret-tops") that, when open, carry a pair of candlesticks. The four cabriole legs carved at the knee indicate luxury, as does the concertina action – a folding frieze frame that supports the table when in use.

▶ **55 Box-top tea table, English, c.1735**. These tables sometimes had a triple top (one for games, the other for tea – the deep frieze concealing a compartment to hold items for either pastime). The earliest type has the veneer to the frieze applied vertically; this changed to horizontal after c.1715.

Born in 1686 the son of a coach painter, William Kent became one of the most famous exponents of the Palladian revival, a form of architecture that dominated grand houses and civic buildings from the 1720s to the 1770s. After spending the best part of ten years in Italy studying the noble orders and befriending Richard Boyle, third Earl of Burlington and "the Apollo of the Arts", William Kent returned to England with an educated talent that was to see him influence landscape gardening and interior furnishings from carpets to wallpaper – as well as the face of the English stately home. His designs for furniture were lavish, building on the rather austere Queen Anne restraint with his own exaggerated curves and carvings of cornucopia, fruit and flowers, fish scales, vitruvian scrolls, grotesque masks, and shells – much of which was picked out from the background walnut with burnished gold leaf, known as part, or "parcel", gilding. Alternatively, whole pieces were painted to represent masonry, again sometimes with gilded highlights. Thankfully we can still enjoy the excesses of this great interior decorator in some of the rooms he created, especially at Holkham and Houghton Halls in Norfolk, where he worked in collaboration with Lord Burlington (*see* Pl. 1, ch.3). Holkham Hall still retains some of the original flock wallpaper imported from France, a development almost forced on to society as a counter to the huge popularity of paper panels imported from China for walls and screens.

Another name synonymous with this period, and an architect in a different way, was that of Robert Walpole. Had it not been for his judicious handling of England's economy after the South Sea Bubble debacle (the first great stock-market crash of 1720), and his establishment of a balance-of-trade account, much of the money made and poured into the building and furnishing of great houses would not have been in the hands of the British elite. As first Lord of the Treasury and Chancellor of the Exchequer, Walpole removed export duties on goods made in the UK, for which there was a demand abroad, and he removed import duties on goods that were needed in manufacture, such as raw silk, dyes, and flax. He also introduced bonded warehouses, giving incentives to traders to import consumer goods by only levying duty when the goods were sold.

The importation craze

At this time London had the greatest concentration of shipping in the world (with the possible exception of Amsterdam), in the Pool of London and the stretch of the Thames River between Deptford and Limehouse. There were as yet no real docks, and the ships from Western Europe, the Mediterranean, the Far East, Africa, the Spice Islands, India, and America discharged their cargoes into small boats called "lighters", which took them to the wharves for customs examination.

▲ **56 Lock and key, German, 17th century.** Every lock must have its key, and only one made with the finest-quality steel and to the highest possible point of accuracy can match those made by the German craftsmen in the 1600s.

▶ **57 Strongbox, German, 17th century**, showing the complexity and ingenuity of German locksmiths. Long established as masters of fine metalwares and intricate mechanisms, German craftsmen were acknowledged as makers of the very best locks in Europe.

DANIEL MAROT

Daniel Marot (1661–1752), the French-born designer and architect who worked for William of Orange in Holland and then England, was the first "interior designer", as we would call him today – well ahead of William Kent in the 1720s and the Adam brothers in the second half of the 18th century. Given a free rein, he would supply rooms complete in every detail, but he is probably best recognized in England for his corner fireplaces, over which receding shelves allowed a display of porcelain or silver (*see* Burghley House Pl. 29). The chair shown below is in the Marot style, *c.* 1690, and has a typically tall back, finely pierced and carved with a curved stretcher below. Despite the numerous scrolls and foliate motifs, it retains a severity that is lightened by the deep and scalloped fringe to the upholstery.

▲ **58 Diagram of Newcomen's steam engine for** *Universal Magazine*, **English, 1747**, described as "the engine to raise water by fire". Optimistic as he was, it is doubtful that Newcomen could foresee the impact this concept of controlled power would have on every branch of industry and manufacture in the near future.

Agents for the nobility anxiously waited for crates of the latest porcelain, furniture, works of art, and *objets du vertu* to be unpacked. These would have been selected by their masters while on the Grand Tour or ordered unseen from the Orient. Alongside them would be merchants eager to procure raw materials to be transported to various parts of the country for manufacture, as the specialized production of household goods was beginning to be localized. Staffordshire for pottery, Sheffield for cutlery, Birmingham for hardware, and East Anglia and the West Country for cloth were areas that were expanding rapidly. The products of cottage industry, such as lace, cotton, hosiery, and leather goods, generally reached the public through a retailer, whether he was a craftsman with a shop or simply an agent. But machinery was beginning to take its place in processing and manufacture.

To aid the deep mining of coal, Thomas Newcomen devised a pump in 1712, which helped to prevent flooding,

and the principles of his device were far-reaching. In 1734 John Lombe smuggled out of Italy a machine for making silk material, which had been a secret closely guarded by the Italians until that time. With it Lombe's brother, Thomas, set up a silk mill on an island in the Derwent River at Derby, and so created a prime example of a factory – a new type of industrial organization.

There were two other subjects that were immensely popular imports but were never successfully made outside their native Italy. One was the Nubian figure, also called a Blackamoor, made from carved wood that was ebonized, painted with bright translucent and solid colours, and burnished gold leaf. These represented a glamorous and highly decorative allusion to the slave trade, which was very much part of life and the economy in Western Europe at the beginning of the 18th century. Indeed, it was fashionable for a grand household to have at least one African servant. Usually slightly less than lifesize, carved

▲ **59** *The Mill*, **French, 1751**, oil on canvas by François Boucher. For centuries society had relied on wind and water for natural controlled power, but throughout the 1700s such advances were made with steam that even the smallest workshops benefited, and people were literally "moved" by the power of steam.

Nubian figures could be torsos, head and shoulders, or full figures, swathed in simulated rich cloth robes and turbans. The full standing figures were formed as bearers of a small tray to hold a light or an ornament and were given pride of place in entrance halls or wall niches. The earliest and finest were made in Venice, and the leading exponent was Andrea Brustolon, whose workshops were operating after the mid-1680s. These figures became extremely popular once again in the 19th century, and there are many varieties from the Victorian period available today. However, most of these are inferior to the originals and can be identified by the poor quality of the carving and the lacklustre decoration.

The other subject was the art of marble cutting and inlaying to create pictures in *pietra dura* (hard stone). The striations of the marble were assessed and, when properly cut and skilfully positioned, created the illusion of perspective and three dimensions (*see* Pl. 61). Sometimes semi-precious stones such as jasper and agate were added, carved as fruit and flowers and applied in relief to heighten the three-dimensional effect. *Pietra dura* panels were often grouped to form the major decoration on the front of magnificent cabinets, which themselves had become the vehicle to display the art of the marble worker. The earliest and finest examples were made in Florence in the workshops of Baccio Capelli at around the same time as Brustolon in Venice. Like the Nubian figures, *pietra dura* has never really lost its appeal, so Victorian and even present-day examples still abound.

Period developments in pictures

In the year 1739 the widow of Charles Bridgeman published her late husband's volume *Views of Stowe*, the gardens of which he planned, planted, and saw to considerable fruition. Bridgeman was the Royal Gardener to George II and, although less well known than Capability Brown, Humphrey Repton, or William Kent, he was a pioneer of the English landscape park. It would be nice to think that he might have had a hand in the delightful view through the window in the family group illustrated opposite. This was painted in 1741 by William Verelst, and shows two members of the Gough family. Certainly the view is of a mature landscape, so the timing is right, but it is unlikely to be the work of Bridgeman as he scarcely left his royal patronage.

The interior setting for the Gough family painting has many clues as to the origins of the items in use. The ladies are no longer bewigged, their caps are much flatter and closer to the head, and the dresses, of the most beautiful silk, are plainer than those of earlier years. The central tea table has a column turned in a plain tapering cylinder known as a "gun barrel" stem and bears a Chinese *famille rose* porcelain tea service on a tray. Behind this is a tea-caddy box containing three silver caddies of a type most popular between *c.*1730 and the 1760s. Most illustrative

of the period is the tea kettle on its salver and tripod kettle stand. The shape of the body of the kettle is a slightly squashed ball, plain except for the engraved coat-of-arms, but its open-frame base, containing the heater lamp, and its upper handle are a mass of scrolls, one leading into another intermittently broken by short straight sections. This shows an early adherence to the transition between Baroque and Rococo designs, as the straight sections had disappeared by the 1750s. A similar pattern can be seen on the border of the salver, which was very typical of the 1730s to mid-'40s. The little tripod stand is a gem, so rare to find today, not surprising when one considers the disproportionate weight it is carrying. This model was new to the early 18th century, and as the family is so evidently fashion-conscious and wealthy this one would have most likely been made of Virginia walnut or mahogany. Note its baluster stem, which in this case is inverted.

When a picture has no signature and date it is the items depicted in it, the style of the scene, and the fashion of the dress that will help in establishing its date. Given a signed and dated picture, the reverse happens, as we then know without doubt the period at which certain items appeared in daily use. There have been instances in the past 50 years when an item has been shown in a painting several years before its first mention in written records, and accepted history has had to be adjusted and our knowledge improved. This particular portrait reveals much about the period.

◀ 60 Detail from *Sir Henry Gough and his Family*, English, 1741, oil on canvas by William Verelst. Mother and daughter both wear the fashionable closer-fitting hairstyle beneath a little cap, and take tea from a kettle on a stand and tripod table with plain tapering stem, all pointing to the 1740s.

▲ 61 *Pietra dura* panel, Italian, late 17th century. The marble is cut to reveal striations that can be placed so as to create a 3-D effect. This highly skilled technique was perfected in Italy during the late 17th century and is still used today, on single panels such as this, or on vast and lavish cabinets.

A WORLD
OF ANTIQUES

1740–1785

Compared to the peaceful landscape of the 16th century, Europe was by now abuzz with activity, invention, and development. In England alone harnessing the power of steam and the creation of the canal system revolutionized manufacturing and transportation. Discoveries in Italy changed the shape of domestic items and new scientific instruments opened the oceans to ships and the heavens to enquiring eyes.

◀ **1 Holkham Hall, Norfolk, England,** built between 1734 and c.1760 for Thomas Coke, Earl of Leicester. In collaboration with Lord Burlington and William Kent, Coke created one of the great Palladian Houses of England. Here, in the Saloon, the crimson velvet wall covering is original, as are the Sicilian marble chimney pieces.

An endless round of dining, dancing, balls, parties, gambling, and horseracing occupied the time of the elite, whose numbers were swelling daily in the prosperity of the mid-18th century. Many from humble backgrounds were elevated to acceptability as artisans, artists, architects, businessmen, bankers, physicians, and scientists, and thus became rich. The importance of their contributions to a better life for all were recognized by the established gentry and aristocracy.

Any hint of restraint had disappeared by this time, as a position in society demanded a suitable display in what people wore, where they wore it, whom they were with, and how they entertained. Expensive imported cloth was used lavishly on men and women's clothing, wall-coverings, and curtains while, conversely, English knotted carpets from Axminster, Kidderminster, and Wilton cost more than imported Oriental ones. A woman' s skirt was enlarged to 1.8m (6ft) round the hem, a man's cuffs turned back as far as his elbows, and full-length curtains were now being drawn together from the sides rather than pulled up to the top of the window in festoons.

Although transport and carriageways were improving, easier journeying from the country estate to London, or the obligatory stay in a spa town, was achieved only in the summer months, so a London house for winter was an absolute must. Here there were numerous leaders of fashion, advising on what furnishings to hire for the season, the "in" shops to frequent, and the very latest in this or that, whereas in provincial cities it was usually down to one character. In the early 18th century Richard

"Beau" Nash (1674–1762) was the prime example of such a person. In 1705 he went to Bath and became "Master of Ceremonies", organizing events throughout the summer. He opposed duelling and smoking, and generally instructed would-be polite society on how to behave. Under his strict regime of etiquette Bath became the most fashionable spa town in England, a position it continued to hold for many generations after Nash's death.

I wonder if Beau Nash ever imagined that his achieving in Bath a "general society among people of rank or fortune" (Oliver Goldsmith on Nash) would change forever the social mores and tenets in England to such an extent as to influence daily life across the classes and thereby change the fashion and style of the household items we use every day. He, or circumstance, certainly took advantage of what Oliver Goldsmith described as a "general increase in society" to break down the barriers between the nobility and gentry.

The traditional aloofness of the ruling minority, considered the natural order of things until the end of the 17th century, began to collapse. This was given impetus by

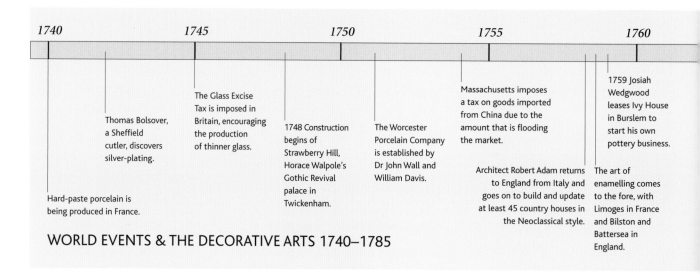

1740	1745	1750	1755	1760

The Glass Excise Tax is imposed in Britain, encouraging the production of thinner glass.

Thomas Bolsover, a Sheffield cutler, discovers silver-plating.

1748 Construction begins of Strawberry Hill, Horace Walpole's Gothic Revival palace in Twickenham.

The Worcester Porcelain Company is established by Dr John Wall and William Davis.

Massachusetts imposes a tax on goods imported from China due to the amount that is flooding the market.

1759 Josiah Wedgwood leases Ivy House in Burslem to start his own pottery business.

Hard-paste porcelain is being produced in France.

Architect Robert Adam returns to England from Italy and goes on to build and update at least 45 country houses in the Neoclassical style.

The art of enamelling comes to the fore, with Limoges in France and Bilston and Battersea in England.

WORLD EVENTS & THE DECORATIVE ARTS 1740–1785

◄ **2 Oil painting on canvas, English, 1742**, by Allan Ramsay. The subjects are Thomas, second Baron Mansel of Margam, and his half-brothers and sister. The informality of the composition, and the warm expressions between the sitters and out to the artist reflect the newly relaxed atmosphere in fashionable society at that time.

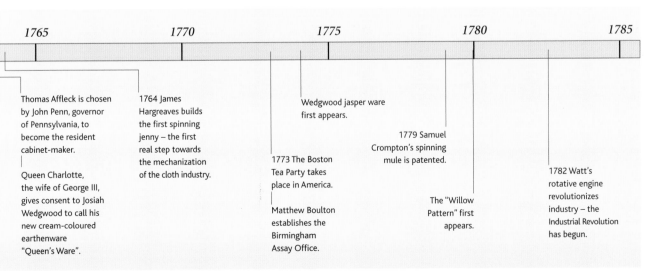

1765   1770   1775   1780   1785

Thomas Affleck is chosen by John Penn, governor of Pennsylvania, to become the resident cabinet-maker.

Queen Charlotte, the wife of George III, gives consent to Josiah Wedgwood to call his new cream-coloured earthenware "Queen's Ware".

1764 James Hargreaves builds the first spinning jenny – the first real step towards the mechanization of the cloth industry.

1773 The Boston Tea Party takes place in America.

Matthew Boulton establishes the Birmingham Assay Office.

Wedgwood jasper ware first appears.

1779 Samuel Crompton's spinning mule is patented.

The "Willow Pattern" first appears.

1782 Watt's rotative engine revolutionizes industry – the Industrial Revolution has begun.

▲ 3 Drawing for the Wilton House Pavilion by Sir William Chambers, English, *c.*1750. The Palladian style that reigned supreme in British architecture throughout the middle 50 years of the 18th century is exemplified in this drawing. Its influence on cabinet and library furniture is also very clear – a good example of which is shown opposite in Pl. 4.

◄ **4 Mahogany china-cabinet, English, c.1745.** Important cabinet and library furniture from the middle 50 years of the 18th century was usually architectural in style, varying in degrees of accuracy according to its cost. The expense of this particular piece is evident: as confirmation the Rococo-style foliate sprays on the spandrels and stiles are an added luxury.

► **5 An ormolu furniture-mount, English, c.1760,** showing how international Rococo decoration could add life and lustre to the severe lines of an English chest-of-drawers. At this period the best ormolu (gilded bronze) was acknowledged as coming from France, with its elements of delicacy and femininity.

also the drum and the rout, both musical entertainments, and the *ridotto* and the *ridotto al fresco*. These were a combination of music and concerts, and the rout, a particularly hectic mixed-media event, gave its name to the wooden-seated hall chairs (known as rout seats or rout stools) used by exhausted dancers to recover in the coolness of the hall despite their lack of comfort. Many rout seats have their seats dimpled from the studs of boots being put on/taken off on their surface. However, the most important innovation was the assembly. This involved several activities being conducted at the same time: conversation, music, card-playing, tea drinking, and so on. At the beginning of the century an assembly was commonly held in one or two rooms. However, it quickly became a vehicle for mass entertainment, involving many rooms in a house or, more importantly, a gathering in a public place ideally suited for the purpose such as the Vauxhall or Ranelagh Gardens for outdoors, or a civic building for indoors.

European hard-paste porcelain

In Germany Johann Friedrich Bottger, an alchemist, discovered a means of making hard-paste porcelain good enough to compete with that of China and Japan. By 1719 a factory was established at Meissen near Dresden, which made very beautiful vases and tea services decorated in polychrome enamels and fine gilding. By the 1730s Meissen was producing figure groups of people and animals on scrolling bases that reflected the latest Rococo style (*see* pp.74–5). In France a factory producing a

Nash's code of conduct, which appealed to the aspiring. It was no longer unthinkable that an impoverished lord might let his daughter marry a wealthy upstart banker or merchant. But, however well intentioned and theoretically preferable this was, a lowering of high standards was inevitable. So by the 1740s the buds of informality started to shoot and artifacts that fitted a more relaxed atmosphere were invented and brought into daily use. This was particularly true in the service of food and refreshment (*see* box, p.88), as entertainment grew in variety. As well as formal and family mealtimes, there was the ball, a term that could denote a dance with as few as a dozen couples early in the century, but which became a huge affair. Then there was the option of the masquerade, doubtless an import from Venice, where guests wore masks at least for the first part of the evening. There was

similar-looking soft-paste porcelain was established at Vincennes in 1740, moving to Sèvres in 1756. Here they made vases and plates and the famous biscuit (unglazed) figures. English factories were still in their infancy with regards to technique, but by 1745 the Chelsea works were established (closed in 1769), followed by Bow (1746–76), Derby *c.*1750, and Worcester in 1751.

From Baroque to Rococo

Little of the luxurious Baroque style affected anyone outside the most wealthy and grandest of people, but out of it came the lighter yet even more fanciful Rococo. The term is a word based on the French *rocaille*, indicating the inclusion of simulated rockwork and inorganic matter, but also shells of every variety, seaweed, waterfalls, flower sprays, "C" and

"S" scrolls, and, to my mind the most beautiful and hardest to recreate, the raffle scroll (*see* Pl. 8).

The Rococo style was, without doubt, a direct import from France, with Pierre Lepautre, Claude Audran, Nicholas Pineau, and J.A. Meissonier among its leading exponents. The main feature was its total asymmetry, with one scroll leading into or abutting the next, leading the eye continuously along and around the design. The style remained fashionable from *c.*1715 until the 1760s, with some decorative features still to be seen in the late 1770s. Rococo took European high society by storm, and the light-hearted style was used for exotic shapes for silver cups and jugs, chair backs, picture and mirror frames, tradesmen's cards and labels, the finely modelled bases for pottery, and porcelain figures. It was also found on the

▲ **6 Open-arm chair, English, c.1760.** The general appearance of this chair is one of total deference to Rococo decoration. It displays admirably the identifiable look and style of the period, especially when compared and likened to the motifs on the tradesman's card in Pl. 7.

▲ **7 Business card of Benjamin Cartwright, English, c.1755,** with a frame, or cartouche, that epitomizes the overall influence across a range of items of Rococo design in the mid-18th century. The illustrations of the teapot, tankard, and clock within the frame also provide important confirmation of what domestic items looked like at this time.

surrounds, or *cartouches*, of coats-of-arms – especially important in establishing whether or not such engraving on a piece of silver is original, as the fashionable cartouche shape was dramatically different before and after the Rococo period (see pp.136–7).

The widespread appeal of the Rococo style stemmed from the fact that just one small element of it could be applied to the plainest item and thus lift it into fashionable status – a "C" scroll bracket on a plain table, an acanthus leaf on the handle of a simple jug, or a raffle scroll on a clock face can gladden the heart of a collector scouring a boot sale today. It was this use of adornment that enabled the period from the mid-1720s to the 1770s to have an instantly recognizable "look". It could be incorporated into the formality of Classical architecture (*see* Pl. 3), the Gothic taste (*see* Pl. 9), Chinoiserie (*see* Pl. 10), or a chaotic blend of all three – such as is shown in the side chair in Plate 15.

By the 1740s it had become common practice to send English items and designs to China to be decorated or copied. The results were often charming cross-breeds, among which some of my personal favourites are pieces of Chinese porcelain made to European shapes and bearing European decoration yet retaining a certain indeterminable quality that makes them unmistakably Oriental. Take, for example, the central dish in Plate 19, and compare it with the Continental silver dish of the same date below it. Both have that continuous scrolling edge, with one curve leading into the next. You will notice there are no intersecting straight lines as there would have been 30 years earlier, and which are so clearly visible in the tea kettle and salver in the Gough family portrait on page 66. The dish on page 81 is *famille rose* porcelain at its prettiest, *c*.1750 and made in what we refer to as a "silver" shape. Similar decoration on dishes of a perfect plain oval shape appeared after the 1780s.

American furniture

On page 80 a mid-18th-century Continental walnut two-door cupboard (Pl. 16) is shown in contrast to an American highboy of a similar period. The total unrestrained carving of the former is clear to see and shows the European pleasure in interpreting the Rococo designs. It is in fact more fun than its English equivalent, and I have yet to see a good-quality piece of Continental furniture, silver, or, porcelain that doesn't raise a smile, and so it should. It would seem, therefore, that Britain

▲ **8 Etching of a raffle leaf, French, *c*.1750**, one of the most popular and pleasing motifs in the Rococo repertoire, and among the earliest to emerge. Each lobe is called a raffle, and, easy as it may look, the motif is particularly difficult to draw. As such, it was a standard test of artistic ability.

▼ **9 Design for a chimney piece, English, 1754**, drawn by cabinet-maker John Linnell (1729–96). It shows the emerging element of Gothic taste in the central feature above the fireplace; the asymmetrical placement of objects is countered by the balance of the crocketed arches and foliate spire.

▲ **10 Four-poster bed, English, c.1755**, displaying mid-18th-century Chinoiserie at its height. It is a totally western piece of furniture presented in a Chinese manner: it has a pagoda top with mythical winged creatures at each terminal, and a headboard made of Chinese-type fence patterns, decorated throughout with red and black lacquer.

18th-CENTURY CHINOISERIE

The 18th-century Chinoiserie (at its peak 1730–70) was more than just a fashion – it was an invasion. Italy, France, Germany, Britain, Spain, and the Scandinavian countries were all prey to the onslaught of westernized Oriental emblems, printed on cloth, painted on walls, enamelled on porcelain, and carved over doors, in alcoves, and on furniture. Herein lies the essential difference between this Chinoiserie and its predecessor; rather than import and copy the authentic article, Western objects were decorated in the Oriental manner. There was no Chinese or Japanese prototype for the bed illustrated on page 76 or the carved panel at Claydon House, Buckinghamshire, shown here, but the sheer exuberance of the decoration caught the mood of the time, especially when interwoven with the Rococo style. The widespread attraction was that even a little Chinese calligraphy on a tea caddy, or a corner bracket formed as a piece of Chinese fencing on a chair (p.79), could elevate the most humble object to being *à la mode*, and give the owner the status of a person of taste.

passed on some of its reticence to the New World cabinet-makers. But look again at the highboy. That outrageous swan-neck cornice, the solid block of drawers, and then those absolutely perfect legs – certainly it has ten times more character than its English counterpart (*see* pp.228–9).

By the 1740s American furniture had taken on an individuality, not just as opposed to English or European, but an individuality to a city, town, or even a certain maker. It embodied sobriety and vitality, practicality, quality, and good looks. It had to fit houses less palatial than the European originals and is therefore, if one can generalize, smaller in drawer size and seat width. This vast continent had to be conquered by the plough and so as yet a display of ornate and fanciful carving in the Baroque manner was not in keeping with most working men's lifestyles. The birthplace or family background of a silversmith or cabinet-maker gave him or her the natural style for their work, be it German, Dutch, Swedish, Spanish, Italian, or French, but England was the chief source for the main elements of quality manufacture in America, although these too saw increasing variations as time went on. The Dutch forms, which had so transformed English furniture in the Queen Anne period, remained firmly embodied in America long after Queen Anne died in 1714. Hence so much of the furniture made in America

▲ **11 Lower section of a mahogany bedpost, English, c.1755.** An example of the ultimate carved bedpost in the Rococo manner. Here, the base column, with its lion mask-head below a lambrequin frieze, supports a perfect baluster shape, decorated with gently spiralling panels of guilloche ornament and raffle leaves.

▲ **12 Upper section of a mahogany bedpost, English, c.1755.** The post tapers to the top and is carved to represent foliage and berries, wrapped around with ribbon, before bursting out with a spray of stylized and naturalistic scrolls, leaves, and feathers. The rails of the tester bed are carved wood covered with crimson velvet.

► **13 The Strawberry Room at the Victoria and Albert Museum, London, c.1783–94.** This High-Gothic-revival interior was designed by James Wyatt for Thomas Barrett's home, Lee Priory in Kent. Barrett's close friend was Horace Walpole and his house, Strawberry Hill at Twickenham, was obviously the inspiration for both name and style. Most elements of early ecclesiastical architecture are combined in the mirrored end-panel, ceiling, and fireplace.

◄ **14 Carved chair-back, English, c.1765**, showing a combination of Gothic and Rococo in the pointed arch and segmented circular framework with raffle leaf sprays at the junctions. These details indicate mid-18th-century design, confirmed by the proportions, which are larger than those of 19th-century revival pieces.

▼ **15 Mahogany side chair, English, c.1765**. The ultimate combination of Chinoiserie, Gothic, and Rococo designs are seen, respectively, in the pierced central back-panel, the ecclesiastical cluster-column legs, and the outswept top back rail terminating in foliate carved ends. Any one of these details will indicate this style period, or a copy of it.

before the Federal Period is referred to as Queen Anne, and furniture made after the 1750s is referred to as "Chippendale". American Chippendale is, to date, the best description of a style that showed the transition from Dutch-influenced to French-inspired in the New World, succeeding the historically inaccurate "Queen Anne" and lasting from the 1750s to the 1780s. In general it was far more restrained in decoration than the drawings of designs by Thomas Chippendale in his *Gentleman and Cabinet Maker's Director*, which was published in Britain in 1754.

This suggests that, in fact, American furniture remained, during this period, very particular to any given area. Generally, curved "cabriole" legs terminated in club, pad, or slipper feet. They were sometimes joined with stretchers, as were the later straight taper legs. Chairs had fanciful scrolling backs or stick-backs, and there were plenty of practical desks, tables, and cabinets. The latter rarely had glass doors, being fitted instead with attractive solid or "blind panels". The Rococo style did arrive in America with Chippendale's *Director*. Its main influence was on chair backs, where the cupid's-bow top rails replaced gentle curves. Splats pierced with modest ribbons, raffle scrolls, or a subtle element of Chinoiserie or Gothic motif appeared. The cabriole legs became bolder, the knees were carved, and the legs often terminated in claw-and-ball feet.

Many pieces developed that were unique to America – the Rhode Island block-front secretary, the Philadelphia "Chippendale" highboy, and the Duncan Phyfe sofa table among them. Thankfully, the lifelong high regard in which they have been held has meant that careful note has been kept of their provenance, which adds enormously to their historic and monetary value, and makes some priceless.

The earliest-known American furniture-maker was Nicholas Disbrowe (1612/13–83), who was born in Walden, Essex, England and to whom the so-called Hadley chests are attributed. John Goddard (1723/4–85), who has been credited with creating the block-front and shell-carved cabinet pieces that today are so much associated in our minds with American furniture, was an eminent maker and influential citizen in Newport, America, where he married the daughter of his master Job Townsend.

Just as the great *ébénistes* (cabinet-makers specializing in veneering) of France and the fashionable cabinet-makers of England rose in the ranks of society, so did selected makers of silver and furniture in America. In 1763 Thomas Affleck from Aberdeen, Scotland was chosen by the commissioned governor of Pennsylvania, John Penn, to join him and become the resident cabinet-maker in Philadelphia. By the time he died in 1795, Affleck counted among his patrons and friends such luminaries as Benjamin Franklin.

▲ **16 Walnut side cabinet, French, c.1755**. Although provincial in form, this cabinet is lifted into a more desirable category by the fine and free style of the carved decoration. The asymmetrical panels are flanked by the traditional type of elongated pin hinges, and centred by extended pierced escutcheons.

◀ **17 Bonnet-top highchest, American, c.1760**, which is relatively plain by European standards of the time. However, American highchests had tremendous character in outline and proportion, giving them the look of a sturdy citizen of the middle years of the 18th century. Construction, timber, and any decorative details allow accurate provenance and dating.

◄ **18 Base of a silver entrée dish, English, c.1767**, illustrating the degree to which Chinese potters copied the designs of European silversmiths, as displayed in the dish in Pl. 19. With the benefit of the hallmarks on English silver we can more accurately date the Oriental products as well.

▲ **19 Large porcelain dish in European "silver shape", Chinese, c.1765.** A precise replication of contemporary silver, thus enabling accurate dating. This dating is also aided by the coat-of-arms, or crest, that was popularly applied, as in this case, giving such pieces the name "armorial" porcelain.

The high value of pieces by known makers naturally arouses the interest and speculation of anybody when presented with a piece they think might be American, either by the nature of its design or by its construction. However, simpler forms of Irish furniture often have much in common with contemporaneous American. This isn't surprising when one considers the fact that the cosmopolitan population of Charles Town (named Charleston after the Revolution), which was the most flourishing area south of Philadelphia, contained a great number of Irish people among its English, Dutch, and French Huguenots.

So how can you be sure that a piece is indeed American? The most satisfactory method is by analysing the timber, remembering that while American makers had mahogany, as did everyone else, they were the only ones that had the huge variety of woods for secondary construction available to them. There are too many of these to list here but maple, cedar, pine, and cypress all have several varieties that made wonderful drawer linings and carcases, and it is the definitive identification of a timber peculiar to America that can make a piece valuable.

The Gothic revival

The term Gothic was used in the 18th century to describe the various forms of ecclesiastical architecture that flourished in Europe from the mid-12th to the end of the 15th century. It emanated in France, where the cathedral of Notre Dame epitomizes the genre. In England the different styles within that period have been grouped together chronologically as follows: Early English (c.1200–c.1300), for example Lincoln Cathedral; Decorated (c.1300–c.1370), as in Exeter Cathedral; and Perpendicular (c.1370–c.1540), as found in Winchester Cathedral.

▲ **20 "Queen's ware" cup-and-saucer, English, *c*.1768**, with Rococo-style decoration in the form of shell-shaped borders, which would start to disappear in the 1770s. In 1763 Wedgwood was allowed to name his cream-coloured earthenware "Queensware", so beginning a long relationship with the royal family.

Pointed arches, flying (open) buttresses, crocketed (a bauble-like embellishment) spires, and a general impression of vast height were mixed and attached to furniture and other objects from the 1730s until the age of Classicism in the 1780s, and again from the early 1800s and throughout the Victorian era of religious zeal, fading in the 1880s. The Gothic revival movement gained popularity in the early 18th century with the formation of the London Society of Antiquaries but there was little actual physical representation until the most important extant example, Strawberry Hill – Horace Walpole's fabulous palace at Twickenham – began to be constructed in 1748 (it was completed in 1777).

To find a piece of 18th-century furniture (for example a mirror or a clock case) or an item of porcelain or silver totally formed and decorated in the Gothic manner is extremely rare, but, in a similar way to the Rococo style, a simple element of it can frequently be found on pieces from that time. This may be in the form of a carved bracket representing a crumbled arch, or the supports for a cresting rail or pediment formed as cluster-columns. This decorative addition is enough to enliven the spirit and give a positive indication of the piece's original environment and date (*see* Pls. 13 and 14).

Clocks

By the 1750s both the clock and the barometer had become fashionable items in the well-appointed home. House clocks, as opposed to transportable timepieces, were of three main types, either spring-driven or weight-powered. The first type is known as a bracket clock due to its compact design and suitability for standing on a wall-mounted, specially made bracket or mantel; it is spring-driven. The second is the longcase, or "grandfather", clock, which is weight-driven. (Longcase clocks ceased to be made in large numbers after about 1845 and their manufacture was not revived until the early 20th century, hence the name "grandfather's clock", because they usually belonged to the older generations.) The third type is the wall clock, which may be driven by spring or weight. Depending on the quality of the piece, they could combine the visual recording of time with a striking movement chiming on a bell, or series of bells, on the hour and the quarters. By the early 1700s (the golden age of British clock-making is reckoned to be between 1660 and 1730), the most expensive longcase clocks could run for a year before needing rewinding. The simplest had a 30-hour movement, the most popular ran for eight days, and others ran for a month to three months. It is possible to determine the length of such non-stop timekeeping by the position of the winding holes in the front of the clock face, as such clocks at this time were key-wound. A year-long clock will have the key holes at the base of the dial, three-month and one-month duration progressively higher, and these are all wound anti-clockwise. An eight-day clock will have the holes level with or slightly below the III and the IX and will be wound clockwise.

Most of the best period English clocks have a square face with – particularly in London – an applied chapter ring on which the hours and minutes are engraved. After the 1720s an arched dial appeared, which could accommodate a calendar or perhaps the phases of the moon. Faces could be flat engraved brass, or silvered, or have a combination of silvered chapter ring on a brass face. The corners were filled with applied cast, and pierced and chased "spandrels" (*see* p.48), the decoration of which can help determine their date. They followed current designs, such as a winged cherub *c*.1665–*c*.1720, a crown flanked by two cherubs or putti *c*.1700–*c*.1715, a Rococo scroll *c*.1740–*c*.1780, and a classical motif *c*.1780–*c*.1810.

Dutch and French clock faces at this time were often covered with material, usually velvet, and French faces were round, enamelled, and slightly convex, becoming flatter after the 1780s.

All clocks depend on the controlled "escape" of their weight- or spring-driven power, hence the name "escapement" given to the various types of mechanisms that perform that function, such as the "verge" and the "anchor". However, it was the use of the pendulum's regular oscillation and the compensation provided by the "fusee" that allowed accurate timekeeping to develop after the middle of the 17th century. Nevertheless it is extraordinary that by the 1720s George Graham had built a "regulator" longcase clock that was so accurate it was used to time astrological observations and set other clocks and timepieces. He incorporated a "dead beat" escapement, which was an improved version of the anchor, and a mercury pendulum. Regulator clocks became the requirement of leading clockmakers, astrologers, enthusiasts, and collectors of scientific developments throughout the 18th and 19th centuries. A dead beat escapement can be spotted from the front of the clock by looking at the second hand. On a normal anchor escapement the second hand shows a slight recoil at each stroke; with a dead beat there is no visible recoil.

▲ **21 Silver two-handled cup, American, early 18th century.** The technique of applying extra pieces of silver to create a 3-D effect, known as cut-card work, came from France in the late 17th century. A French influence is evident in the simple but effective leaves on the lower part of the cup.

◄ **22 Silver beaker, English, 1784,** with a pastoral-themed decoration that shows the raised and depressed effect of embossing, visible on the inside. Chasing is a lighter and finer form of the same technique.

WORKING WITH SILVER

Items of silver are made in three basic ways. The first is by rolling out a sheet of silver from an ingot and making a cylinder to which a bottom is attached; with a handle, lid, and spout a mug, tankard, jug, or pot can be formed. Molten silver can be cast in a mould; this method is used to make spoons, forks, candlesticks, handles, feet, and finials. Finally a silver sheet can be beaten by a hand-hammer to be "raised" to make hollow vessels.

Silver items can then be decorated in three main ways. The first is engraving: this is done entirely by hand and the work does not show on the reverse. Next is chasing and embossing, or *repoussé* work. Chasing may be used alone or to add fine detail to embossed work. It is done with a hammer and a variety of punches and can be seen on the reverse. Embossing is created by pushing the inside out towards the viewer and the outer surface in to create high relief. This is also done with a hammer and punches. To prevent the whole thing collapsing when pushing in, the vessel is filled with pitch. The inside-to-outside effect is created with a snarling iron. This is an elongated right-angled "z"-shape tool that the silversmith in the illustration is using. He is seen to be striking near the end of the iron fixed in the vice. This will cause the other end of the iron that is in the vessel held in his left hand to vibrate or "snarl" violently enough for the smith to press down on it and enforce the desired pattern to be raised. Finally there is cut-card or strapwork (*see* Pl. 13, ch.1). This is the application of additional pieces of silver to the surface of the vessel.

▼ **23 Carved mahogany paterae, English, c.1775.** An early interpretation of Neoclassical design, carved in wood and embossed in silver. Oval and round architectural motifs such as this were used on friezes, particularly at the tops of legs, during and after the 1770s.

▲ **24 Carved detail on a side table, English, c.1770**, illustrating the use of gilded and painted decoration, which was expensive and reserved only for the greatest pieces. The use here of pastel as well as bright colours is confirmed by years of restoration and conservation in the 20th century.

▲ **25 Marquetry paterae, English, c.1770.** The import of exotic timbers encouraged a revival of marquetry. Classical designs were applied with contrasting veneers on furniture, and delicate "bright-cut" engraving on silver. Detailing was etched on, rather than cut-through as it was in the 1600s.

Barometers

Following the discovery that atmospheric pressure indicates forthcoming weather patterns, and that mercury in a sealed glass tube will react to its changes, developments were swiftly made in the production and accuracy of household barometers, although they remained available only to wealthy patrons well into the 18th century. There were three main types of case, all reliant on mercury but with slightly different mechanisms. They were: the column, or "stick", barometer; the wheel barometer (later nicknamed the "banjo"); and the signpost, or "yard arm", barometer. The latter was by far the most accurate, as by extending the glass tube and bending it at an angle the mercury was made to travel along rather than up and down, giving its slightest movement a greater effect and therefore scope for more definitive measurements (*see* p.48).

The decorative arts

The 1750s were hectic in the world of decorative arts. Robert Adam was studying in Italy, and in England Chippendale published *The Gentleman and Cabinet Maker's Director*, Josiah Wedgwood partnered the master potter Thomas Whieldon prior to founding his own business in Burslem, Staffordshire, and in London Eliza Godfrey became acknowledged as the leading female goldsmith of the day. In France and Italy there were early signs of Classical influence in the structure of furniture, ahead of Britain, while in America there were innovative clockmakers established in Connecticut and Philadelphia. At least ten glass factories were operative near Salem, New York, and Boston, and the Philadelphia-born master potter Andrew Duche had discovered the raw material source and the technique to create "as good porcelain as is made in China". Imports from China continued to grow at an alarming rate, to such an extent that in 1754 a tax was imposed on such goods in Massachusetts, by which time Duche had become a wealthy merchant and landowner in Norfolk, Virginia.

The rise of English craftsmen

Under the reigns of the first two Hanoverian Kings, George I (1660–1727) and George II (1714–1760), it was more parliament than monarch that decided the course of strategy adopted by England either in conflict or in partnership with her European neighbours and her disparate colonies. So while we refer to antiques as being "Georgian" this is a little vague, spanning as it does over 100 years until the death of George IV in 1830.

The 18th century was the time for the names of designers, architects, makers, and sellers to be associated with a "look" or style. English craftsmen came to the fore as they started to publish their ideas. Thomas Chippendale was among many designer/makers who produced catalogues in series and part form, to be bound in a single volume eventually. We think of Lord Burlington and William Kent as synonymous with Palladianism but we describe overt and elaborate Baroque furniture as being "Kentian". We refer to light, Classical-inspired interiors as being "Adamesque", and the furniture therein as "Hepplewhite" or "Sheraton". Wedgwood is automatically coupled with any pale blue jasper ware, and every political cartoon is, a collector would hope, by Rowlandson.

In recent years, and in some attempt to be more precise with attribution, we use the phrases "in the manner of", or "in the style of", much more. Naturally there was a fair amount of plagiarism, but it does not take long to recognize the subtle differences between a mirror made "in the manner of" one of Thomas Johnson's illustrations in his *Twelve Girandoles* in 1755 and his *One Hundred and Fifty New Designs* 1756–8, from one made "in the style of" Chippendale's *Gentleman and Cabinet Maker's Director*.

▼ **26 Mahogany side or serving table, English, c.1770.** This has a transitional style: the pure architectural Classicism of the legs and frieze and pierced gallery with honeysuckle motifs mix with the Rococo-period angled gadroon design of the edges to the top. Flanked by a pair of pedestals, this would have made a perfect serving table in a dining room.

▲ **27 Pair of dining-room pedestals and urns, English, c.1770**, showing a combination of Rococo and Classical influences in shape and decoration, typical of the transitional period. One pedestal contains a heater compartment, the other a cooler; they were used either side of a serving table in a dining room to hold hot and cold food.

▶ **28 Mahogany sideboard, English, c.1790**, combining the three pieces shown above as one piece for the smaller dining room. One end is usually a cupboard, the other a cellarette drawer. Turned legs were introduced as an alternative to square legs and became more popular after 1800.

American silver

Until the early 18th century there was considerable Dutch influence in the beakers, boxes, and salvers produced in America, particularly when decorated with *repoussé* work (*see* box p.83) depicting tulips, birds, and animals – as indeed there was in England at the same time. The Continental style of "wriggle-work" (a continuous zig-zag engraved line) does not appear on English silver but does on American silver of this time.

After 1700 American silversmiths closely followed English and some French patterns for the rest of the century, with the exception of the high-style elaborate Rococo decoration. There was a strange survival of the shallow bowl with a single side handle (*see* Pl. 36), known in England as a bleeding bowl and, probably more correctly, as a porringer in America. The shape has a "puritanical" look and disappeared from the British inventory after 1700, but remained popular stateside for the next 150 years.

▲ **29 Pair of ormolu-mounted blue john two-light candelabra, English, c.1770**, in a style that was used in the 1770s and for some time afterwards. The candle branches, attributed to Matthew Boulton, clearly overshadow the lower mounts in scale and exuberance. For more on blue john *see* page 87.

Another exception to the English influence can be seen in American braziers, or chafing dishes, that show some French characteristics in their curving shape, drop-in divisions, and wooden screw-in handles. Otherwise there are few, if any, pieces showing other foreign or even Irish or Scottish traits. In the 19th century there was a change to an amalgam of styles, forms, and decorative motifs from Italy, Scandinavia, Germany, and Eastern Europe, no doubt reflecting the influx of settlers from many other countries. However, generally speaking, American silver is plainer than that from elsewhere. It's as if the silversmiths took the best parts of ideas and left the superfluous embellishments alone – as they did with their furniture.

GLASS AND CHANDELIERS

By the last decade of George II's reign Britain's glass industry had developed a style of its own and indeed had begun to influence Continental makers. A tax on glass by weight, "The Glass Excise Act", was imposed in 1745 and this encouraged the production of thinner glass. Such glass was more suitable for engraving, which was still the main method of decoration – although some shallow cutting, gilding, and enamelling was used and subsequently flourished. This was also the time when drinking glasses were made with trumpet shapes or conical bowls atop a plain or baluster stem, with a wide, slightly raised spread foot.

At the luxury end of the trade, improved techniques in manufacture and decoration made it possible to imitate polished rock crystal, a skill that had been practised in France since the 13th century. Glass chandeliers were recorded in England as early as 1725 in an inventory of contents at Cannons for the First Duke of Chandos, and three years later the *Daily Post* displayed an advertisement for "Crystal Cut Lustres" (chandeliers). By 1752 the leading glass seller in London, Jerom Johnson, was advertising that he sold in his shop in the Strand "branches" (chandeliers) and "brilliant lustres diamond cut and scalloped". The form of these early chandeliers followed that of the brass ones, in that the arms were double curved but plain and the body comprised one or two large balls interspersed with rings, parts of which were diamond cut. It was in the age of Neoclassicism (1785–1810) that the grand chandelier, bejewelled and festooned with faceted drops, arrived in every house of note.

▲ **30 Cut-glass chandelier holding eight candles, English, c.1775.** This displays a clear Neoclassical influence in the form of the "covered vase" shape, prominent in the centre column, and the swags, festoons, and pendants – motifs popularized by Robert Adam – created in facet-cut glass drops.

Derbyshire Spar

In 1743 Lord Duncannon's horse struck a piece of rock and stumbled while they were journeying in Derbyshire, England. Dismounting to examine the cause, His Lordship discovered the rock to have curious colours and qualities. What he discovered was a piece of radix amethyst, better known today as "blue john" – a coloured crystalline stone ranging from blue, green, and yellow to deep purple, which could be shaped and polished to produce ornaments.

Unwittingly the horse had founded a huge industry, exclusive to a remote part of England, for blue john is found only in the caverns of the Tray Cliff, Castleton. As far as we know today, that is still its only source in the world. Very soon the material was in great demand and it was

mined and exported to France, where its colours prompted the name *bleu-jaune* – hence blue john. Once there it was mounted with fine cast-and-chased gilt bronze (ormolu), and the finished candelabra, perfume, or pastille burners and casollettes were exported back to England. Casollettes are metal-mounted vases, the tops of which may be taken off and reversed to form candlesticks; they appeared after 1760. To combat this new market, English manufacturers needed to equal and, if possible, improve on the quality of

DINING FURNITURE

By the mid-18th century a dinner party was run on much the same lines as today, with a reception in an anteroom or drawing room, a procession into the dining room, and allotted seating – although there were more staff in attendance. However, it became increasingly popular to dispense with staff once the food had been brought to the dining room. It is from this period that the serve-yourself dining room emerged.

At this time a serving table was flanked by two freestanding cupboards (see Pl. 27, p.85). One had a zinc lining and held heated iron ingots in the base to keep plates hot, with open grill shelves to allow the air to circulate; the other cupboard had a lead lining and held ice to keep food cool. Each cupboard supported a wooden, lined bucket or decorative urn to hold and dispense drinks. By the 1780s these three pieces were combined to create the Georgian sideboard as we know it (see Pl. 28, p.85). The 1750s were also the earliest years when bottle sliders, wine coasters, or decanter stands appeared. Prior to this, wine glasses were taken by footmen to be rinsed and replenished at the serving table by the butler. In their absence small wooden trays were introduced to protect the table or the fine linen cloth from the base of the bottle and its drips. Cheese trolleys also appeared in the middle of the 18th century, the earliest being of fairly plain form, such as the one shown on page 89.

When all the staff had been dismissed, service or at least assistance was still required; surely the most symptomatic piece of furniture of the period was the tripod-based, two- or three-tiered stand that held extra plates, some fruit, more cutlery, and napery, and which could be wheeled around the room for everyone's convenience. It is called a "dumbwaiter" and is shown here.

the French ormolu. This was achieved by one notable character, Matthew Boulton (1728–1809) – see p.102.

A novelty in the 1750s

The art of enamelling is ancient and takes many forms (see p.95), but at the height of the Rococo movement it came to the fore in Europe as a means to decorate novelty items such as *etui*, *necessaires*, snuff, pill, patch, and needle boxes, candlesticks, and wine labels. In France it was the

◄ **31 Pair of silver wine coasters, English, c.1786**, which are typical of the most popular form of coaster. They are simply made, with minimum pierced and engraved decoration, in the Neoclassical style, confirming a mid-1780s date. Silver rather than wooden bases were more expensive, and thus more valuable today too.

▶ **32 Blue glass decanter, English,** *c.***1780**, with stone or iron wheel cutting to the neck and body in typical Neoclassical patterns, which sit happily on the shouldered tapering body. The stopper may be a contemporary or later replacement, but it is of the correct shape and therefore acceptable, as stoppers were so often broken or lost.

▼ **33 Mahogany cheese coaster, English,** *c.***1800**. An example of coasters that were made with little variation in design from the 1760s to the 1820s. Some were fitted with leather castors, others with brass, and some had adjustable divisions. The pattern of turning that forms the handle at each end here suggests a later rather than earlier date.

defeated the French and their allies in Germany, the Caribbean, Canada, and India. Britain was rich and getting richer so everything was flourishing. After such a long preceding reign it seems natural that there would be some aura of change, and so there was. Developments in science, technology, commerce, and industry that had been in the bud came to full bloom over the next 25 years.

The King, wrongly credited with losing America (it was surely the arrogance of Parliament that did that), was a well-educated, well-rounded character, fluent in several languages, competent at riding, shooting, dancing, and fencing. He also had a deep knowledge of, and keen interest in, the arts and sciences. He was an accomplished horologist and astrologer, and the greatest bibliophile of all the British monarchs. He bought over 67,000 books on every conceivable subject, thus creating the nucleus of what was to become the British Library. These were first stored in Buckingham House, which later became the royal London residence Buckingham Palace. It may well have been from here that the Queen, Charlotte Sophia, in 1763 gave her assent to Josiah Wedgwood to call his new cream-coloured earthenware "Queen's Ware" after he won a competition to supply her with a tea service, and advertise himself as "Potter to Her Majesty". This royal connection was cultivated and served Wedgwood well, for in 1773, with the help of the British Ambassador to Russia, his company was commissioned to supply Empress Catherine the Great with a service of 1,000 pieces.

The King's interest in horology brought to his attention one John Harrison, who for many years had striven to prove that a ship's position at sea could be established by using a clock with a perfect mechanism. A prize for the first "chronometer" was offered by the government in 1713, and for more than 40 years Harrison built successively more brilliant movements attempting to win it, with powerful competitors thwarting each attempt. However, in 1773 the King intervened, and after a private court decision Harrison was awarded the full £20,000 prize. This was proved to be more than justified as Harrison's life's work allowed fellow pioneers within 15 years to make the marine chronometer in the form that has been used ever since.

At Kew the King built a larger observatory than the one already established at Richmond, in order to watch the transit of Venus across the sun. This was made possible by his patronage of William Herschel, a remarkable astronomer who discovered the planet Uranus in 1781.

Limoges factories that led the field, while in England Bilston and the surrounding Staffordshire areas created the greatest production. There are two main types of enamel finish: one has painted decoration, the other is decorated by transfer. The latter has always caused the greater interest and, as its production was from one factory only – Battersea – this has become a generic name for all English enamel wares. But true Battersea enamels are rare, as the factory lasted for only three years (1753–6).

Developments during George III's reign

George III was proclaimed King of England on 26 October 1760. This coincided with a period of national jubilation following the Year of Victories in 1759, when Britain

PAUL REVERE

Until 1776 any concerned Englishman considered America as much a part of England as the Northern Counties, and deplored the imposition of restrictive taxes placed on the colonies by the Whig Parliament. One of the best-known characters in this sad affair was the established American gold- and silversmith Paul Revere (1735–1818). While there is no doubt he would have made his mark in history through his manufacturing skills (an example of his work is shown opposite in Pl. 36) and his proficiency as a copper engraver, it is for his midnight ride from Charles Town to Lexington on the 18–19 April 1775 to warn of the approaching British Troops from Boston that he is best remembered. After the war he pioneered the manufacture of copperplating in America and died a prominent citizen in Boston.

As an ardent botanist the King was happiest at Kew, where the work of one of his appointed "Architects of His Majesty's Works", William Chambers (knighted in 1770), added pleasure to the joy he found in plant life. Chambers created the orangery, temples, and pagoda from his deep understanding for architecture across different periods and cultures. He had arrived back from his travels in 1755, having spent the last five years in Italy, three years before his rival and co-appointee to the King, Robert Adam. Chambers was already known to the King as he had been recommended as a suitable architectural tutor to George when he was still Prince of Wales. But despite whatever close ties Chambers may have had, there is no question that Robert Adam was to have a greater lasting impact and influence.

Robert Adam (1798–1892) was the best-known member of a family of architects. One of four sons born to father William and mother Mary in Kirkaldy, Scotland, Robert went to study in Italy in 1755 and returned in 1758. From then until his death he was involved in the erection or updating of at least 45 country houses in the Neoclassical style. To begin with Adam's version combined

▼ **35 Louis XVI-period carved and giltwood chair, French, c.1780.** Gone now are the gentle curves that had dominated furniture design for most of a century. Neo-classicism came earlier to France than England and was well-established by the 1770s. However, the low seat-frame and enormous cushion remained, here covered with Beauvais tapestry.

▲ **34 Oil-on-canvas portrait of Queen Charlotte, English, c.1765,** by Johann Zoffany (1733–1810). The Queen looks natural, her dress is densely frilled and ruched, with a lace modesty piece and contrasting bow above. The front panel, or stomacher, became known as *échelles*, as it looked like a ladder; this style remained popular until the 1780s.

the lighter elements of the Rococo movement with the purest Classical ideals (*see* Pl. 26), but by the mid-1780s most elements of Rococo had disappeared. He worked with his brother James in their London practice and, like Marot and Kent before him, left no detail unattended in the furnishings and interior decoration of his projects. There is no end to the list of household items that reflect the "Adam" look, for the style allowed affordable fashion in furniture, silver, porcelain, glass, common metal wares, pottery, and treen. It also lent itself admirably to the recently developed Sheffield Plate industry (*see* p.119).

Coinciding with the advent of mass production, the elegant straight lines, perfect symmetry, delicate ovals, swags, and festoons could all be achieved with less consumption of raw material. As to be expected, the first signs of the new order were executed in raised form, that is to say in relief, being carved in wood, embossed in silver, in cameo or *intaglio* in ceramics, cast and chased in bronze, or cut and engraved on glass. After 1785 the import of exotic timbers and the demand for flat surface decoration led to the revival of marquetry and the introduction of painted decoration on furniture and flat engraving on domestic silverware. Robert Adam popularized such motifs as the anthemion (honeysuckle flowers), the palmette (formalized palm leaves), paterae (oval discs), swags, festoons, and pendants, often with the adornment of rams'-head terminals.

▲ **36 Silver porringer, American**, by Paul Revere (1725–54). An example of the American resolve to retain what was best in functionality and design, irrespective of the latest fashions from Europe. Sometimes referred to as "barber's" or "bleeding" bowls, porringers went out of fashion in Europe, but remained popular throughout the 18th century in America.

◄ **37 Coloured lithograph showing the "Boston Tea Party"**. On the 16 December 1773 colonials protested at import taxes imposed by the British by dumping the cargo of tea from an East India Company ship into Boston harbour. This contributed to changing the course of British influence on American decorative arts.

AN AFFLUENT SOCIETY

1785–1830

When the rich and educated formed the ruling classes, it was their decision as to what was current fashion. For the first time a young generation asserted itself, and out of the Classical revival they created a style we know today as Regency, which set the scene for much of the 19th century.

◄ **1 Reconstruction of Robert Adam's extraordinary and magnificent Glass Drawing Room for Northumberland House, London, 1773–6.** The room was rescued from demolition in 1874. It is the most exotic interpretation of Classical taste, and a section is on display in the Victoria and Albert Museum, London.

𝒮tudying the Rococo style, with its forays into Chinoiserie and Gothic, makes it clear that it represents the greatest period of ultimate focus and concentration. Every scroll and leaf came from imagination and was placed with meaning to create an effect. Neoclassicism, on the other hand, looked to history and relied on its contrast to its predecessor rather than inventiveness. Even so, at the high end it was a period of elegance in interior decoration, liberated but monitored etiquette, and industrial development.

It is easy to imagine the dismissive attitude taken by the Neoclassical followers of fashion towards the previous Rococo style, because each generation does the same, and we are still doing it today. Inevitably something once loved then reviled is loved again, and by the end of this chapter, *c.*1830, sure enough a non-historic style was sweeping the board in a retro-Rococo craze known as *Tous-les-Louis*, (which incorporated every known style from 17th- and 18th-century France). However, it is hard to see a greater contrast in all walks of life throughout Europe and America than that from the Rococo of 1755 to the Neoclassical of 1785. Change seldom means total improvement, and the emergence of a style that could be mass-produced for the

common people had to mean a dilution of quality in a large proportion of the supply. It is particularly important that from this period onward age is not confused with merit. Much of the household merchandise made in the Neoclassical form and period has little more to commend it than that it has survived; a lot of it was inferior.

As each major leap in European expansion had spawned a characteristic look, so too did this one. But in England and America it was not from a single source. Since 1710, when the Italian-influenced Louis XV ascended to the throne of France, it was his profligate patronage of the arts that enabled the English to enjoy their modest version of elaborate Rococo décor. With the accession of Louis XVI

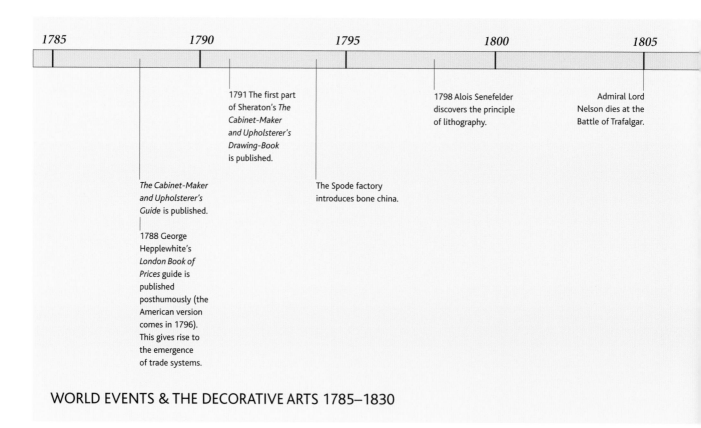

| 1785 | 1790 | 1795 | 1800 | 1805 |

1791 The first part of Sheraton's *The Cabinet-Maker and Upholsterer's Drawing-Book* is published.

1798 Alois Senefelder discovers the principle of lithography.

Admiral Lord Nelson dies at the Battle of Trafalgar.

The Cabinet-Maker and Upholsterer's Guide is published.

The Spode factory introduces bone china.

1788 George Hepplewhite's *London Book of Prices* guide is published posthumously (the American version comes in 1796). This gives rise to the emergence of trade systems.

WORLD EVENTS & THE DECORATIVE ARTS 1785–1830

in 1774 the only thing that changed was the form, from curvilinear to rectangular, on which the excessive elaboration continued. To a degree this was copied and assimilated by Robert Adam in his Neoclassical drawings of the designs discovered following excavations at Herculaneum in 1748, and ten years later at Pompeii. So during 1774–94 English designs were mainly modifications of French-adapted Italian and, to a lesser extent, Greek designs.

The single most important visual clue to this turn-of-the-century age is the shape of the urn, which was seen in jugs, vases, pots, chair backs, and table stems after the 1770s (*see* p.96). While not so evident in clothing as other shapes had been in previous periods, it is clearly the identifying "look" of the time. Nevertheless after the 1780s women's fashion certainly took on a historical form with the unbolstered "Empire" line (*see* p.131), while men, who dressed in wool cloth for the day and fine silk or velvet for

▶ **2 Fashion plate, English, c.1800**, showing two well-dressed men a century apart. Although the figure on the right is of heavier build than his companion, his clothes are closer fitting and less cumbersome, an element that was reflected in the furniture of the later period in contrast to that of the early 18th century.

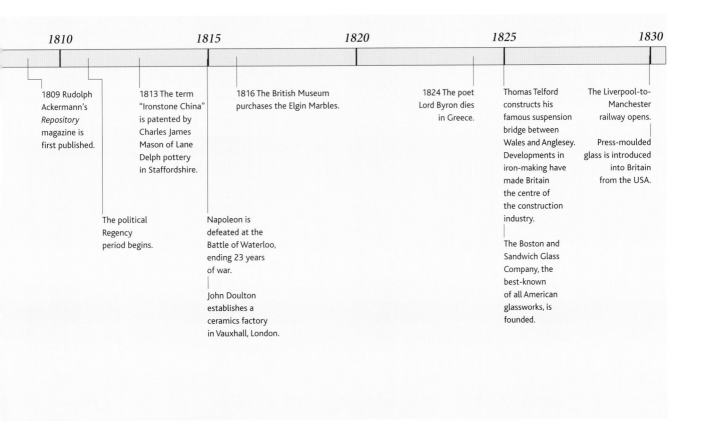

1810	1815	1820	1825	1830

1809 Rudolph Ackermann's *Repository* magazine is first published.

1813 The term "Ironstone China" is patented by Charles James Mason of Lane Delph pottery in Staffordshire.

1816 The British Museum purchases the Elgin Marbles.

1824 The poet Lord Byron dies in Greece.

Thomas Telford constructs his famous suspension bridge between Wales and Anglesey. Developments in iron-making have made Britain the centre of the construction industry.

The Liverpool-to-Manchester railway opens.

Press-moulded glass is introduced into Britain from the USA.

The political Regency period begins.

Napoleon is defeated at the Battle of Waterloo, ending 23 years of war.

John Doulton establishes a ceramics factory in Vauxhall, London.

The Boston and Sandwich Glass Company, the best-known of all American glassworks, is founded.

URN SHAPE

The Classical urn form that became so popular during the last 30 years of the 18th century gives us an immediate style identity and a guide as to date, in the same way as had the baluster shape and the earlier Elizabethan cup and cover. While it cannot be related in outline to clothes as closely as the former two, it reflects the poise and elegance that people adopted during that period, and it can be seen in a variety of ornamental and domestic items, from works of art such as the Wedgwood specimen piece shown in Plate 6 to a humble salt cellar of pottery, pewter, or silver (*see* Antiques Analysis pp.230–31).

3 Detail from an inlaid marble fireplace, English, *c*.1785. The style of the decoration denotes the period, but the medium, known as *scagliola* (literally scales or chips of marble ground to a fineness), is more ancient. The process was improved in mid-18th century Florence by an Irish friar, Henry Hugford. Among the chief exponents of the technique who travelled to England and Ireland were Richter and Bossi (*see scagliola* pp.99–100).

4 Silver two-handled cup and cover, English, 1774. A perfect example of early Classical-style silver, the formal decoration is embossed and chased with an applied cast border. The inclusion of handles cast in the Rococo style is typical of this transition period in the 1770s.

5 Satinwood and painted armchair, English, *c*.1785. Part of a well-known suite by the firm of George Seddon – at that time the largest cabinet-maker in London. The urn or shield shape can be seen in the form of the back. The use of cane for the seat and painted satinwood confirm the date.

▲ **6 Jasper ware two-handled vase, English, c.1785.** Made famous by Josiah Wedgwood, the earliest examples of jasper ware,1774–77, are solid colour; after that date a coloured slip on a white body was used. Pastel green, yellow, lavender, and black were all used to great effect, and are still in production.

▶ **7 Interior at Heveningham Hall, Suffolk, England, completed 1784.** This room was designed by James Wyatt (1746–1813). It exemplifies the Neoclassical taste of the period, bringing from ancient Italy the fan-vaulting that was to become so popular as a decorative motif on even the humblest of domestic items.

the evening, had altogether more neatly fitting garments (*see* Pl. 2). Both these fashions looked better on the young, and, for the first time, this age group's style became separate from its seniors', which was exemplified by the relationship of the Prince of Wales and his father, the King (*see* p.113).

Another major style arose, which was to run concurrently with that of Hepplewhite and Sheraton (*see* p.107), encompassing Graeco-Roman, contemporary French, Egyptian, Gothic, and Chinese in forms not seen

before. Its chief protagonist was George, Prince of Wales, later to become George IV, who in 1811–20 was Prince Regent, and whose title is attached to the style, the English Regency. In design terms this describes the period when the Prince's taste, sometimes referred to as "High Style Regency", dominated the fashion adopted by him and his close circle of friends, and later when it became affordable to a wider public – namely from when he became 21, in 1783, until his death in 1830. Those designs he favoured during his years as

► **8 Detail of overmantel mirror, English, *c*.1800**, with three panels of *verre églomisé*, an ancient method of securing gilt decoration to glass using varnish or metal foil rather than firing. This skill was revived in the late 1700s by Parisian art dealer Jean-Baptiste Glomy.

◄ **9 Mahogany pole screen, English, *c*.1780**. The shape of the banner and the finely turned stem immediately give a date of not before 1775. The tripod base, in "umbrella" form, also appeared at this time; the banner fabric is later.

► **10 Fireplace with mirror over, English, *c*.1800**. A style of inlaid marble fire surround, triple plate mirror, and fire grate that became popular during the last decade of the 1700s and into the early 1800s.

king, from 1820 to 1830, are called "Late Regency". So, the term Regency Furniture is used to describe those pieces made in the styles that refer to antiquity in Egypt, Rome, and Greece, or exhibit naval paraphernalia, projected by Henry Holland, Thomas Hope, George Smith, and shown in Ackermann's *Repository* (*see* p.122). Although Chinese furniture and decoration was popular at the same time, the name Regency is not used to describe it. Nor is it used typically to describe the existing earlier French style that the Prince of Wales also enjoyed at Carlton House (*see* pp.116–17). In the context of the decorative arts English Regency describes a certain style from a 45-year period and does not describe everything made during the political nine-year Regency. Any future references to Regency in this text will be concerned with the style and period 1783–1830.

New rooms

In the well-to-do home the closet, which for three generations had been the inner sanctum where privileged guests and friends were entertained, had given way to the (with)drawing room, and the master of the house had a library in which to study, away from the hurly-burly of the family. Reading had become widespread, and collecting books on a vast range of subjects was a desirable passion. As well as freestanding cabinets of fine mahogany, fitted shelves were made either open or with wire-grill doors, the woodwork of pine and often painted. Leather flaps

were fixed to each shelf to fend off dust, while Classical busts or other mementos stood on top. A pair of large globes, one celestial and the other terrestrial, showed one's interest in astrology and geography, and a billiard table suggested that the room was also for recreation. A new type of large, open-kneehole desk with drawers each side, called a pedestal or partner's desk, became fashionable and indicated a note of grandeur.

One of the best examples of a Neoclassical interior is at Heveningham Hall in Suffolk (*see* Pl. 7). In the main hall the illusion of great space is created by proportion and decoration, for it is not a large room. It was used as a "parade" room, where guests and day visitors could walk and view the décor and latest acquisitions from the Grand Tour, and see, and be seen by, everyone else. Sprouting from the tops of the columns are the fan-type vault motifs. It is now known some original Roman mosaics were found in Fishbourne, Sussex, so there was no need to go to Italy for inspiration. These mosaics were replicated on carved Hepplewhite and inlaid Sheraton pattern furniture, ceramics, metalware, and carved and inlaid mantelpieces.

Fires and fireplace designs

By 1785 coal had replaced wood as the domestic heating fuel in all smart town houses and contemporary country mansions. The containing grate had become the subject for fashionable form and decoration, as well as being capable of creating great heat. Standing on four legs, the basket comprised a tall fire back, two solid sides, and serpentine-shaped bars at the front. Below these was a

frieze, usually pierced to simulate fluting, flanked by the front legs formed as square or turned tapering columns, topped with urns. Surrounding this and the fireplace opening was the Classical-style carved wood or carved or inlaid marble of the surround and mantelpiece.

For marble versions the ancient craft of *scagliola* found additional popularity as it was a means of creating three-dimensional images on or in the flat surfaces of the

▼ **11 Carved-wood and gilt picture frame, English, *c*.1771.** The picture is a collage of hand-painted wallpaper. The frame is a beautifully drawn oval with a stylized honeysuckle supported by leaf-capped scrolls. The combination of early carved Classicism and Rococo is perfect for an item dating from this transitional period.

ROCOCO TO NEOCLASSICAL

The change in style from Rococo to Neoclassical influence is well illustrated when comparing these two table candlesticks. On the left is a typical Rococo model made between 1730 and 1765. It is cast and chased, with a stepped and wavy-edged base below a stem that has a knop and a baluster, below a shoulder and waisted sconce. The separate nozzle is flared and shaped to conform to the outline of the base. There are no vertical straight lines, and with one curve leading into another it has all the elements of a pre-Classical piece. It was made in London in 1744.

By 1785, when the second candlestick was made, all such erratic curves had disappeared, to be replaced by sweeping lines that give an illusion of height and elegance. It is cast and chased as the other one, but here the decoration is of fluting within a beaded border. The base is circular and dished, before swelling up to the tapering stem and elongated, vase-shaped sconce. The nozzle is so perfectly plain as to almost disappear, but it has a beaded border to match the base. When held upside down the base replicates the fan vaulting in the ceiling at Heveningham Hall, pictured on page 97.

▲ **12 Two silver candlesticks, English, *c.*1740 (left) and *c.*1785 (right).** These show the easy-to-recognize difference between the standard Rococo period and style fashionable prior to the 1760s, as depicted on the left, and the Classically inspired model from after the 1770s, on the right.

surround. The term derives from the Italian *scaglia*, which means "scales or chips of marble". A delicate shading of colours was produced using finely ground fragments of marble mixed with pigments, and a superb example of a mantelpiece in this style is at Burghley House (*see* Pl. 10). A much-venerated exponent of *scagliola* was Dr Bossi, an Italian known to have worked in Ireland from 1785 to 1798 but who, due to his being implicated in the Irish Revolution, "deemed it advisable to leave Dublin". Not much is heard of him after that point, which is a great shame as his work was superb.

The heat from the smaller and better-contained coal fires was as fierce as any wood blaze. The use of heavy and poisonous make-up was no longer necessary to disguise the ravages of the pox, as these had disappeared through the last two generations, but it was still considered unbecoming to appear flushed and so the fire screen, albeit a smaller version, remained an essential item. Here another clue to the instant recognition of the date of an item presents itself in its very shape. Plate 9 shows a pole screen that is definitely post-1780s, with its delicate "umbrella" tripod base and vase-shaped banner. A pair

or more of these would have graced every fireplace, and they were used especially after dinner, when it was the practice of the ladies to withdraw in order to prepare tea. The gentlemen remained at the table to drink wine and discuss matters of state and importance before joining the women later when the tea was brewed. In fact it was more the habit for them to continue to drink toasts to one another and the absent ladies in increasingly (to the offence of any French guests) intimate and bawdy terms, while circulating the wine clockwise around the table – a ritual still observed with port today at more traditional dining occasions.

European porcelain

From the late 16th and throughout the 17th century European nobility had spent the equivalent of millions of pounds acquiring Oriental porcelain, so it is not surprising that leading alchemists gave up their quest to make gold in favour of discovering the secret of making hard-paste porcelain. At their head was Johann-Freidrich Bottger (1682–1719), who, in 1709, produced a hard, white porcelain from a kaolin base and, in 1710, a calcareous glaze. In the same year Bottger was appointed director of the recently formed Meissen factory in Germany. After a period of research and development in improving the body, modelling techniques, gilding, and colouring with enamels, Meissen established itself as the leading producer of fine hard-paste porcelain in Europe. Its greatest period of exclusivity was between 1725 and 1740, when the vogue for Rococo style allowed the imagination and skills of such great masters as Johann-Joachim Kandler (1706–75,) Meissen's chief modeller, to create breathtakingly beautiful figures and groups of lovers, musicians, comedians, gardeners, shepherdesses, animals, and his famous set of models of street vendors calling out their wares – "Cries of Paris" – to delight wealthy patrons.

Although stunning in the white, these pieces were further enhanced with the most brilliant colours ever seen, largely due to the work of Johann-Gregor Horoldt (1696–1775), who, by 1731, had 78 painters, associates, apprentices, and colour grinders in his Meissen workshop. To protect knowledge of the ingredients and precise methods of production from being leaked to other factories, those employed at Meissen were subject to strict rules of confidentiality and severe isolation, and any "holder of the secret" who attempted to run away was punished if caught. However, it was inevitable that such a valuable asset would eventually spread, and by 1769 hard-paste porcelain was being produced at Sèvres in France, a factory that had capitalized handsomely on the market for soft-paste wares. It was at Sèvres that the most celebrated "holder of the secret", Louis-Victor Gerverot, served his apprenticeship before moving on to work all over Europe, gaining recognition and status but not staying anywhere very long. Such men as Gerverot, genuine masters of every stage of fine production, were rare and so were treated as nobility, with entreaties to stay in a town with a factory long enough to teach its workforce how to make it the new Meissen.

▼ **13 Silver tea and coffee service, American, c.1800**. It is immediately identifiable from the shape as being after the 1780s, as it does not show the English interpretation of Classicism. The teapot, from Boston, and the coffee pot, from Baltimore, both have a double-tiered upper body; the sugar vase is covered and without handles, and the cream jug has a hinged lid.

Developments in the decorative arts

Building on his previous successes (*see* p.89), in 1768 Josiah Wedgwood marketed a new, fine, black stoneware with which he produced tea sets and ornaments moulded in Neoclassical form. This was called basalt, or "Basalte"; a rougher form, known as "Egyptian black", had been produced in Staffordshire for some years by a number of potters. Wedgwood's version proved a popular export, particularly to America, but was largely superseded by his next triumph – pale blue "jasper ware" (*see* Pl. 6). Still made today, it first appeared in 1774 with the Classical decoration in white applied to a solid blue body. In 1777 a white body was used, then dipped into a blue slip before being decorated. Other body colours were introduced, including yellow, lavender, pale green, and black. All the above are best known by their traditional matt or "biscuit" surface, being unglazed, but more unusual examples can be found that were polished to a soft shine.

▶ **14 Federal gentleman's secretary, American, c.1793–1811**, made in Salem, Massachusetts in mahogany and mahogany-veneer. The top shows glazed doors with 13 panes – a number preferred by the superstitious English. In contrast, the deeply swept cornice with four vase finials is typically American in style.

Another great name of the period is Matthew Boulton (1728–1809) of Birmingham. The son of a successful "toy maker" (*see* below), Boulton junior became the leading manufacturer of all fine metalwares, responsible for establishing the Birmingham Assay Office in 1773. Through the endeavours of his works in Soho, Birmingham, he ensured the city's place in the register of industrial centres in Europe. It can be claimed that his finest ormolu bettered the French. (Ormolu is the English corruption of the French *or moulu*, which literally means "ground gold". In fact the term is used to describe bronze articles, such as mounts for furniture and clocks, finely cast in bronze and then delicately chased to a high degree of detail before being gilded by the mercurial process. In this process gold and mercury are mixed together to create an amalgam, which is then applied to the surface of the bronze. The article is next heated until the mercury evaporates, leaving the gold firmly affixed to the surface. This can then be burnished to give mirror-like highlights. The fumes from the evaporating mercury are extremely noxious to the point of being lethal, and the process was officially superseded by electro-gilding in the mid-19th century.)

The word "toys" in the 18th century described small objects: buttons, buckles, fine steel chains, sword hilts and other mounts, enamelled novelties, and accessories. Using machines already in operation, Matthew Boulton's takeover of the family business coincided with the development of the technique of silver-plating on copper,

◄ **15 Federal treble-elliptic trick-leg card table, American, c.1810**, in fine carved mahogany. The shape of the top is not at all English in style, rather it is distinctively American. The Classical influence can be seen in the vase shape in the centre of the table stem, here carved with the universal motif of a formalized acanthus leaf.

▲ **16 Portrait of George Washington, American School, 19th century.** The President's clothes owe more to French fashion than to English, and so does his furniture. The table leg and the details visible on the chair show clearly empirical motifs, such as ribbon bindings and foliate sprays, in painted and burnished gilt finish.

known as Sheffield Plate (*see* p.119). Although it was first invented during the Rococo period, it was the coincidence of improved techniques and a simplified fashionable design that enabled large-scale production and consumption. The production of "toys" was not limited to metal and enamelware, as both porcelain and pottery makers were producing miniature figures to hold bonbons, bodkins, needles, and perfume.

The Chelsea factory, which had excelled for a while in fine tea wares, started to decline along with the Bow factory, and by the 1770s it had been taken over by the Derby Porcelain Company. However, the Worcester Porcelain Company, which had been started by Dr John Wall and William Davis in 1751, went from strength to strength, and entered one of its many great phases with the introduction of a body that was less susceptible to hot water, making it a market leader in the sale of tea and coffee services from the 1760s. At the luxury end of the trade the role models were still the porcelains of Meissen and Sèvres. In 1783 the "First", or "Dr Wall",

period of Worcester came to an end when Thomas Flight bought the company for his sons to operate. In 1792 Martin Barr was co-opted, and from then on there are various references to "Flight and Barr" wares – the best known is "Flight Barr and Barr", which was used after 1813. The word "Royal" was added to the firm's title after a visit to the factory by George III and Queen Charlotte in 1788, and a crown was added to the crescent mark. A rival factory in Worcester, which was started in 1789 by Robert Chamberlain (a former apprentice to Dr Wall), was merged with Flight's factory in 1840, and the extant "Royal Worcester" company was founded in 1862.

The third Chinoiserie period, *c*.1800–30, which is epitomized in the Royal Pavilion at Brighton (*see* Pl. 29), reflected the continuing import of artifacts from China and, at a slower pace, a few pieces from Japan. Thomas Minton, a potter, had the ingenuity to take advantage of the new transfer printing methods being applied to chinaware and is credited with being the first to take a Chinese legend and decorate tableware with it for the Caughley pottery

▲ **17 Diamond-and-pearl brooch, English, *c*.1790**, with three miniature portraits encased behind diamonds. This beautifully drawn brooch has an unmistakeably late-18th-century design of ribbons of diamonds topped with a bow, and suspending a pearl pendant.

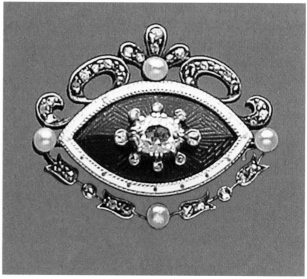

▲ **18 Enamel lozenge brooch, English, *c*.1800**. The overall outline is similar to that in Pl. 17, but there the likeness stops. Here a more dramatic effect is created by the royal-blue-and-white enamel, centred with a cushion-cut diamond within the diamond-and-pearl-encrusted border.

KNIFE BOXES

Before the great silver canteen chests of the late Georgian and Victorian periods, which held every type of utensil imaginable, it became fashionable to retain knives, forks, and spoons in small boxes that could be kept on display in the dining room. They had sloping tops so that, when open, the silver could be seen to its best advantage. By the 1760s these boxes were made in pairs and of fine quality timber; the detailed design of their escutcheons, handles, and feet, in fashionably shaped brass or hallmarked silver, is the best indication of date. By the 1780s an alternative model in the form of a vase-shaped container emerged, with a lid supported by a central column. It was at this time that this pair, of exceptional quality, was made, complete with cutlery; the classic shield-shaped silver escutcheon is confirmation of the date. Sadly during the 1930s, and after World War II, knife boxes were considered useless, and many were gutted and converted into stationery boxes.

in Shropshire *c*.1780. With its essential ingredients of a willow tree, a pagoda, two birds in flight, and figures on a river bridge, it became so popular it was copied by the Chinese potters and then exported back to England! It was known as the "Willow Pattern" and is still produced in large quantities today.

The European production of fine ceramics changed after 1794 when the Spode factory introduced "bone china", wherein the body consisted of approximately 50 percent bone ash. This enabled a type of hard paste, rather than soft paste, to be produced at a much-reduced cost. In the early 1800s another new and improved body was introduced called "stone china", which was used to make heavy-duty dinner services, often decorated in big and colourful foliate patterns. The term "ironstone china" was patented in 1813 by Charles James Mason, son of Miles Mason of Lane Delph pottery in Staffordshire. Miles Mason was the first in the family line of famous potters and, despite his son being granted the patent, it is his name that is most commonly associated with it. However, it is far from being "china" or porcelain as it is an opaque and hard earthenware. By the 1820s the choice and variety of English and imported ceramics was vast, from the finest and most sophisticated to the comical; the latter often came from Staffordshire, where "Toby Jugs" and "Flat-Backs" (*see* Pls. 20 and 21) were in full production.

▲ **19 Oil-on-canvas portrait, English, 1785**, by Sir Thomas Gainsborough. There had been an increasing softness in women's clothing, culminating in the style seen here: gauzy fabrics added to necklines and wrists and thin drapes over the skirt. A big hat with quivering feathers was popular, as was the gentleman's soft cravat. The suit is formal and enriched by gold buttons.

▲ **20 Derby porcelain figure of a shepherdess, English, c.1770**. The grand dress of the shepherdess was intended to delight the owner and display the skill of potter and decorator. Impromptu fancy-dress parties were popular among the young, wealthy elite, and the simplest conversion for a girl was to become a flower-seller or shepherdess; boys became gardeners.

▲ **21 Ralph Wood pearlware figure group, English, c.1790**, entitled "The Birdcage". This continues the theme of shepherd and shepherdess. Pearlware is the same fine earthenware body as creamware, but with a bluish glaze that had the appearance of expensive porcelain. It first appeared in the 1780s.

The influence of cabinet-makers

Tax records from 1772 prepared by the cabinet-maker William Savery in Philadelphia show that all cabinet-makers in America were still being listed as joiners, yet as early as 1714 there is evidence of the two being separately defined. This shows that a country focused on agriculture, and under the umbrella of the United Kingdom, could remain content with the status quo, allowing its citizens' good taste and probity to control steady and tasteful changes in fashion. When the 13 American colonies merged into a single nation the focus, certainly on the Eastern seaboard, changed to commerce, manufacturing, and trade. With hindsight it may be considered fortunate that the sweeping changes advocated by Robert Adam and his contemporaries in England were not published in America, for they were certainly not to be welcomed in the years leading up to 1776, and by the time peace was declared in 1784 and mutually beneficial trading began, Adam's patterns were on the wane in England. They were replaced by the published drawings of George Hepplewhite and, later,

Thomas Sheraton. Hepplewhite was a practising cabinet-maker, but we have no evidence that Sheraton ever was. Considering Hepplewhite's importance in the development of English and American furniture, we know very little about him except that he was apprenticed to Gillows of Lancaster, a leading furniture company, and that he died in 1786 – two years before his widow, Alice, published his *The Cabinet-Maker and Upholsterer's Guide.* So popular was this, with its 300 illustrations, that a second edition was published in 1789 and a third in 1794. The oval paterae, carved swags and festoons, delicate raised mouldings, bell flowers, and fluting in evidence were certainly from the Adam repertoire, but in Hepplewhite's hands were used only as an understated adornment that could be successfully executed by average as well as the finest cabinet-makers, and which appealed to the American good taste. He is credited with introducing the Prince of Wales feathers as a chair-back motif – with the alternative spray of wheat ears if the patron was an advocate of the King. Such is the material of folklore, and

▲ **22 Enamel wine label, English, *c*.1775, and silver wine label, Continental, *c*.1800.** Most English enamel objects, often referred to as *objets du vertu*, came from the environs of Bilston in Staffordshire. After the 1760s wine labels became extremely popular and followed the outlines of current style. Here an early date is evident from the reference to a Rococo border. The silver label has a Neoclassical form, and is decorated with a man tucking into a meal of fish.

◄ **23 Group of enamel snuff boxes, English, *c*.1760–70,** of regular shape but with decorative borders and costumes on the figures that are definitely from the Rococo period. The proliferation of snuff boxes is explained by women as well as men partaking of snuff on a large scale. The range of finely painted subjects had no limit, with scenes from well-known pictures, studies of birds and flowers, group activities, and portraits. Importantly all give us firm evidence of a way-of-life conducted in western Europe during the mid-18th century.

LINKING ITEMS THROUGH PROVENANCE AND HISTORY

There need be no restrictions on the diversity of a collection. Indeed, it is possible to link even the most disparate items together, albeit tenuously, to add a further dimension to their interest. The three objects shown here, for example, would appear at first sight to have little in common, but on closer inspection there is a link between all three.

The rare and beautiful Meissen porcelain teapot (Pl. 25) has a detailed estuary scene within a gilt Rococo border, showing figures in the foreground and shipping beyond. One figure is a man wearing the long coat fashionable in the early 18th century, similar, no doubt, to one worn by the trader Jean Martell when he travelled south to Cognac in France to establish his distillery there in 1715. In its deep hems he would have carried samples of the cork and rabbit pelts he intended to trade, as entrepreneurs used to do.

Travelling tutors would similarly have loaded their coats, this time with drawing instruments, mathematical tables, and a pocket globe (Pl. 26). The globe was an indispensable piece of equipment to show what details were known of the world's geography, and it was protected by a shagreen (leather) or mock fishskin case. This was papered inside with a map of the heavens, thus providing celestial as well as terrestrial information.

These little globes also showed the latest voyages of discovery, and, after 1780, the routes followed by the legendary explorer Captain Cook. So legendary was he that Josiah Wedgwood created a silhouette portrait miniature of him in his pale-blue-and-white jasper ware in 1784 (Pl. 24). By this time Wedgwood was himself a national figure (see p.102), known for his decorative and domestic ceramics. In the early 1760s he improved on the production of a cream-coloured lead-glazed earthenware, which had been developed in Staffordshire in the 1740s. Its new lightness and durability appealed to all and sundry, including Her Majesty Queen Charlotte, who in 1765 allowed Wedgwood to name his product "Queen's Ware". Within a few years queen's ware had replaced most Chinese and European porcelains – including Meissen – as everybody's favourite tea-set.

◄ **24 Jasper ware portrait plaque, English, 1784**, of Captain James Cook by Wedgwood and Bentley. The uniform and wig conform to the post-1750 period, the material dates it after 1774.

▼ **25 Meissen porcelain teapot, German, c.1724.** The squat shape countered by a delicate curvilinear spout and handle is typical of this period. The everted lip gives a distinctly oriental "mandarin" look.

▲ **26 Pocket globe and case, English, early 19th century.** Miniature globes were originally more necessity than novelty, and could be carried in the deep pockets of long travelling coats worn into the mid-19th century. They were made in the same way as table and standing globes, with plaster over a skeleton cage covered by papers cut into "gores".

if it sells antique chairs so be it. Thomas Sheraton (1751–1806) published his designs in *The Cabinet-Maker and Upholsterer's Drawing-Book* in three parts from 1791 to 1794. In it he advocated use of the same Classical features, but this time depicted with inlays of the newly imported exotic timbers in a revival of the art of marquetry cutting. This had an even greater influence in America during the Federal Period.

The Federal Period (1788–1825)

Duncan Phyfe (1768–1854), a well-known American cabinet-maker, settled in Albany in 1784 before moving to New York in 1791. His name is synonymous with the Federal Period in American history, but in truth his contribution to the advance of design and manufacture went beyond the parameters of that style. Due to the hostilities between America and England, the published works of Robert Adam were never distributed in America; their popularity was on the wane by the time a truce had been declared in 1784. Instead, the drawing books of Thomas Sheraton and George Hepplewhite were the main source of English influence in the newly independent continent. Combined with these were designs from contemporary French taste and historic Italy, Greece, and Egypt. Duncan Phyfe successfully blended Sheraton with Thomas Hope (*see* pp.122–4) to create Egypto-Roman Classicism that had comfort and utility (*see* Pl. 53), which lasted well into the end of the Federal Period.

Always to be relied upon to display the very latest fashion, Phyfe's showrooms in New York displayed the *Tous-les-Louis* Rococo-revival style of the late 1820s, and the Gothic revival of the 1830s and '40s. Less well known now, but equally lauded at the time, was another émigré craftsman in New York, Honoré Lannuier (1779–1819). Unlike Phyfe, Lannuier kept a low profile, but his influence on New York taste was considerable. Having trained in Paris as an *ebeniste*, the top class of cabinet-makers, he arrived in New York in 1803. Here his work was more closely defined than that of his competitors, as he showed the subtle differences between French designs of the *Directoire* (1793–99), the French Consulate (1799–1804), and the French Empire (1804–15). However, influential as he may have been in his exclusivity, he also succumbed to combining any of these to conform to the needs and tastes of a wider clientele. It was more the practice of French manufacturers to attach a label or impress a stamp with their name to their furniture than

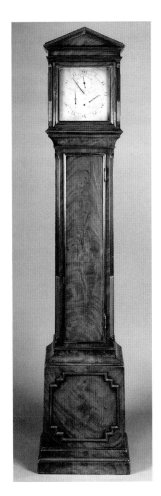

◀ **27 Regulator clock, English, c.1790**. The austerity of the case gives a clue that the clock would have a regulator movement. The emphasis is on accuracy, usually powered by weights controlled by a temperature-sensitive pendulum and a deadbeat escapement. Regulators were made by leading clockmakers for their own workshops, as well as for eminent, and wealthy, clients.

it has ever been with the English (or Scottish). Lannuier continued this tradition in America, and identification of a piece by Lannuier is easier and more positive than that of a piece supposedly by Duncan Phyfe.

Meal etiquette

Toasting had become increasingly popular as a means of keeping glasses replenished throughout the meal, as unless a person had struck a deal with a footman or the butler, the serving of wine was slow. During a meal, particularly at the "removes" (*see* below), respectful toasts were made to absent notables such as the King and other leading public figures and friends, as well as to those around the table. At this point the art of flirting with eye contact over a glass of wine was refined to a subtlety that matched that of the Elizabethan court, made more effective with the fashion of seating men and women alternately.

The term "remove" is not recognized much today, although it did appear on some Edwardian menus and still does on pretentious modern ones. Again due to the

slowness of service, a light, decorative dish was brought to the table to bridge the gap between the first and main courses, and to follow the main course before the dessert. It was used to create an entertaining diversion during the removal, or "remove", of the used plates and cutlery and the positioning of their replacements. There was usually some hidden reference to the course to come, in either the decoration or the content of the remove, the second one being more lavish than the first. In fact, so lavish was it that it often cost as much as the entire meal. However, without doubt the most expensive item on the table was the centre-piece plateau. This followed the outline of the table, and was a mirror-based platform on which a series of models were placed to create a miniature garden or landscape. A folly, temple, waterfall, or foliage, made of a variety of appropriate materials and hedged in by a silver or silver-gilt border,

▲ **28 Detail of cast-iron balconies, Cheltenham, England, c.1824**. The use of cast iron in architecture, much encouraged by George, Prince of Wales, in the early 19th century, affected every spa town in Britain, giving a light tracery in Classical and Gothic patterns to the fronts of fashionable rows, or "parades", of houses.

▶ **29 Illustration of the Royal Pavilion at Brighton, England, 1838**. A "farmhouse by the sea at Brighthelmstone (Brighton)" was redesigned for the Prince of Wales by Henry Holland in 1787. Successive architects and designers, including William Porden, Humphrey Repton, and, finally, John Nash, changed the Palladian villa between 1817 and 1824 into the "Hindu"-style palace we see today.

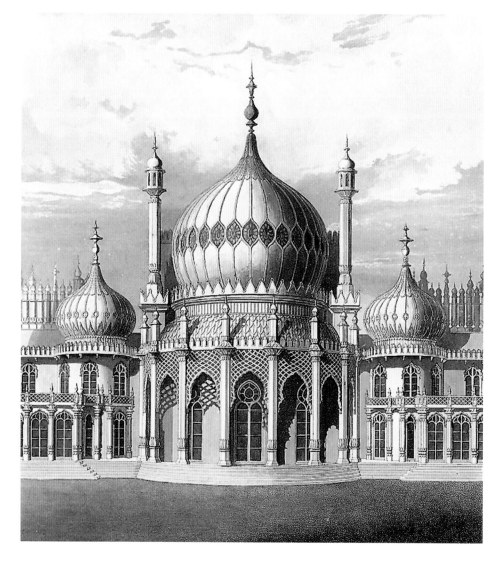

formed the background for the careful display of the current greatest luxury: fine porcelain figures of musicians, comedians, lovers, gardeners, shepherdesses, and animals that could be played with and admired during the meal.

An alternative to the centre plateau was the epergne, an elaborate dish raised on legs, with branches extending from it to take smaller dishes for sweetmeats, fresh or candied fruits, and nuts (pistachios were renowned for their benefits to digestion). The epergne became popular during the 1730s and lent itself well to the exotic Rococo style, but found equal suitability to display the classic shapes of the Adam period. The finest examples have branches with optional candle sconces instead of small dishes. The earliest were exclusively silver, sometimes gilded, then came silver plate, and, rarely, enamelled metal. In the 19th century various designs on the same theme were made in glass.

Cutlery designs

Until the 19th century the variety of cutlery design in Britain and America was limited compared to the

▲ **30 The Iron Bridge at Coalbrookdale, England**, built from 1777 to 1781 to designs by Thomas M. Pritchard under the supervision of Abraham Darby III. This huge achievement, spanning the Ironbridge Gorge, revolutionized the perception of iron as an architectural material, as well as affecting industry, transport, and the domestic market, and throughout the world.

imaginative use of agate, malachite, and other semi-precious stones, bone, carved bone, ivory, and decorated wood so popular for handles throughout Europe. Until the 1760s British spoons and forks had a tapering handle with a rounded end that turned up the same way as the bowl, known as the Hanoverian pattern.

Both spoons and forks were laid on the table face-down and the forks had three prongs or tines. Knives had a scroll at the end of the handle (known today as a "pistol handle") and steel blades. From 1760 spoon handles turned down at the end and were laid on the table with the bowl face-up. The shape of the handle remained plain and tapering, and forks appeared with four prongs. Knife handles became plain and tapering and the difference is noted by the new name, Old English pattern. Also around this time the hallmarks became smaller, more

DATING ITEMS BY USE AND SHAPE

As an example of dating an item from its use and shape, this pair of chestnut urns could not be bettered. The process of decorating items made of tinned iron with japanning had been used in parts of Europe, particularly Britain, since the late 17th century, and is described in detail on p.44. So to narrow our date lines we must look to the shape of the urns and the fact that they were intended to hold, and to keep hot, cooked chestnuts, which became most popular during the last quarter of the 18th century. The nuts were boiled, then roasted, and presented at table to be eaten with salt and served with coffee. The earliest examples of such containers are of a plainer vase shape, whereas these, with their large goblet form and elaborate handles, must date from the early 1800s.

uniform, and were moved up the handle away from the bowl or prongs, where they had been struck previously.

By the 1780s a shoulder appeared at the junction of handle and bowl or prongs but otherwise there was little change until virtually the end of the century, when the Fiddle pattern came in (*see* spoon-handle analysis, pp.224–5). This had various added motifs, such as a shell at the terminal and a lined edge known as a "thread". The Fiddle pattern was soon followed by King's, Queen's, and Prince's patterns, which had elaborately decorated handles with an hourglass outline.

Cutlery was still kept separate from other serving utensils, as the great canteen containing everything from knife rests to soup ladles had not yet been invented. It was contained, instead, in "knife boxes" kept in the dining room. Indeed it had been since the 1730s, but examples from this early period, which are usually covered with polished sharkskin (shagreen), are rare. The great age of the knife box was after the 1760s (*see* feature box on knife boxes, p.105).

Condiments and their containers

The variety of condiments to enhance or disguise the flavour of food increased during the 18th century from the traditional salt, pepper, nutmeg, mustard, oil, and vinegar in the 1730s to over a dozen different essences, peppers, and spices by the 1790s. Mustard was still served dry but sauces, such as soy, were also popular. These were contained in silver casters and silver-mounted bottles,

grouped together in a cruet for grander tables. The earliest and best known is the Warwick cruet, which, in the 19th century, became a generic term for any specially made tray on legs with a central handle that contained either five casters or three casters and two bottles. At that time it was believed the Earl of Warwick commissioned the first one to be made, but earlier examples have since come to light, thus debunking the legend. The caster, with its pierced top, could cast its contents evenly over the plate, while a similar-shaped container with a solid unpierced ("blind") top needed a spoon to serve its contents.

Salt, which by now had lost much of its ceremonial significance, was served separately from the cruet in small dishes, or cellars, that were placed between guests or sometimes one for each. The first were rectangular and shaped rather like small jelly moulds with sunken tops. These were known as "trencher" salts (*see* Antiques Analysis pp.230–1). From the 1730s a circular bowl with an everted "gadroon" border and raised on three scroll feet was popular, until the Neoclassical style took over. The boat shape in its various forms was an elegant replacement and could be made to a variety of qualities and costs, enabling even the less affluent to dress their table in the height of fashion. This was encouraged even further by the advent of Sheffield Plate (*see* pp.119–21).

Salt will eat into silver and scorch the surface in the same way as a burn on wood if it is left for many days – a fact soon learned and remedied by coating the insides of cellars with gold, which is impervious to salt. An alternative was the introduction of blue-glass liners in the 1760s as their production became easier and more affordable. Although useful for the circular cellars, the boat shape, which came in with the Neoclassical style after the 1780s, lent itself admirably to the coloured glass – particularly when the sides of the cellar were pierced, allowing the contrasting blue to show through the cut-out patterns (*see* Antiques Analysis p.231). During the Victorian period the variety of designs for cruet sets defies description here, but by the early 1900s a small set of the three main condiments (salt, pepper, and mustard) became the smart accoutrement to have, and remains so to the present day, with less accent on the salt.

▼ **31 Enamel portrait miniature of the Prince of Wales, English, 1753**, by Jean-Étienne Leotard (1702–89). The future King George III is pictured here at 19 years old, wearing the fashionable short curled powdered wig and black wig-bag, with a plain, moderate cravat and lace jabot.

The Neoclassical style

No aspect of life in an increasingly affluent society was left untouched by the Neoclassical style, from the most delicate jewellery (*see* Pls. 17 and 18) to a common teacup. The age of Neoclassicism is therefore easy to spot. For example, look at the shape of the overmantel mirror in Plate 10. Long rectangular mirrors, usually with three plates (the centre one larger than the two ends), had been used in this position in a room since the early 18th century, but with a scrolling frame to conform with the rest of the décor. Here the architectural theme of end columns supporting a deeply moulded cornice, often with balls spaced within it over a deep frieze, was a totally new concept. The frieze

▼ **32 Oil-on-canvas portrait of George, Prince Regent, by Sir Thomas Lawrence, English, 1814–20**, in which the future King George IV displays the post-1790s fashion for natural hair cut short, and an excessively high cravat with collar points protruding. This dramatic picture illustrates well the theatricality that he enjoyed and surrounded himself with.

could take a number of forms. For example, sometimes it was a scene with Classical figures in slightly raised plasterwork, at other times a simple geometric all-over design. But the most exotic was a technique known as *verre-eglomise*. This is an ancient skill that was practised centuries earlier in Damascus and then Italy, before being popularized in France, then England and America, by a framer and designer in Paris, Jean-Baptiste Glomy (*d*.1781). With this technique a dramatic effect is achieved by drawing or painting on the reverse of a glass panel and then backing the picture with metal foils, usually gold or silver, and black or brown insets. It was much used in the 1780s and thereafter until the middle of the 19th century, and can be seen used in decorative borders on small pictures, miniature portraits, and on the tops and sides of mirrors.

Frames for pictures also changed dramatically at this time and the one on page 99 is a perfect example. The whole body of the frame became one simple moulding decorated with fluting. This occurred on square and rectangular frames as well as ovals and rounds. The cresting on the one in Plate 11 reveals the adherence to Robert Adam's use of the formalized honeysuckle motif, which continued with various interpretations throughout the ensuing high-style Regency period.

Despite trade restrictions on British exports to America, the economy continued to boom thanks to the battles with Napoleon from 1793 to 1815, enabling tradesmen and women, as well as gentry, to equip themselves as nobility. A fine example of this is the painting on page 105, *The Morning Walk* by Thomas Gainsborough. The subjects of this elegant portrait are

◄ **33 Interior of Otis House (now a museum), Boston, America, c.1796**, designed for Harrison Gray Otis by Charles Bulfinch. This interior shows the similarities and differences between English and American decoration at this time: there is a pleasing mixture of British Sheraton and French Empire styles, particularly in the dining chairs and the pier table.

◄ **34 Portrait miniature of a lady by George Engleheart, c.1775**. The art and popularity of miniature painting reached new heights in the last quarter of the 18th century. The general softening of women's costume at that time encouraged a more romantic look, as shown here.

► **35 Portrait miniature of an officer by John Smart, English, 1786**. This still depicts the fashionable powdered hair and lace jabot that had been the fashion for a generation or more. However, this fashion changed in the 1790s to hair worn naturally, and cut quite short above a deep cravat tied higher to the chin.

William Hallett Jnr and his wife. Hallett was the grandson of the cabinet-maker William Hallett, who had emerged during the middle of the 1700s as a leading manufacturer. His wealth overcame his lowly background to allow acceptance and inclusion for him and his family into polite society. So as well as multi-racial (in fact, truly cosmopolitan, especially in London), this society was also multi-class. It was therefore natural that as soon as George, the headstrong and hedonistic Prince of Wales, gained his majority in 1783 he should choose for his coterie of friends men and women from disparate

▲ **36 Interior scene, Swedish, 1830**, by Carl Johan Ljunggren. The empirical form of much Scandinavian furniture and decoration is well documented, but little appreciated in comparison with that of the rest of Europe. It is elegant and often understated, with references to France and, to a lesser extent, Italy: note the freestanding stove, and the chandelier in the far hall.

▼ **37 Design for a house to be built on Clapham Common, London, c.1810**, by Humphrey Repton. By the early 19th century the ideal house in the country was of pavilion rather than palatial concept. The main reception rooms were at ground level to facilitate walking into the garden, and iron pergolas supported climbing plants.

backgrounds. Once away from the dullness of his father's court at Buckingham House, the Prince consorted with anti-establishment figures at Brooks's Club in St. James's, London, and embarked on creating a sumptuous palace at Carlton House in Pall Mall, not many steps away, which his father had allocated to him on his 21st birthday.

Although the influence of Robert Adam, Hepplewhite, and Sheraton designs was overwhelming, there was still appreciation for many objects of the previous Rococo period, particularly *objets d'art* that were treasured as heirlooms in the same way they are today. As examples we only have to look at the forms and decoration of enamel boxes for snuff, patches, and needles, as well as other "toys" as described on page 103. The Prince of Wales retained his admiration for the French styles of the pre-Revolution court, and furnished much of Carlton House in this manner. The plush upholstered chairs, with frames elaborately carved and gilded, were in contrast to, and reflected in, the huge pier mirrors made in the latest Neoclassical style, which were designed and put in place by Henry Holland.

Holland's designs had drawn the attention of the Prince when he completed alterations to Brooks's Club. Holland's elevation to such prestigious company was certainly helped by his marriage to Brigitte Jones, only daughter of Lancelot "Capability" Brown, the renowned landscape gardener to the aristocracy. But it was entirely merited, for he became, justifiably, the next most

▲ **38 The Trafalgar vase, English, 1804–9.** There were 66 of these vases made, 15 of which were presented by Lloyds Patriotic Fund to the captains who had served closely with Nelson at Trafalgar. Designed in the Neoclassical style by John Flaxman, they were made by Digby Scott and Benjamin Smith for Rundell, Bridge and Rundell.

SOFA TABLES

It was during the last 15 years of the 18th century that there was another influx of new furniture: ladies' work and writing tables, chiffoniers, canterburies, small individual writing desks called davenports (*see* p.134), and sofa tables.

The fashion for Empire-style clothes for women and the new informal atmosphere of the drawing room encouraged the gentle and highly posed attitude of reclining on the sofa, which was a modern version of the earlier daybed. Ladies now required something other than a lap-desk to support their writing, so a rectangular table was constructed, wide enough to pull over the sofa, and which stood on a single pedestal at each end with two swept legs terminating in castors. A shallow, hinged leaf, or flap, at each end over the pedestals became a standard fitment, along with two drawers in the frieze below the top (*see* pp.232–3).

Until the 1790s this was the pattern, but by 1800 a bar running from one pedestal end to the other was added to give stability, unfortunately denying access to the reclining lady and defeating the original purpose. Nevertheless, the elegant proportions of the top of the sofa table ensured it a lasting place in household furniture, and by 1810 it became a fashionable alternative to have it supported by a single central pedestal. This ended just over halfway to the ground on a square or rectangular platform that had a curved leg extending from each corner terminating in a brass cap castor. This took the form of a lion's-paw foot after *c.*1810.

The heavier and more cumbersome a sofa table is, the later it will be, but it never really went out of fashion.

influential interior designer and architect in English history. The effect of Holland's design was so lavish that Carlton House became known as one of the most enviable new palaces in Europe, with dignitaries from all corners of the globe vying for an invitation to attend. Holland worked in a simplified version of the latest French Empire style (*see* p.122), as well as using his Graeco-Roman and Chinoiserie patterns, and he also introduced the practice of making room settings less formal. Reception rooms were no longer set with furniture around the walls to be brought into use when necessary; rather, tables, chairs, and large settees were placed seemingly at random (while being carefully arranged to look so) for people to relax and enjoy separate pastimes, and from which positions they were rarely moved. As an example of this, the interior of Southill in Bedfordshire (the home of the Whitbread family, which was rebuilt 1796–1800) still contains the original furniture designed by Henry Holland, and all remains very much placed where he decreed.

▲ **39 Oil-on-canvas painting of the death of Admiral Lord Nelson, English,** by Henry Singleton, RA (1766–1839). This historic event affected every walk of life for the next 50 years, as anything connected to naval campaigns and memorabilia was immediately saleable, such as the curved "sabre leg", and, morbidly, the sarcophagus shape so popular on tea caddies.

The emergence of trade systems

The demand for furnishings and household items continued to increase along with the population, making the use of machinery and a factory system inevitable. Trade societies and livery companies agreed to the publication of price lists for all manner of goods, which protected both the manufacturer and the buying public by announcing the equivalent of today's *Recommended Retail Price Index*, although they were not universally accepted as being a good thing at first, particularly in America. In 1788 the *London Cabinet Book of Prices* was published, with many illustrations to show standard models of furniture with suggested prices attached. On 1 August 1796 the first-known American version was published and appeared in Hartford,

▲ **40 Rosewood and brass inlaid sofa table, English, c.1820,** the inlay of brass stringing and the angled corners plus a central column support giving us instant recognition of a post-1810 date. Here it would be advisable to look carefully to ensure that all the parts are original.

Connecticut. Two years later *The Philadelphia Cabinet and Chair-Makers' Book of Prices* was published, closely followed by a "second edition, corrected and enlarged".

In England, leading furniture-makers had for more than 30 years recognized the benefits of combining separate but allied crafts under one roof. Major companies, such as those of Ince and Mayhew and George Seddon (1727–1801), employed joiners, carvers, gilders, mirror-makers, locksmiths, and upholsterers on their premises. According to the German traveller Sophie von La Roche, Seddon's workshop housed 400 such artisans – incidentally with a turnover inventory of £118, 926 ($190,282), an astronomical figure in 1786.

In America there was no less development, albeit on a smaller scale, when we learn that in 1792 T. Bradford and Henry Clements, upholsterer and cabinet- and chair-maker respectively, joined together in partnership to best accommodate their clients with "all kinds of upholstery furniture made up, or old altered". Antique furniture was altered for the most innocent of reasons, such as a change of use, as well as being improved to increase its value.

The price books established some uniformity in the acceptable wage for a specific job, and took their early levels from those in London. However, by 1795 these had

risen in America to 50 percent higher in Philadelphia and 75 percent higher in Charleston. The Federal Period also saw an exaggeration of the imported patterns from England and the rest of Europe, in contrast to the restrained domestic and decorative arts designs prior to the American Revolution. As can be seen in Plate 13, a fashionable silver tea and coffee set had the body of each main pot given an extra waisted section above the vase-shaped lower part, and below the cover and finial. In Plate 14 the secretary cabinet has a swept and curved cornice that is both convex and concave, giving it an extraordinary undulating contour with some bulk at each end. This magnificent and charming example shows, in its combination of such a variety of design features, that its origins are in more than one area and from more than one period of English styles, making it un-English and in this case unmistakably American. The top of the centre section is taken straight from Thomas Sheraton's *The Cabinet-Maker and Upholsterer's Drawing-Book* (1791–4), but the ends have a Scottish feel to them and would be ten years later in British design, *c.*1810. The doors each have 13 panes of glass, a pattern made popular by Hepplewhite's *The Cabinet-Maker and Upholsterer's Guide* (1788–94). The designs for the lower doors, with their oval inlaid panels, were described in both publications. All of this shows an extended adherence to several important and rapidly changing features on fashionable English furniture over a longer period of time than one would expect to see in England. However, such combinations often did occur in English provincial furniture. Take, for example, the situation where some of the latest patterns were suggested to a highly skilled, local, but elderly cabinet-maker, set in his ways and disinclined to modernize. This could create such anomalies. Of course this is possible but unlikely in the case of Plate 14 for the following reasons: the finest and most expensive cuts of timber, which are so clearly evident on this piece, combined with the wide range of different skills required to make it, lift it out of the provincial workshop status. Provincial furniture from any country has its own charm and quality, but just as a country tailor makes a country suit best, so his equivalent cabinet-maker makes his individual furniture, and the difference from higher-quality goods is always discernable.

A new type of folding table, used for games or tea when open, travelled quickly across the Atlantic. Instead of one or two legs hinged at the back to swing out and support the open top, the lower leaf of the top was made

▲ 41 Coloured woodcut of Napoleon's grave on St Helena, French, reprinted in 1813, by François Georgin. The *acroterion* (plinth) to each top corner is formed as a stylized honeysuckle within a solid quarter-circle tablet. This ancient device became a standard motif in High-style Regency design throughout Europe.

▶ 42 Lady's bookcase of mahogany and kingwood, English, *c.*1822. This clearly shows the architectural influence on Regency furniture in the pediment and the *acroterions*, which replicate those on Napoleon's grave. The free-standing columns, which are equal top and bottom (a persic pillar), give a later-Regency feel to this piece.

to swivel, allowing the table to have an elegant central support. In Plate 15 the base is taken directly from the English Classical style, while the top has an extra sweep to its shaped edges and frieze. This is not an English pattern at all, but if proven through timber analysis not to be American then the verdict on its provenance would be Scottish, the home of one of America's most celebrated cabinet-makers, Duncan Phyfe (*see* p.109).

Sheffield Plate

During the last quarter of the 18th century the development of Sheffield Plate made a huge impact on the appearance of the middle classes and their homes. This was because it enabled them to adorn their clothes with buckles, buttons, and brooches that looked like silver but which actually cost a fraction of the real thing. They could also dress their tables with candlesticks, candelabra, cake baskets, coasters, and cruets in the same way.

Applying a thin layer of a precious metal onto an object made of base metal, called "close plating", is a skill that had been known for centuries, but its disadvantage in a world already anxious for speed and efficiency was that it was an additional and expensive process. The advantage of Sheffield Plate was that the two metals were fused together prior to the manufacture of an object. An ingot comprising a block of silver and one of copper was rolled out into a thin sheet, the gauge of which allowed it to be made into an object by stamping or hand-raising, just as if it was solid silver. So instead of requiring an additional craftsman to aggrandize the object, it could be made by any accomplished silversmith. The process had been discovered almost by mistake in 1742 in the workshops of one Thomas Bolsover, a Sheffield cutler who, the story goes, was mending a silver handle with a copper coin under pressure in a vice when he allowed his work to overheat and found the two metals inseparable.

It was 40 years before the process came to the fore, encouraged by another Sheffield company, Messrs Tudor, Leader, and Sherburn, who used horse-power to power their rolling mills in 1762. By this time there were 22,000 people in Sheffield making knives and scissors, and the

town was established as the cutlery centre of Great Britain. Meanwhile Mr Bolsover's method had attracted the attention of London manufacturers, and of Matthew Boulton in his Soho, Birmingham works (*see* p.102). At the age of 17 Boulton had invented a means of making inlaid steel buttons, charms, trinkets, chains, and "toys", which he exported in vast quantities to France. Here they were bought by English beaux as the latest French delights and brought back to England as souvenirs. Having had such success in the "small" market, Boulton had a great interest in any technical innovations in this field, and when he set up business with James Watt in 1775 to build steam-powered engines for their own factory production (as well as for sale to others) the Sheffield Plate concept was a natural vehicle.

Various improvements were made in the production, including the application of a layer of silver on both

▼ **43 Mahogany cellarette, English, c.1825,** with heavy angled gadroon borders and split-turned moulding to the front, indicating a date after 1815. The monumental form of the sarcophagus became popular for furniture after the death of Nelson in 1805. Cellarettes of this type usually stood under a sideboard.

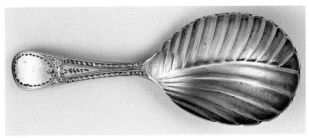

◀ **44 Brass tea caddy, Continental, c.1835.** This still has a sarcophagus shape but is now rounded. This is a most desirable collector's item due to its charm and untouched surface. In certain circles this is a patina to die for, and it must never be cleaned away.

▲ **45 Silver caddy spoon, English, 1789.** The earliest recorded caddy spoons date from the 1770s, necessitated by the common practice of chopping the leaves of tea into fragments. The variety is endless, from leaf-pattern bowls, as here, to miniature jockey caps.

sides of the copper, but the most significant was the development of the roll-over edge. Unless disguised in some way the outer edge of the finished object would show the core of copper and so it was cut at an angle to enable the top layer to overlap and turn under, thus concealing the edge of copper and producing a neat rounded finish. This left a visible line around the border, which was also detectable to the touch and is a good indication of Sheffield Plate period manufacture, although it is far from proof. Alternatively, a hollow wire like a miniature hosepipe was split lengthways and applied to the edge; this created a visible line on both top and bottom surfaces. Both methods were obsolete after the introduction of electro-plating in 1840, wherein an object fully formed of copper was plated with silver by means of electrolysis.

By the 1780s platers began to apply marks of identification. Some were highly distinctive, such as Matthew Boulton's two eight-pointed stars, but others became increasingly similar to the hallmarks on solid silver to such a degree that to the untutored eye – that is, most of the buying public – they looked the same. Legislation established restrictions but these were only partially workable, and close scrutiny is still advisable (*see* Silver Marks on p.154 for further information).

Another problem for buyers today is that French manufacturers quickly and successfully adopted the Sheffield Plate method but they continued to use it long after Britain had changed to electro-plating, hence the fact that the roll-over edge is not definite proof of genuine Sheffield Plate.

The emergence of various styles

The differences between father and son, King George III and the Prince of Wales, were not dissimilar to any such frictions within a family, but the status of the parties involved meant they were aired in public. They extended beyond mere family spats into the world of artistic appreciation, and were highlighted by the Prince's flamboyant rejection of modesty and restraint in such matters. Many examples of the furnishings he chose for his London residence, Carlton House, are extant and can be seen only at Buckingham Palace and Windsor Castle, as Carlton House was found to be unsafe and pulled down in 1827. However, thanks to the work of a succession of dedicated curators since World War II, we can still visit and enjoy much of the original grandeur of the exterior and interior of the Royal Pavilion at Brighton (*see* Pl. 28). Here Indian architecture, Chinese décor, and French Empire-inspired artifacts create a fantastic jewel in the crown for English heritage. Whatever his critics may say about him, had the Prince of Wales not been such a profligate spender on his surroundings Britain would have been a much duller place today, especially in the Brighton area.

In the intervals between the Napoleonic Wars the rich English maintained a dialogue with their French counterparts, and so French taste was dominant in high-society decoration. Following the excesses of the Rococo period the design pendulum swung unsustainably the other way in France, where the Neoclassical style became plainer and more severe. The strictest adherence to this occurred during 1793–9, a period known as the *Directoire*. Like the wine at that time, this style did not travel too well

▲ **46 Carved wood and gilt open armchair, English, c.1805,** with a design and decoration similar to several that can be attributed to Henry Holland – for example, the way the front face of each back support flows forward into the seat frame. So we can date this chair within the period of Holland's influence.

▲ **47 Dining room in The Royal Pavilion, Brighton, England.** This room displays a cosmopolitan influence, as the walls are typically Chinoiserie in style, but the curled-over tops of the chair frames, bottom left, are distinctly English, and the candelabra are very much in the French taste. Meals would have been comfortable, well-lit, and perfectly served.

nor last too long, and by the beginning of the 1800s a lighter, more decorated approach was receiving acclaim on both sides of the Channel. This is described as *Empire* and is pronounced in the French manner in order to distinguish it from the English Empire style, which lasted from *c.*1760 to the 1820s and which, for once, Britain had adopted first. It is worth mentioning here that the French *Regence* was from 1715 to 1723 and therefore totally different in date to the English Regency.

At this time, therefore, there were not one or two styles but several, variously appealing to different classes and ages of people. The King's generation and followers stuck to the pleasing and non-challenging designs for furniture of Hepplewhite and Sheraton, often because the sweeping changes of the 1780s had been expensive and only the very rich could afford to re-furnish yet again. But the Prince and his set followed the styles decreed by Henry Holland, the Prince's chosen architect and confidant (*see* pp.116–17).

These comprised New French, Old Mediterranean in its various forms, and Chinese. Greek and Roman designs were heavily accented and often coupled with strong naval themes, such as simulated rope backs for chairs, cannons and cannon balls, anchors, and capstans following Nelson's achievements, and, particularly after the Battle of the Nile, the odd alligator. Following Nelson's death in 1805 the ancient sarcophagus shape of his coffin was widely adopted for household items such as tea caddies, as well as for monuments in memoriam (*see* Pls. 42 and 43).

Fashionable people read the innovative Rudolph Ackermann's *Repository* 1809–29, a magazine showing and explaining the latest in everything, as well as a growing number of catalogues produced by connoisseurs, manufacturers, and retailers. One such connoisseur was Thomas Hope (1769–1831), a Dutch-born, wealthy, highly educated, and multi-talented patron of the arts. His *A Collection of Designs for Household Furniture and*

▲ **48 Interior from the house of Thomas Hope, English, c.1807.**
Hope was a connoisseur of antiquities and good taste, and introduced
a new style to London with the publication of his book *Household
Furniture and Interior Decoration* in 1807 (*see* pp.122–4).

▶ **49 Design for a convex mirror by George Smith, English, 1808**,
with a Graeco-Egyptian flavour that dominates the frame. The flying
bat carrying the mirror is a play on Bat, the Egyptian goddess of fertility
(*see* George Smith p.124). Convex mirrors became popular in the late
18th century and remained so during the Regency period.

▼ **50 Drawing for a throne, by Thomas Hope, English, c.1807.**
Although something of a hybrid, this drawing shows the strict
adherence to ancient style adopted by Hope.

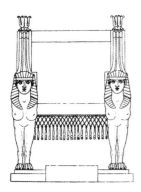

▶ **51 Ormolu and cut-glass dish light, English, c.1810.** A style of hanging light that replaced the centrally supported chandelier of the 18th century in fashionable Regency interiors. Note the elongated drops suspended from two or three rows of buttons, compared to those on the chandelier in Plate 31, chapter 3.

Interior Decoration (1807) became the standard reference book for high-style cognoscenti, and showed interiors inspired by his travels to Ancient Greece and Egypt, as well as his huge collection of genuine antique sculpture and vases.

Such Classical accuracy as advocated by Hope was restricting, but George Smith (*c.*1786–1826), a leading London furniture-maker, saw commercial potential in the style. In 1808 Smith published *A Collection of Designs for Household Furniture and Interior Decoration*, which was a compilation of 158 drawings dating from between 1804 and 1807. This was the first publication to show the Regency style as a possible and affordable alternative. His last book, *The Cabinet-Maker and Upholsterer's Guide*, was published in 1826, and the change from light to heavy ornamentation that became popular during the late Regency period (1820–30) is so clearly evident that it is Smith's books that are used today as much, if not more, than any others as points of reference (*see* p.129).

The French *Empire* style was as stately as one would expect an Emperor to relish, with more display of polished mahogany enriched with gilt metal mounts than the English version. In America, where the regularity of line and proportion was appreciated, the style became adorned with more natural motifs (such as flower sprays), imaginative and topographical scenes, and the American Eagle. By 1820 the delicacy of the Hepplewhite/Sheraton styles had all but disappeared, to be replaced by the more opulent but still Classically inspired Regency, which became ever more fleshy and foliate.

The famous Regency stripe in fabrics gave way to floral and scenic patterns, encouraged by rapid advances in the cloth-making industry, especially cotton, making fashionable fabrics available in larger quantities and to more people. New techniques in printing wallpaper by block or roller meant that fabric patterns could more easily be replicated, and, as fashion changed so quickly, the expensive effect of matching walls and curtains could be achieved at a fraction of the previous cost.

The mystical world of the East and the mythical aura of the Ancient civilizations spawned an age of Romanticism, with paintings by Ben Marshall, Thomas Lawrence, J.M.W. Turner, and John Constable hanging beside the Old Masters. The latter, if not inherited, could be bought at auction in London, which was now considered the centre of the European art market. In literature it was the age of Wordsworth, Coleridge, Byron, Shelley, and Keats. Looking at the new style of "romantic" house in Plate 36, or the interior in Plate 53, it is easy to relate their writings to the environment of the time. It is also easy to understand a revival of the Gothic taste, accompanied by a harking back to the "Age of Chivalry", which was to set the scene for all manner of objects being adorned with maidens in distress, and knights in shining armour slaying dragons, in the decades to come.

The construction industry

In 1811 King George III was deemed unfit to rule; a Regency was declared, and the Prince of Wales became the Prince Regent. During this period the benefits of the developments in iron manufacture during the last quarter of the 18th century became apparent, and made England the centre of the construction industry. In 1779 Thomas Telford (1737–1834) constructed the famous Ironbridge at Coalbrookdale (*see* Pl. 29), and his suspension bridge over the Menai Strait linking Wales and Anglesey in 1825 became a role model for the rest of the world (it is still in use today). The rapid changes in fashion, and the countrywide knowledge of them, was due to the further improvements to Britain's roads, and here again Britain led the rest of the world.

It is extraordinary that the first great pioneer of professional road-building was blind. John Metcalf (1717–1810), or "blind Jack of Knaresborough" as he was commonly known, was responsible for over 320km (200 miles) of soundly built roads in Yorkshire, England – some of the most difficult terrain in the country.

Metcalf's ideas were furthered by Telford, who built over 1,600km (1,000 miles) of roads and 1,200 bridges in Scotland, and by John McAdam (1736–1836). McAdam

▲ **52 Mahogany dining chairs, English, *c*.1795**, to a design associated with Thomas Sheraton. The stylized "x" frame backs, oval paterae to the centre, and entablature on the top rail confirm their date and superior quality.

▼ **53 Interior of house in Edgewater, USA, *c*.1820**. The Federal style predominates here, with chairs made to an English pattern but with "Grecian Cross" legs attributed to Duncan Phyffe and New York manufacture.

◄ **54 Pair of silver-gilt wine trolleys, English, 1823**. The sheer lavishness of these trolleys, in the form of vine leaves and grapes, makes them a typical luxury enjoyed by wealthy courtiers of King George IV. Trolleys did not appear much before the 1790s, and even plain examples are highly sought-after today.

improved the road surfaces by pressing down broken stones bound together with a tarry liquid. His roads were said to be "macadamized", and the liquid later became known as "tarmac". At precisely the end of the period covered by this chapter, in 1830, the Liverpool-to-Manchester Railway was opened, and so was England opened up, as a new age of transport began.

Work- and leisure-dictated fashions

The daily life of the middle and upper classes was very much as we would recognize and fit into today, being of two main forms: the working day and the weekend. The first revolved around the trade or profession of the master of the house, with breakfast and dinner and an interval for luncheon somewhere in between. The weekend is much

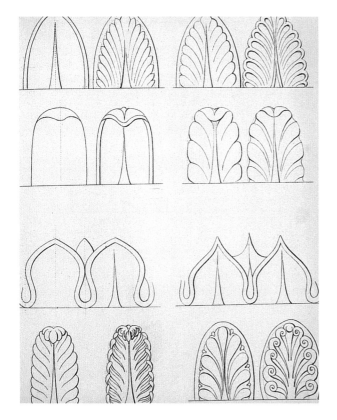

▲ **55 Leaf drawings by George Smith, English, 1826**. Smith produced three important books of designs, of which the first, in 1808, and the last, in 1826, are the most significant. His early work was influenced by the Egyptophile Thomas Hope, but his later style became eclectic and foresaw the Victorian heaviness.

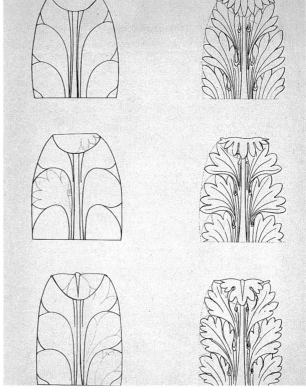

▲ **56 Leaf drawings by George Smith, English, 1826**. These can be compared with the type of leaf decoration favourable in early Regency design shown in Plate 55 – where the leaves are highly stylized and formal. In these drawings from the 1820s, shown above, the acanthus leaf has almost become a raffle leaf, reflecting the Rococo revival of the late-Regency period.

▲ **57 Detail of ormolu shelf-support, English, c.1825**, in finely cast and chased gilt-metal combining pure Classical square section scrolls, and Rococo-revival leaf-capped ornamentation.

◄ **58 Regency cabinet, English, c.1825**, with marble columns, top, and shelf, and wood painted to simulate rosewood. The mounts (*see* Pl. 57) show a French influence, popular at the time.

more fun to relate to as it inevitably involved a collection of guests for the "house party". Guests would have a huge and late breakfast at about 10 or 11 o'clock, followed by pastimes according to country or town situation and the time of year. Internal activities included board games, needlework, music, painting, and drawing – in fact all the things we do today, except watching television of course.

These pastimes were carried on in one or two of the several reception rooms, which were open throughout the day, and in the early afternoon a lunch was served. Alternatively, a buffet was laid out for guests to help themselves and then wander around with plates of food, perhaps into the garden or onto the roof terrace.

Clothing was considered informal, but by present-day standards would have required far more preparation than we would cope with. For the men, fine boots and breeches,

close-fitting short-tailed coats over a vest or waistcoat, an impeccable cravat with white linen shirt, and natural but carefully groomed hair, rather than a wig, was expected. Empire dresses were the norm for women, and much attention was paid to hair, complexion, and accessories such as purses, fans, and jewellery.

Dinner began at around 7 o'clock, and continued the traditional formality with a gathering in an anteroom before the procession into the dining room. This was conducted in strict pecking order, the highest-ranking guests being the first to follow or accompany the hosts. By now it was the norm to have four or more servants in attendance, and the meal was long and the menu varied, consisting of several courses and many dishes. Large dinner services were made to include specific items, such as asparagus trays and custard cups, and numbered

◀ **59 Late-Regency-period centre table with marble top, English and Italian, c.1825.** The definitive design of the table is precisely in the style of the late-Regency period (c.1820-30). The base refers closely to the designs of George Smith (see p.131).

▼ **60 Italian marble table top, c.1825.** It is made of a variety of specimen pieces using the *pietra dura* inlay technique. Examples of this craft had been brought back to England since Elizabethan times, and furniture-makers made suitable stands to display them.

from 12 to 36 place settings. As many as 500 pieces were sometimes required for a formal meal.

In town, men carried umbrellas rather than swords, and wore shoes with laces. Horror was expressed at first by the "establishment", but when the clergy adopted both these fashions there were no more protests. In wealthier circles, particularly that of the Prince of Wales, dressing became a pastime in itself, with meticulous attention paid to detail. An extreme example is that of George Bryan "Beau" Brummel (1778–1840), who, at the age of 16, was introduced to the Prince and his circle. Already elegant and keen-witted, he became an instant favourite and an arbiter of fashion. Brummel is credited with inventing the "evening dress" for men – a black tailcoat and long black trousers worn always with the finest white linen shirt, a stiff white collar, and an immaculate cravat. His dress code was simple but meticulous, to which end he would spend up to five hours preparing for the day, inching into skin-tight breeches, having boots polished with champagne, and tying innumerable cravats until perfection was achieved. Brummel was not unusual in having a different snuff box for every day of the year, many of which were

gold, gilt, silver, or enamel, and all extremely expensive. This whole way of life, especially when coupled with the costs of gambling, entertaining, building, and constant redecorating, could only be supported on an enormous disposable income, and indeed most of the affluent friends of the Prince, or young "bucks" as they were known, had £30,000–60,000 ($48,000–96,000) per annum to spend. While many, like Brummel, spent it quickly enough – he was bankrupt by 1816 – and ended up penniless, many others provided us with the legacy of the magnificent houses and collections that we can experience today.

Through the wider broadcasting of national and international affairs, and the heroes and villains involved, public figures were increasingly praised and lampooned according to the population's perception of their actions. A general improvement in education and the circulation of pamphlets and news-sheets encouraged this development, building on the satirical and immensely loaded drawings of William Hogarth (1697–1764) and a steady growth in general interest in the goings-on of the rich and famous. In the world of political journalism one man stands out as being responsible for the freedom

GEORGE SMITH

Decorative details became heavier during the late-Regency period. This enables us to differentiate and date items quite accurately as being either pre- or post-c.1815–20. The third and last publication by George Smith, *The Cabinet-Maker and Upholsterer's Guide* in 1826, is among the best illustrations of recent past and current taste, as seen in Plate 65. The use of even the smallest identifiable feature, such as a simple scroll or leaf, can make it possible to identify a designer, possibly a maker, and certainly a period.

► 61 Carved foot of table, English, c.1825, made en suite with the table in Plate 66. The triform base sits on a foot clearly taken from Smith's designs (*see* Pl. 65), with the drawn acanthus leaf replaced by the type shown on page 126.

► 62 Late-Regency stool, English, c.1825. The ancient "X" frame form is almost lost in the huge Lion's-Paw feet, heavily capped by a single wrap-around leaf. This type of late-Regency style was innovative at the time.

► 63 Part of a late-Regency brass mount on a sideboard, English, c.1820. Note the difference between this scroll support and the one in Plate 57, which shows some Rococo-revival leaf decoration; this is purely Classical in style.

▼ 64 Decorative detail from a design by George Smith, English, 1826. Drawn as a vignette in a text, which explains its purpose, this stylized bell flower can be used to great effect, as seen in the brass mount above in Plate 63.

▲ 65 Page from a book by George Smith, English, 1826. Nine variations for feet show popular motifs such as the Lion's Paw, Vitruvian Scroll, and Stylized Acanthus Leaf. Smith did not invent these, but recorded in his own style what was then popular.

▼ 66 Base of an important late-Regency library writing table, English, c.1825. The paw feet and leaves are realistic and fleshy, the scrolls are architectural. Such fineness is only achievable when the best quality timber, in this case rosewood, is used.

PLATE CXI.

The outlines in this plate are compounded more or less from those given in the preceding plate : for instance,

Fig. 18, will be seen to partake of the outlines marked 8 and 9 in the preceding plate. It is chiefly used in ornamental work to fill up the vacant space betwixt two scrolls as rising one out of the other : thus, as in the wood cut.

◄ 67 Design for a writing table by George Smith, English, 1826. There may be many variations on this idea, but the essential form is sufficient to establish a starting point for research.

◄ **68 Wheel, or "Banjo", barometer, English, c.1835.** The sharp outlines of the case offer an alternative to the earlier gentle curves of wheel barometers in the late 18th century. The inclusion of a detachable hygrometer and barometer and a spirit level at the base will also indicate a 19th-century date.

▶ **69 Mahogany and gilt-mounted bracket clock, English, c.1825.** The lines of this clock case are quite severe and architectural with a round, convex glass door, in contrast to the square or rectangular door of the 18th-century clocks. The best examples have the gilt enrichments in metal, rather than gilded gesso.

the press has enjoyed for over 200 years – John Wilkes (1727–97). He was an agitator, journalist, politician, reformer, and one-time Lord Mayor of London. During the American Revolution he championed the colonial cause, and in April 1763 he published the 45th edition of his *North Briton*, in which he accused the British Government of lying in the King's Speech.

For the next 30 years his career was to secure freedom of choice for the electorate and freedom of the press, but it is his "No. 45" edition for which he is best remembered. On drinking glasses, snuff boxes of silver and brass, and bowls of pewter and porcelain were engraved the words "Wilkes and Liberty" and "No. 45", sometimes with a caricature portrait showing the unfortunate cast he had in one eye. Any genuine example of one of these will be rare and valuable. So too will similarly engraved or decorated pieces pertaining to any famous person or event. For example, Admiral John Byng (1704–57) was executed for failing to do his utmost to relieve Minorca when it was under attack from the French navy. Although this was later re-appraised as being an unduly harsh punishment, at the time Byng was

popularly depicted as a coward, and shown on drinking glasses hanging from a gibbet – he was actually shot to death.

Navigation

Captain James Cook (1728–79) is known today as the great British navigator and cartographer. His work in observing planetary movements for King George III, his discoveries of unknown lands, and his prescribed diet, high in Vitamin C, for his crew – which virtually eliminated scurvy – earned him a special place in the hearts of the British people, and as well as having the Staffordshire potters create a seated figure of him, a jasper ware plaque by Wedgwood was produced in his honour (*see* Pl. 24). Travelling with Cook on his second voyage was another seafarer whose future career was to show an extraordinary variety of fine qualities, talents, and flaws: my namesake, Captain, later Admiral, Bligh (1754–1817). The famous mutiny aboard the *Bounty* and its aftermath made his name as a remarkable navigator, eclipsing his gifts as an artist, cartographer, and botanist. His mission on the *Bounty* was to transport breadfruit from Tahiti to the West Indies. Aside from the several known portraits of Bligh, commemorative items ascribed to him are rare.

Captain Cook's voyages are recorded in detail in book form and on all contemporary and later terrestrial globes – standing, table, and pocket-size. Globes were an integral part of education, and from the late 17th century can be found as small as a cricket ball, often contained within a shagreen case, the inside of which is lined with a map of the heavens, providing the viewer with celestial information. Legend has it that these miniature globes were carried by the itinerant tutors that roamed Europe well into the 19th century, as well as by portrait and topographical artists, music teachers, dancing instructors, letter writers, attorneys, preachers, and quack doctors. This probably has a factual base, for a good knowledge of geography was highly important to the educated classes. With its study came an understanding of scientific instruments, from the telescope and compass to the astrolabe and orrery (*see* scientific and teaching instruments, below). The marine chronometer (*see* p.89) played an important part in navigation, making accurate timekeeping a principal means of determining position at sea.

No single person was untouched by the death of England's greatest naval hero, Admiral Horatio Nelson (1758–1805), and few artifacts were not made to commemorate his life and tragic end (*see* Pl. 38). Every conceivable item made of gold, silver, wood, brass, iron, steel, glass, pewter, stone, tin, and papier-mâché bore some allusion to him, either emblematic or narrative, or both. But he and other war-heroes were not alone in being the subjects of such adulation, for politicians, writers, painters, and inventors were also publicly acknowledged, together with certain captains of industry.

Scientific and teaching instruments

The magnetic compass has been in use since the 2nd century BC and can be found in any degree of antiquity, fineness, and historical interest. In common with other such instruments, there are many aspects to its intrigue: it may be the rarity of the piece itself, or it might be a mundane example from a ship with a great history. Or of course it may be by an important or interesting maker, such as Richard Glynne of London (*c.*1706) or F.W. Lincoln Jnr & Co., of Boston, Massachusetts, USA (*c.*1850).

A simple "pocket" example from the 18th century in a plain wooden case can also be fascinating without being

costly and can easily start a collecting "bug". There were great improvements in the manufacture of fine glass for telescope lenses in the late 1750s, which means that those made after that date are more usable today. The names associated with the best telescopes during the last half of the 18th century are those of John Dollond (*d.*1761) and his two sons Peter and John, and an example by them will cost considerably more than one by any other contemporary maker. This was recognized at the time and from the early 1800s there are telescopes signed "Dolland", no doubt in an attempt to mislead unwary buyers. Note the use of an "a" instead of the second "o" to avoid copyright infringement. However, such copying was short-lived as by this time P.L. Guinand, a Swiss glassmaker, was making fine-quality optical flint glass, and within five years Britain's opticians had lost their pre-eminence.

Equatorial ring-dials, octants and sextants, nocturnals, and backstaffs are all instruments used at one time or another in assisting men to traverse the globe, and all have an intrinsic, visual appeal in addition to their other qualities. But collecting them must be undertaken with

▲ **70 Fashion print, French, *c.*1810.** This shows a move in women's fashion for the elite, after the French Revolution, to the greatest simplicity that had been known since the times of ancient Greece, led by Mesdames Recamier and Tallien. This "Empire" line became popular throughout Europe, although for colder climes more layers than a single chemise were needed.

the whole solar system. There are two types of armillery sphere: one is as described, with the earth at the centre, known as the Ptolemaic; the other has the sun as the centre and is known as the Copernican (universe).

Of all scientific instruments probably the most captivating is the orrery. This is a mechanical model of the solar system, with the planets as miniature-scaled spheres on rods that rotate accordingly when powered by turning a cranking handle or a clockwork motor. Most were made to stand on a table, usually with a tripod base and central column supporting the "drum" top that housed the mechanism. The name is said to come from the Earl of Orrery, who commissioned an early example to be made in 1713, but they were most popular in the later 18th and the 19th centuries, when they would have been found in private libraries, studies, and schoolrooms. The later an orrery is, the more complex it becomes. For example, between 1781 and 1794 the planet Uranus, six of its satellites, and two more satellites for Saturn were discovered, all of which had to be included in the orrery's display.

▲ **71 Regency-period coverlet, *c*.1820**, created from various chintz pieces, showing the delightful patterns and colours of fabrics in favour during the late-Regency period. Its arrangement of *broderie perse* (appliqué chintz) birds and butterflies is reminiscent of the new hobby of scrapbook-making with specially printed images that had become popular.

supervision and expert advice for it is a highly specialized subject. Nevertheless, as most were made to be used or to educate, it is still possible to go back in time and, gently, try them out today. An important teaching instrument was the armillery sphere. Appearing in the late 15th century, it comprises a series of open rings of different sizes set to swivel at different angles around a central sphere, supported on a single column and a wide base to be set upon a table or stand. The sphere is the earth and the rings represent the paths of the celestial equator, the solstitial and equinoctial colures, the tropics, and the elliptic. Originally constructed of silver and brass for the wealthiest families, they were later (in the 18th century) made with cardboard rings, particularly in France, for general use. From the late 16th century additional rings represented the planets, the moon, and the sun, to present

▼ **72 Stipple engraving by Paul Tessaert, French, *c*.1810**, in which the dress, hair, and mirror all identify the date and provenance. The fashion for hair taken off the neck began during the Revolution, when it was worn short in a style known as a *la victime* – to ensure a clean cut for the guillotine! To emphasize the message a thin red ribbon was worn around the neck.

Mechanization

We think of the Industrial Revolution today and tend to assume that suddenly everything from curtains to cabinets was mass-produced, but in the manufacture of household items this is far less accurate than in the case of cloth. Certainly Britain was the first country in the world to adopt machinery in respect of its major industries, but the beginnings of this can in many cases be traced back to the middle of the 18th century, and the integration of mechanization continued well into the 19th century. The true factory system is best illustrated in the cotton industry, which, over a number of years, introduced various technical developments, such as James Hargreaves' "spinning jenny" (1764), Arkwright's water-powered spinning frame (patented in 1769), and Samuel Crompton's spinning "mule" in 1779. The latter was called a mule because it combined the best parts of both the other two, and the "jenny" was probably so called as a derivative of "gin" – as in "engine". Romantics would have us believe it was the name of the inventor's wife. The word "cotton", we know, comes from the Arabic word *qutun.*

The main essence of mechanization was that one human operative could, by means of a mechanical device, control dozens of identical processes. It was not until the late 1840s that this was successfully applied to the furniture industry, but since the early 1700s a system of line manufacture had been well established. In major potteries and furniture and silver workshops specialist "part" workers were employed; just as pottery decorators sat at their benches painting just one part of a scene, so in a line of carvers one man concentrated on the back legs and another on the front. At the silversmith's, one specialist applied handles and spouts, while another fixed the lids.

While it can be claimed that spinning jennies and seed drills (horse-drawn seed planters that sowed seeds in straight lines) made the British victory over Napoleon possible, so too did advances in manufacturing create more accurate cannons by successfully boring cast iron. This was achieved in 1774 by John Wilkinson of Bradly, whose name ranks among Abraham Darby of Coalbrookdale, Roebuck of Carron, and Walker of Rotherham as leading iron masters of their time, revered throughout Western Europe. It was Darby's method of smelting using coke as the fuel, instead of the heavily restricted supply of timber, that ensured the future of the iron and steel industry in Britain, and made millionaires out of owners of coal-rich land.

▲ **73 Large earthenware platter, English, c.1825.** At first glance this is a fine but standard example of blue-and-white willow-pattern Staffordshire pottery. However, a closer inspection reveals the names of the owner and his hotel, which makes it a rarity. It was presumably intended to discourage a guest from packing it in with the towels and the coat hangers.

▼ **74 Pair of porcelain vases with covers, Chinese, c.1700,** with later overglaze "clobbered" decoration. To encourage sales it became common practice during the mid-18th century, particularly in the Netherlands, to decorate Oriental blue-and-white porcelains with bright enamel colours. This continued into the 19th century, with diminishing quality irrespective of the age of the original piece.

◄ **75 "Bamboo" chair from Brighton Pavilion, English, c.1818.** Chairs of beechwood, carved, turned, and painted to simulate bamboo, first took this form in the Regency period and remained popular throughout the Victorian period. The same applies to Chinese rattan cane and genuine bamboo furniture, some of which was imported "flat-packed".

approximately 71cm (28in) high in elevation. This supported a sloping-top writing desk with a hinged lid, made to slide towards the sitter to provide knee room. The first record of such a piece appears in the late-18th-century accounts of the furniture-makers Messrs Gillow of Lancaster, and was ordered by a Captain Davenport. So, legend has it, the "Davenport Desk" was born. Since then it has undergone many variations, from a simple school-type desk to elaborate curved lid or "piano-top" versions

Accurate boring of iron and steel meant more efficient engines powered by steam, and here the names of Matthew Boulton and James Watt appear once again. In 1782 Watt's rotative engine proved the most reliable to date, and the age of iron mania had begun. The iron bridge was built over the Severn River (*see* Pl. 30) in 1779, and an iron boat sailed under it. To complete the picture, an iron aqueduct was built in 1803. All this activity caught the attention of George, Prince of Wales, who enthusiastically championed its use, particularly in Britain's spa towns, such as Bath and Buxton, and, of course, his beloved Brighton.

Developments in furniture and architecture

Each period sees the introduction of something new whose useful and decorative qualities retain popularity thereafter. In furniture the end of the 18th century saw two such items. One was a small, individual-size writing desk comprising a stack of drawers, square in plan, and

DEVELOPMENTS IN MATERIALS

The early 19th century saw further developments in materials as well as manufacture, and novelties as well as necessities. Papier-mâché became the subject of a massive industry, as did Tunbridge ware (*see* p.149) and coiled springs for upholstery (after *c.*1820). By the time he died, Joseph Bramah (1748–1814) had introduced an hydraulic press, an ever-sharp pencil, a water closet, and, importantly for the furniture industry, a lock that no one was able to pick open in his lifetime and which to this day will require a specialist locksmith to undo and a key more expensive than average to open it. In 1805 the first patterns for Berlin embroidery (*see* p.146) were available in England, and by 1830 this had joined the ranks of papier-mâché and Tunbridge ware in popularity.

By the middle of the century the zinc alloy spelter had become enormously popular, although it is doubtful if most people who bought it knew what it was. It is fragile, light in weight, and when fractured reveals an aerated body. Its advantage was that it could be cast to a reasonable degree of accuracy and detail, and plated to resemble a more valuable material – ormolu (gilt bronze), bronze, silver, enamel – or painted to look like stone or wood. It was the answer to the mass-demand for decorative items, such as figures for the mantelpiece, lamps for the hall, or great cups and platters for the sideboard at an affordable price. Copies of famous bronzes of any subject and any size were suddenly available to all, and remained so until World War I. A good way to test whether something is made of spelter is to pick it up: if you can pick it up with no effort then it is most likely made of spelter.

after the 1860s, with "secret" compartments that rise up from the top at the press of a hidden button.

The other piece, or rather set of pieces, is the nest of four small tables, each one being of a slightly different size to enable them to fit together as one. They were approved by Thomas Sheraton in his *Cabinet Dictionary* (1803) when he stated they are "made to draw out of each other, and may be used separately", and by George Smith (*Household Furniture*, 1808), who recommends them for drawing rooms where they "prevent the company rising from their seats, when taking refreshments". We know that these "quartetto" tables, as they were called, were also made by Gillow, and have remained popular ever since. Today they are sometimes made in sets of three.

The days of Dr Johnson's Britain had seen Italy as the role model for architecture, but Greece took on that mantle for the cogoscenti during the Regency period. This was much encouraged by Lord Byron's delight in the country (he died there in 1824), and by Lord Elgin's acquisition of the famous marbles from the frieze of the Parthenon while the building was being used as target practice by the Turkish forces occupying Athens. The Elgin Marbles were sold to the British Museum in 1816 for £35,000 ($56,000).

But it was not a totally overriding change, and the main architect of the day, John Nash (1752–1835), remained distinctly Roman in influence when he designed Regent Street, Regent's Park, and Carlton House Terrace.

◄ **76 Paint-decorated dressing table, American, c.1830**. Paint had long been a popular decorative medium for American furniture, and the ring-turned pattern to the legs was fashionable in the early 1800s. The set-in drawer section and the scroll backboard to this New England piece show a contemporary Scottish influence.

A swing away from the more minimal, restrained interiors in the Thomas Hope Egyptian style (*see* p.123) began after 1815, and, as can be seen in George Smith's last book (*see* p.129), which was published in 1827, decoration became heavier, with greater, fatter foliage and a look of Etruscan and Graeco-Roman solidity. This remained the mainstay of interior design for the masculine rooms of the well-appointed house, while the feminine apartments and general reception rooms saw a fundamental change back towards the old French Baroque and Rococo decoration of the mid-18th century.

In 1827 Philip and Benjamin Dean Wyatt were responsible for the redecoration of Crockford's Club, using deeply fringed velours in great voluptuous swags, with cherubs and other elaborate stucco work to walls and ceilings. This interior had a great impact on those who were ready to show their knowledge of the latest fashion, and had the wealth to have it executed.

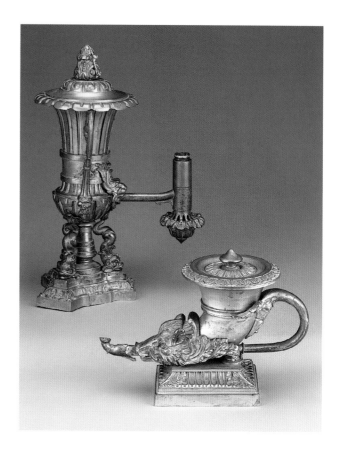

▶ **77 Two late-Regency colza oil lamps, English, c.1825.** There were many variations of gravity-fed lamps from this period. The boar's head and dolphins are ancient characters. Colza is a vegetable oil, originally from Sweden, hence the popularity of these lamps in Scandinavia. The best English examples were made by Thomas Messanger of Birmingham.

CANTON *FAMILLE ROSE* PORCELAIN

The ever-increasing demand in the West for more colourful porcelain led the early-19th-century Chinese potters to smother the surfaces of their wares with decoration. Among the most popular was the all-over pattern that has become known as Canton *famille rose* porcelain. The surrounding area of the great port of Canton was occupied by potteries, and the name *famille rose* derives from the dominant pink colour. The random arrangement of birds, butterflies, flowers, and insects shown on the service below is one type of Canton; another has panels of garden scenes with figures set within dense borders of colour. All were made to follow European shapes.

FLUTING AND LOBING

Vertical moulded decoration of a curved section has been applied to architectural columns, legs, and other upright members of furniture, garden vases, and a wide range of silver articles since such objects came into being. If the section is concave, that is, sunken away from the viewer, it is called fluting, if it is convex and comes out toward the viewer it is called lobing. It became popular during the late-18th-century revival of Greek and Roman Classicism, and again in the late 19th century when the style was revived once more. At this time it was particularly prevalent on silver tea services, as shown here at the workbench in Plate 78, and the sugar basin in Plate 81.

78

80

78 Craftsman creating lobing (graduated flutes). This technique is similar to embossing: a snarling iron (see p.83) is used to raise the outer surface and the vessel is filled with hot pitch – resilient enough to hold its shape against the impact of hammering but pliant enough to take the design.

79 Georgian silver wine cup, English, 1825. A classic example of design crossing the boundaries of material, as this useful and enjoyable cup is in the precise style of the original, massive exterior vase shown in Plate 80.

79

80 Large stone garden vase of a type made in Italy and England, 18th and 19th century. The design is based on an antique shape, and has majestic proportions. Some vases have a more slender body, similar to the wine cup in Plate 79. The top rim is decorated in a pattern known as "egg and dart".

81 Silver sugar bowl, English, 1884. The lobed decoration on the lower body was used on tea services throughout the Victorian period, and remains popular today. The inclusion of cast foliate terminals on the handles indicates a date approaching the revival of past styles, which occurred in the 1890s.

81

CRAFT & INDUSTRY

1830–1860

Following the ribald decade of George IV, England had seven years of benign rule under William IV before the accession of Queen Victoria. She was a fairytale figure who captured the hearts of the people. A close and more insular family life became the aspiration of all classes, reflected in the comfortable furnishings with which all except the poorest surrounded themselves.

◀ **1 The American Exhibit at the Crystal Palace in 1851,** which showed that nation's enthusiasm for the project. The items on display were of great variety: fine and decorative art was combined with a piano large enough for four players, a machine for turning pages of music, a model of a floating church, and the introduction of the "American System" of interchangeable parts in rifle manufacture, subsequently adopted by the new Enfield Armoury works.

At the time of his death it would seem that few mourned the passing of King George IV on the 26 June 1830, for the Georgian era holds more pleasure in its encapsulated history for us now than it could have done for the majority of people who lived through any part of it. During his last ten years the profligate and undisciplined character of the king overshadowed the benefits he bestowed through his enthusiasm for innovation and tradition alike.

When George was 15 years old his tutor, Bishop Richard Hurd, had said of him that he would be "either the most polished gentleman or the most accomplished blackguard in Europe – possibly both". He was right on both counts, but, whatever the praise or the criticism of him, the death of George Augustus Frederick was more than the end of a reign; it was the end of Georgian England.

Acceding to the throne in June 1830, William IV, third son of George III, had little effect on the galloping development of design and manufacture of household goods, imports and exports, travel, and transportation. Indeed it was a while after the succession of young Queen Victoria in 1837 before the royal household had any influence on the outside world, and even then it was her consort, Prince Albert, who had the most impact.

So from 1830 the next dozen years of activity in the arts, which saw huge strides in variety and commercial production, were without inspiration or intervention from the royal family. It was more the growth of Britain's empire, European and American trade, and a continuing fascination with the goods from (and the way of life of) the exotic Middle East that influenced developments. In manufacturing areas throughout Europe and America the production of even the simplest things affected and contributed to people's comfort. For example, by the mid-1830s coiled copper springs were being produced in Birmingham, which revolutionized upholstery. Until their use, the webbing that supported the stuffing and covers of a chair seat went over the top of the seat frame, and the upholstery itself was shaped to compliment the shape of the chair. When coiled springs are used, the webbing goes under the seat rails to allow space for the springs, and then the stuffing and covers are added. As the period progressed, and fashionable furniture could be made increasingly

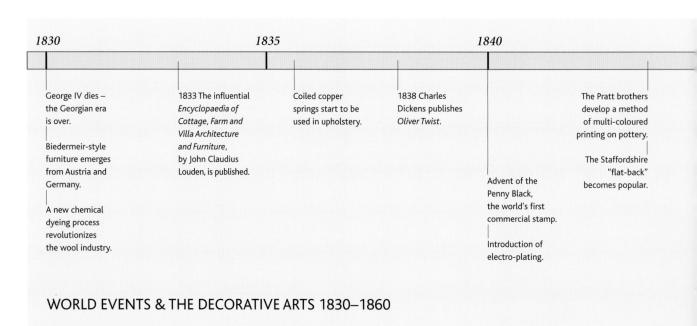

1830

1835

1840

George IV dies – the Georgian era is over.

Biedermeir-style furniture emerges from Austria and Germany.

A new chemical dyeing process revolutionizes the wool industry.

1833 The influential *Encyclopaedia of Cottage, Farm and Villa Architecture and Furniture,* by John Claudius Louden, is published.

Coiled copper springs start to be used in upholstery.

1838 Charles Dickens publishes *Oliver Twist.*

Advent of the Penny Black, the world's first commercial stamp.

Introduction of electro-plating.

The Pratt brothers develop a method of multi-coloured printing on pottery.

The Staffordshire "flat-back" becomes popular.

WORLD EVENTS & THE DECORATIVE ARTS 1830–1860

▲ **2 His Royal Highness Prince Albert, English, 1850.** An oil colour portrait published by George Baxter (1804–67). An earlier version shows the Prince in long blue trousers, but at his behest these were changed to buckskin breeches and top boots. Baxter was accredited with perfecting colour printing in a method he patented in 1835.

▲ **3 Her Majesty Queen Victoria, English, 1850.** An oil colour portrait published by George Baxter, who was so highly regarded he was invited to make prints of the Coronation and the Opening of Parliament, and to attend the christening of the Prince of Wales. Sadly, his printing process proved too cumbersome to succeed and his business folded in 1860.

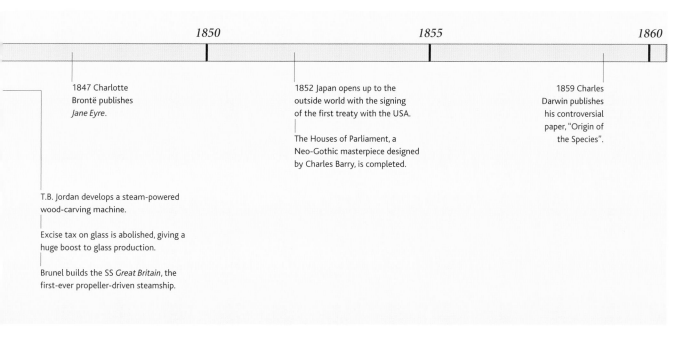

1850   *1855*   *1860*

1847 Charlotte
Brontë publishes
Jane Eyre.

1852 Japan opens up to the
outside world with the signing
of the first treaty with the USA.

1859 Charles
Darwin publishes
his controversial
paper, "Origin of
the Species".

The Houses of Parliament, a
Neo-Gothic masterpiece designed
by Charles Barry, is completed.

T.B. Jordan develops a steam-powered
wood-carving machine.

Excise tax on glass is abolished, giving a
huge boost to glass production.

Brunel builds the SS *Great Britain*, the
first-ever propeller-driven steamship.

cheaply by mass production and machine, so materials for upholstery were also subject to price control. Fine horsehair was used for the best work, but anything to hand was used to fill the cheapest seats – infested straw, grass, newspaper – even the sweepings from the workshop floor, so it is no wonder that a large number of Victorian chairs and sofas made for poorer families have simply rotted away. In the 1950s it was still the practice, certainly in the provinces in England, to dig a pit in the garden and throw such items into it. We shall never know how much 18th-century furniture handed down from servants of grand families to successive generations went into the pit. The result of the use of coiled springs was the appearance of a seat looking more like a marshmallow on legs, as upholstery became disproportionately large in relation to the shape of the frame. During the last half of the 18th century there had been a practice of stitching through a seat or stuffed chair-back, the upper or outer end securing a button or "tuft" – a small piece of fabric. In the 19th century this was continued but made much deeper, giving a dimpled look. So universal was its popularity that at first glance it is difficult to tell where a settee or upholstered armchair from 1830–50 was made.

The general influences of the 1830s were ancient (Greek, Roman, Egyptian), historical (Gothic and Medieval), and Arabic (Moorish and Saracenic) for the masculine apartments, and a continuation of the Rococo revival, *Tous-les-Louis*, for ladies' boudoirs.

Tous-les-Louis is a derogatory term coined later in the 19th century to describe the Rococo revival of the 1825–50 period, which was particularly prevalent in England at that time. However, it is far from historically accurate, as the English taste for Rococo began in the early 18th century, while the Kings of France named Louis XIV, XV, and early XVI covered a period from 1643 to c.1785 that incorporated some early Classicism as well. The term is best used to describe the more flamboyant French Baroque and Rococo revival blend of the early 19th century than the English milder version. A mixture of the two from the 1840s and later, when English makers imported French fittings such as locks and hinges and gilded mounts to "Frenchify" their wares and so make them more attractive to the buying public, is sometimes, and again usually derogatorily, referred to as "Franglaise".

There is always a reaction against any discipline, however lighthearted that discipline might seem, especially with hindsight. So the adherence to the noble orders of architecture, proportion, and style at the end of the 18th century spawned a movement in favour of spontaneous creativity, man's relationship with his environment, and an interest in the irrational rather than proven tenets. Highly educated and cultured minds followed this path in literature, music, and painting, and from the 1790s in France, Italy, Germany, and England the Romantic movement never really disappeared completely. Also the growth of Medievalism called for things reminiscent of the age of chivalry. But there is no question that French-made and French-styled items continued to dominate the English market. So much so that it was commonly accepted that to sell a new line an English manufacturer had to take it to France, where the English tourists would buy it as *à la mode*. However, one English product that continued to buck this trend was porcelain and bone-china dinner and tea ware. The ability to make fancifully shaped and decorated services in the scrolling French style (*see* Pl. 5) ensured the success of pottery factories Coalport, Davenport, Ridgway, Rockingham, and Spode, among many others, who saw their greatest

◄ **5 Part of a porcelain tea service, English, c.1840.** This is typical of the maker Rockingham, displaying all the swirls and scroll of the Rococo revival that set the scene for much of the early Victorian period. A variety of colours were available; these cobalt and yellow bands, under the burnished gilding, were among the most popular.

▲ **6 Victorian fashion plate, English, c.1860.** The wide skirts of the 1840s were still the desired look, but instead of multiple starched petticoats a crinoline or hooped underskirt was introduced, reverting back to the fashions of the 16th, 17th, and 18th century. The difference now was that modern technology enabled the use of lightweight steel hoops.

▲ **7 Victorian fashion plate, English, c.1860.** One problem with such full skirts was that they facilitated shop-lifting, causing objections to their everyday wear. Another was that the light weight allowed them to billow up, so pantaloons had always to be worn underneath. The full puffed sleeves of the 1840s, which had harked back to Elizabethan times, were moderated.

► **8 Rosewood wellington chest, English, c.1845.** The "Iron Duke" is credited with putting his name to the English version of the French *semainier* chest – one with seven drawers to take fresh, small items of linen for each day of the week. One side panel is hinged, and when locked in place it secures all of the drawers.

expansion in this period, while Derby and Worcester continued to create porcelains as beautiful as any made in Europe. (The Rockingham just mentioned is the English pottery established on the estate of the Earl of Rockingham in 1745, which lasted until 1842 – not to be confused with the American pottery yelloware usually streaked or dappled with lustrous manganese brown glaze and made in large quantities from the 1840s until the end of the century.)

The impact of mass production

The greatest changes during this time came through mass production. Throughout Europe and America the burgeoning middle classes were now able to afford comfortable surroundings, and factories could provide them with an unrestricted supply of goods.

For the first time people went shopping and bought household goods on display as an alternative to consulting catalogues of various designs and ordering accordingly. One of the first and largest shops was that of Lamb of Manchester, furniture manufacturers and retailers. There a vast stock was arranged on three floors, each of a different quality and cost to cater for the different strata of local society (who were shown to the appropriate area to avoid any embarrassment). The catalogues, which for a hundred years had informed the educated wealthy classes, were now aimed at, and devoured by, the uninformed and uncertain middle classes, and as such became their manuals for all matters related to good taste: etiquette, colour schemes, crockery, and clothes (*see* Pls. 6 and 7), in addition to the types of furniture and where they should be placed in the room.

Among the most influential authors of such catalogues was John Claudius Loudon (1783–1834). He was an architect and landscape gardener, and his *Encyclopaedia of Cottage, Farm and Villa Architecture and Furniture,* published in 1833, was used as a pattern book throughout the Victorian period. In 1838 he produced *The Suburban Gardener and Villa Companion.* In recent years reprints of many such works have made it possible for anyone interested to see just how much we are still influenced by the designs of this early post-Regency period today.

The Biedermeier style

The 1830s also saw the emergence of a style of furniture from Austria and Germany known as Biedermeier. It had simple, elegant lines in the classical manner, much like the late Napoleonic furniture but without applied gilt decoration. The bed shown in Plate 4 is a typical Biedermeier shape, and also illustrates the Continental fondness for the bed being placed sideways against the wall. The cost of manufacture, kept within the reach of the middle classes by the furniture's plainness, made Biedermeier attractive throughout a vast area of central Europe and Scandinavia, and heralded the growing production of domestic and decorative artifacts in Denmark and, more particularly, Sweden.

For many years after World War II there were various myths concerning the origins of the genre, a favourite being that a "Papa Biedermeier" made it all. In fact, the name of the style came from a fictional character, invented by Ludwig Eichrodt around 1855, called Gottlieb Biedermeier, who epitomized the comfortable, undemanding attitudes of the bourgeoisie. The style was first recorded soon after the British defeat of Napoleon, reached a peak during 1830–55, and faded away after 1860. It had a strong revival among fashionable decorators in London, Paris, and New York in the 1960s and 1970s, and remains desirable through its elegant versatility.

Transportation and travel items

Items for use when travelling or on campaigns gained huge popularity after the naval and military victories of Nelson and Wellington. We have already looked at the davenport desk (*see* p.134), which it is safe to assume was made for the good Captain for use at sea. The upright chest in Plate 8 is an example of another item for use at sea. Known as a wellington chest, it is an adaptation of the French *semainier*, a piece containing seven short drawers to take fresh small linens for each day of the week. Legend states that, because it is such a compact and convenient item, one was adopted by the Iron Duke Wellington, who promptly gave his name to it. Back in Britain, mass production was underway and, in common with brass-bound and brass-cornered campaign chests, portable lap-desks and toilet boxes, Wellington chests were made for people who were unlikely to leave their home town, let alone go on a campaign. These pieces should not be confused with the extremely sophisticated folding and collapsible beds, chairs, tables, canvas baths, and shower units that were produced for officers and gentlemen from the last quarter of the 18th century, and which often represent stunning examples of ingenuity. In fact, the Victorian age saw such imagination totally

▲ **9 Portable water closet, English, *c.*1837.** The late-Regency Classical style is still in evidence on this intriguing piece of furniture in the low-arched panel doors and the carved motifs on the ends. The quality is absolutely marvellous. Presumably, as the disguise is so good, an accurate memory was an advantage when its use was required!

◄ **10 Page from *Robson's Directory*, English, 1837.** It is always fascinating to find an advertisement for a specific object. Here we can date without question the portable lavatory designed by the amusingly named Robert Wiss. Even better is his claim that it can be placed in any room, and disguised as any piece of furniture!

▲ **11 Embroidery panel, English, c.1840.** Although created in England, the materials and the design were imported from Germany, where a development in chemically dyeing wool to vibrant colours transformed the industry. Produced in Berlin, the wool was dispatched throughout Europe and the USA, with paper patterns that could be transposed easily onto canvas.

▲ **12 Embroidery panel of Samuel and Eli, English, c.1865.** Berlin embroidery depicting religious scenes or copies of paintings by leading Victorian artists is less valuable today than that showing floral or animal subjects. By the 1850s glass beads were incorporated, and improvements in printing allowed the designs to be printed directly onto the canvas.

unbridled, unhindered by restraint. For example, some furniture was actually made out of coal and glass.

In the face of the inevitable steam train and its ability to transport people considerable distances without a break, "mathematical underclothing and corsets" were devised that could be "opened instantaneously in the case of emergency" (quotes taken from the official catalogue of the time). Quite what help that would be on a train without a toilet is not recorded, but there was an increased awareness generally of the need to improve sanitation. Thirty years before Thomas Crapper developed his flushing water closet, there were several ingenious machines developed for that purpose. In a catalogue produced in 1837 the aptly named Daniel Chambers advertised a water closet "made in imitation of Bedroom Furniture thus avoiding the unpleasantness of the article proclaiming at first sight its use and purposes". In the same catalogue Robert Wiss advertised that he was the

originator of such beneficial items, and that the public should beware of "unprincipled imitators" who had copied his ideas, which he claimed to have been working on for 12 years (*see* Pl. 10).

An example of a Wiss original is shown in Plate 9 and is as near to the advertised model as one could get. (Being able to trace any item as definitely as this adds considerably to its historical and commercial value.) Its style is distinctly early post-Regency, revealed in the Classical columns flanking the doors, each with an arched inset panel. This design for cupboard doors remained popular until the 1860s. Notice, too, the handles on the sides. Since the Middle Ages the addition of such "carrying" handles to the sides of any piece of furniture have immediately given it that "my owners travel a great deal" look, when in fact they have always been totally impractical. A piece of furniture should never be lifted by means of those handles, particularly if it contains a water tank!

▲ **13 Two pages from a design book of the Spode factory, English, c.1814.** The tapering side with inswept lower body, shown above, is called the "London" shape, which reigned supreme from c.1812–22. These examples incorporate the "Grecian" handle. The colours of the cup and saucer on the right are delightful, and reflect those of contemporary and later printed fabrics.

▶ **14 Sèvres porcelain coffee "can" and saucer, French, c.1790.** This is an early example of the straight-sided coffee "can", which has remained the accepted shape to the present day. The deep-blue ground and fine jewelled and gilded decoration are typically Sèvres, and typically European in style.

Berlin embroidery

By 1831 the firm of Wilks of Regent Street, a fashionable retailer, was selling all the materials and accessories for the home-craft of needlework, and within ten years had 14,000 patterns available for "Berlin embroidery". The first of these had been imported in 1805, and their early popularity was largely due to their simplicity, employing the cross or tent stitch. The wool came from Gotha, Germany, before being dyed in Berlin, and was accompanied by printed colour-chart patterns that could be transposed easily onto canvas. The big breakthrough came in 1830, when a new chemical dyeing process was introduced that enabled bright primary colours to be used. This revolutionized the entire wool industry but its impact on embroidery was no small matter. Every item that could be made of fabric was at one time or another subjected to the Berlin embroidery treatment, whether by hand, by the fireside, or in a factory. Gradually, more complex stitches

◄ 16 Illustration from the *Art Journal Catalogue of the International Exhibition*, London, 1862. These two designs for chandeliers in bronze and silvered metal show total allegiance to the Gothic-revival style. Many churches underwent rebuilding and restoration at this time and were fitted with similar lights, sadly all-too-frequently removed in the mid-20th century.

▲ 17 Oak and bronze book carrier, English, *c.*1850. Even modest functional items can accurately reflect current taste, especially when assisted by mass production. This book tray is made of oak with a bronze border – cast in long lengths, with Gothic-revival geometric windows and crocketed spires.

were incorporated, and different materials, such as coloured glass beads and metal foil, were introduced. The patterns also grew more ambitious, depicting scenes from the Bible and pictures taken from leading contemporary artists (*see* Pls. 11 and 12). However, romantic landscapes, marine subjects, and floral displays remain the most sought-after.

Prior to 1830 many Berlin patterns were executed in silk, often depicting pseudo-Oriental scenes, so the best way to recognize a date is by the harshness of the colours

◄ 15 The Royal Gallery, Houses of Parliament, London, 1847–52. Following a fire in 1834, Sir Charles Barry was appointed to rebuild Westminster and he adopted an Italian Renaissance style. Under his direction was A.W. Pugin (*see* pp.152–3), whose pure Gothic Revival influences can also be seen, from the overall structure to details on door furniture.

and the variety of stitches and materials used. For example, a black background will be after *c.*1850. Berlin embroidery, or wool work or needlework as it is variously called, began to wane in the 1870s, after its reliance on machine- and mass-printing was heavily criticized by the Arts and Crafts Movement (*see* p.186).

Tunbridge ware

Another product that may too easily be dismissed as a novelty is Tunbridge ware. Wooden objects decorated with a specific version of marquetry were first made in Tunbridge in the late 17th century but became mass-produced after the 1830s. From the smallest box to tables, chairs, and desks – particularly davenports (*see* p.134) –

▲ **18 Illustration from the catalogue of the Great Exhibition, London, 1851.** The Chinese exhibit was something of a disappointment as the space was booked but no items were presented, so warehouses and shops in Britain were scoured to make a suitable display, with mixed results.

▼ **19 The Crystal Palace, London, 1851,** an extraordinary achievement by the designer, Joseph Paxton, and his workforce, who created in less than a year a building of glass and iron that covered 19 acres. The exhibition remained open for six months and received just over 6 million visitors.

any piece of treen or furniture could be enhanced by its application. Its origins are said to be from the Tunbridge waters in Kent turning the local Tunbridge timber, particularly oak, an attractive green colour. Given the fondness for colourful stained woods in the late 1600s and again in the late 1700s, items made in Tunbridge were much sought-after at various times in history but never for as long or as strongly as they were in the Victorian period.

The effect of the Tunbridge technique looks very much like mosaic, miniature parquetry, or even fine needlework, but it is none of these. Faceted strips of varying coloured woods are glued and bound together, positioned in such a way as to form a pattern or section of a scene; think of the letters in a stick of seaside rock, as that is the same sort of idea. Dry thin slices are cut from the end of the bundle and applied to the surface of the piece to be decorated in the same way as marquetry (*see* pp.48–9). Geometric and floral patterns were most popular for borders and bands, while pastoral and architectural scenes were, and still are, the most sought-after subjects for central and side panels.

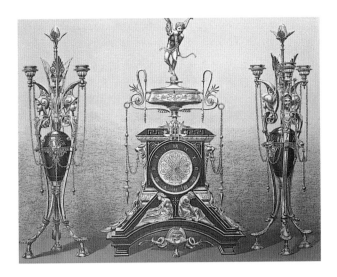

▲ **20 Illustration from the *Art Journal Catalogue of the International Exhibition*, London, 1862,** showing the extreme version of the Italian Renaissance designs popular during the latter part of the Victorian period. Black slate could be used instead of marble, and the zinc alloy spelter stood in for cast bronze. The style was easily adaptable to less elaborate models.

After the 1830s a considerable amount of Tunbridge-type decoration was made in Ireland, and large numbers of boxes with two bands of pseudo-Tunbridge work running across the top, front, and back were imported from central Europe and the Far East. Like Berlin embroidery, Tunbridge ware declined toward the end of the century.

Papier-mâché

A third material to make a huge impact on the contents of the average home in Europe and America at this time was papier-mâché. Pulped paper that could be moulded when wet and decorated when dry had been developed in France – hence the name *carton pierre*, meaning hard composition – during the latter part of the 17th century. It spread into adjoining countries and to England, where it was used as a novel alternative to carved wood for mirror frames. Examples of papier-mâché work from this time are rare and highly desirable. But in 1772 Henry Clay, a furniture-maker and japanner in Birmingham, introduced a method of applying layers of wet pulped paper mixed with glue, chalk, and sometimes sand over a mould, which retained its shape when heat-dried and could then be fired or stoved as many times as necessary in the process of being decorated with lacquer and japanning (*see* p.44).

There had long been a need to create a material that would serve as a cheap alternative to tin plate in the making of small decorative and domestic items like trays, caddies, and decanter stands that were traditionally lacquered in the Oriental style of japanning. Such tinwares were first produced in England in the 1690s at Bilston in Staffordshire and by 1720 in Wolverhampton. This was another product resulting from the need to compete with the demand for Chinoiserie goods, which were being imported (*see* p.22). By 1750 Edward Allgood and his brother had established their celebrated factory in Pontypool, Monmouthshire to such an extent that the name Pontypool is synonymous with the craft to this day. On a visit there Bishop Pocock recorded that there were "only the two (Allgood) brothers and their children making it, it is costly and they keep it (their process) secret". At about the same time, *c.*1740, the Pattisons from Ireland settled in the Connecticut River valley and are credited with starting the tin-plate industry in the town now called Berlin. By the end of the 18th century the craft of japanning had crossed the Atlantic and by the 1820s the decorative style had parted from the Oriental to become very much a vibrant force in the early folk art scene. This incorporated primary colours and the clever use of quick strokes of the brush to create flower sprays, scrolls, and shells. The work was done almost entirely by girls. (Children were employed in all walks of life because of their stamina, suppleness, artistic ability, and quick and nimble fingers.)

So Henry Clay's introduction of pulped paper was the answer to a growing demand for lacquered objects that looked in every way like their more expensive counterpart. To distinguish his method from that of the French he called his product "paperware". This may not seem to us today to have been a particularly smart move, and, indeed by the 1830s the term papier-mâché was used to describe all such wares, however they were made. Nevertheless Clay's paperware was a success, aided in no small way by the demand for lighter transport to fly along the new, improved roads. His patent, which was taken out in 1772, included making in paper "high varnished panels or roofs for coaches, all sorts of wheeled carriages and Sedan chairs", as well as "panels for rooms, screens, 'cabbins' of ships, chimney pieces, tea-trays and waiters".

After Clay the best-known maker was the company formed by Aaron Jennens and T.H. Betteridge, who in 1825 introduced a method of applying paper-thin pieces of pearl shell, known as mother-of-pearl. This was developed by an employee named George Souter, and it is extremely helpful to collectors today as it allows them to

▲ **21 Design registration mark for 14th December, 1847.** To keep track of all the new materials and designs, this mark was introduced in 1842 showing the day, month, and year of patent registration. In 1868 the numbers and letters were moved one space clockwise, and in 1883 the mark was abandoned completely in favour of a registered number.

date with accuracy any piece of papier-mâché that shows pearl decoration. Henry Clay and Jennens & Betteridge stamped their wares, and this evidence will increase the historical and commercial value of an item. Just like Berlin embroidery, the more complex the decoration and varied the materials used, the later a papier-mâché item will be.

Increasing foreign imports of awful quality and a general over-supply meant that papier-mâché lost its appeal, and by the end of the century the industry had all but disappeared. But not before tea tables, chairs, end panels for beds, and even a complete village in Australia had been made out of this extraordinary material.

A new sense of piety and moderation

It is predictable that following any period of excess there is a swing toward moderation, and this happened in the period after the reign of George IV. In the much-expanded middle and upper classes of the mid-19th century propriety, domestic tranquillity and comfort, and a great deal of piety were considered the ideals and essentials in life.

Uncertainty in matters of taste among the newly affluent continued to affect the dominant styles, which, despite the illustrated catalogues of manufacturers showing a range of alternatives, remained for the most part in the safety of the past. Most styles established in previous years held sway, particularly medieval and Gothic. Of the latter the greatest exponent was Augustus Welby Northmore Pugin (1812–52). Given the wider audience and broader field of designs available, it is difficult to relate 19th-century protagonists of taste to their predecessors. Nevertheless it is not unreasonable

WOOD-CARVING MACHINE

With the rapidly increasing demand for household furniture it was inevitable that ways of producing it at greater speed and by cheaper means would be sought. Inventive minds were put to work to solve the problem by improving existing machines and developing new ones. The most important functions in a woodworking shop were dovetailing, mortice and tenoning, moulding, planing, sawing, and carving. Since the advent of controlled steam power, many of these had been done by machine or were already machine-assisted, but carving was the devil to do. Several attempts were made before Thomas B. Jordan patented his Wood-Carving Machine, following a paper he read to the Royal Society of Arts in 1847. As it appeared at the time, and as far as we still know, Jordan's was the first successful machine to enable one operator to create more than one piece of carving simultaneously. This resulted in such advancements to the furniture industry that it merited a gold medal from Prince Albert. The basic principle was that the operator followed the required design on a master pattern, which was replicated by innumerable steam-powered cutters. A later, improved model by Jordan enabled the carving to be undercut, giving the deceptive appearance of the most expensive type of work previously exclusively done by individual carvers. American- and French-made carving machines were less successful, probably because they were over-complicated, and for the rest of the century the machines made in England and Prussia (Germany) were rated the best.

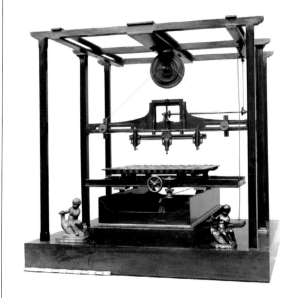

◄ 22 Selection of coloured-glass decanters, showing the vast selection available from the 1840s onwards. In the 19th century, when new shapes developed, it did not mean the automatic cessation of existing patterns. So it is a combination of stopper-shape and colour, plus evidence of acid rather than wheel polishing, that will help indicate a date.

to equate Pugin with William Kent in his importance in furthering one particular style. Pugin was a Catholic convert at a time when Catholicism was just gaining respectability, so his religious fervour gave an intensity to his designs and writings, wherein he insisted that Gothic was godly and Classical was pagan. At the age of 24 he assisted Sir Charles Barry in designing the new Gothic Revival-style Houses of Parliament (*see* Pl. 15). Here, and in all his future work, he advocated much use of crocketed spires, lancet and geometric windows, and most other of the established ecclesiastical decorations from the 11th–14th centuries. In 1841 he published his most widely read and influential book, *True Principals of the Pointed or Christian Architecture.*

In his short lifetime Pugin designed and saw built many churches and houses, and, like William Kent and Henry Holland before him, he designed their interiors and the fitments to go in them – from furniture, silver, and ceramics to stained glass and wallpaper. An attractive example of Pugin's Gothic style applied to a purely domestic item is the book carrier shown in Plate 17.

These religious overtones fitted well into the mindset of the early Victorians of modest and upward means, as they became more concerned with a close-knit family and high moral standards. (Little thought seems to have been given to those working in factories under appalling conditions, or the deprivation suffered by the poorer classes in general.) Of course families were large, or at least started off large, and so a family party was quite a large affair, but, with the exception of the seriously wealthy, the houses for town and city dwellers were no longer designed to cater for grand-scale entertaining.

Advances in medicine and science also had an effect on the interior fittings. Fads and phobias abounded in the

SHEFFIELD PLATE MARKS

There has been no system of marking precious metalwares as accurate or as strictly controlled as that applied by the Worshipful Company of Goldsmiths in London since its inception in the 14th century. But as methods of replicating such wares became available, so markings that may confuse the unaccustomed eye have also appeared. For example, by the last quarter of the 18th century, when Sheffield Plate had become widely used, proud makers were dangerously close to imitating silver hallmarks on their wares, and legislation was brought in to prevent mistaken identity.

By the 1840s two other materials were found that were even more eligible for plating than copper – nickel and Britannia metal. The former, also known as German silver and argentan, was chosen because its similar colour to silver meant that worn parts would not show so readily, and the latter was popular because it was cheap. Both were commonly used throughout the rest of the 19th century and were marked accordingly, giving instant indication of a post-1840 date.

23 Specimen mark on electro-plated nickel silver, English, after 1840. Nickel silver is an alloy of zinc, copper, and nickel, found during the 1840s to be ideally suited to electro-plating. The chief exponent of the process was George Elkington who, in 1840, patented the process and whose company in Birmingham became a world leader.

24 Specimen mark on electro-plate Britannia metal, English, after 1840. Britannia metal is an alloy akin to pewter, but without lead and with a high tin content. It is cheaper than pewter, easily damaged, and has a low melting point, making it difficult to repair. Its mass production was by "spinning": pressing thin sheets onto a revolving pattern or model.

SILVER MARKS

The British system of testing and marking items of silver, gold, and platinum, first established in England in the 14th century, provides a purchaser with the finest and most comprehensive guarantee. From the early 18th century it is possible to tell from these marks the maker (or company responsible for the manufacture or sale), the person who tested the silver and thus its age, the quality of the material (the proportion of pure silver to alloy), the town or city where it was tested, and, from 1784 to 1891, whether or not the legally imposed duty had been paid (*see* hallmarks p.119).

25 Hallmarks on silver, 1300–1720. The earliest, left, is the Leopard's Head (King's mark) for the London Assay Office. Next is the Lion Passant, introduced in 1544 as the guarantee of Sterling Standard silver. The Standard percentage was raised 1697–1720, denoted by a Britannia mark. In London the Lion's Head Erased replaced the Leopard's Head.

19th century – some we may regard as foolish today while others still make good sense. An example of one of these was the danger of house dust and termites. While long fringes and tassels became popular, the great drapes and swags of material over curtained windows were thought to be unhealthy as they harboured such undesirables. So undisguised curtain poles and rings came into vogue instead, together with the unpleated pelmet or lambrequin. To lessen the amount of drapery in the bedroom the half-tester bed (*see* Pl. 39) came back into fashion, often with an elaborate iron-and-brass frame.

By the early 1840s carpets were fitted wall-to-wall, partly for insulation and warmth and partly for fashion. All-over patterns were popular, and were made available to more people through the use of steam-powered looms at the major mills in Axminster, Edinburgh, Halifax, Kidderminster, Kilmarnoch, and Wilton. From these centres Britain was overshadowing the rest of the world in mass-produced carpeting, and exporting accordingly. After 1832 tapestry carpets also became very fashionable.

Men dressed comfortably, with trousers rather than breeches, and frock coats almost to the knee, flared at the

► **26 Parian figure of Ophelia, English, c.1860.** This hard-paste, fine-grained porcelain, which takes its name from the Aegean Island of Paros where marble was mined, is usually attributed to the Copeland factory, but it was made extensively by others after its introduction in the 1840s. Its marble-like surface made it ideal for the mass production of figures and groups.

waist and without the Regency high collar, and they sat on comfortable chairs with their new deep-sprung seats. Women also sat on comfortable chairs but their dress was anything but relaxing. The demand for the slimmest possible waist meant corsets were laced to the point of restricting breath, and swooning was frequent. Upper sleeves to dresses were puffed in similar style to the Elizabethan period until *c.*1840, when a sloping shoulder came into fashion.

Developments in the arts during Victoria's reign

William IV was not a bad king, but he was indecisive to a degree that drove his ministers to distraction and saw the country near to rebellion. Thus the accession to the throne at 5am on 20 June 1837 of a young and pretty girl was a huge relief – she was the right person in the right place at the right time.

Victoria, Queen of the United Kingdom of Great Britain and Ireland and Empress of India (1819–1901), was the only child of Edward, Duke of Kent, fourth son of George III. The circumstances of her being in the position to accede were complex, but she quickly became a role model for families throughout her expanding empire, especially after her romantic marriage on 10 February

▲ **27 Pottery painted name plate, English, c.1840.** The Victorians invented the nursery, and grown-up items, such as this plate, were made small for children to use in their nursery years. The raised floral decoration, overcoloured with this particular combination of red, green, and yellow, indicates a Staffordshire origin.

▲ **28 Pottery transfer-decorated plate, possibly South Wales, c.1855.** The moulded foliate border and the sepia transfer pattern in the centre suggest that this little nursery plate might have been made in the Ynysmeudwy pottery in Wales. This pottery was started in 1845 and within five years was producing similar work to its larger, rival-neighbour, Swansea.

▲ **29 View of Osborne House by Thomas Allom, English, 1851–72.** In 1845 Queen Victoria and Prince Albert purchased Osborne House on the Isle of Wight, and Victoria continued to use it until her death there in 1901. Thomas Cubitt was responsible for the rebuilding. The Queen's role as Empress of India was celebrated by the creation of the Durbar Room in 1891.

1840 to her cousin, Francis Charles Augustus Albert Emmanuel (1819–61), second son of the Duke of Saxe-Coburg-Gotha (whence came the wool for Berlin embroidery).

Albert, Prince Consort of England, had a tough time settling into English society. His interventions in politics and his enthusiastic support for international trade and commerce were seen as superficial at the time, and total acclaim for him came only after his death, when records of the history of the period became accessible. In retrospect it can be seen how innovative and important he was in many ways, not least encouraging the greatest-ever boost to world trade in the creation of the Great Exhibition in 1851. Victoria inherited an age of political and economic unrest, an age of paradox that Albert put great energy into helping to resolve. In 1847 he became President of the Society of Arts, and played a leading part in organizing three exhibitions of "Art Manufacture" in 1847, 1848, and 1849.

As far back as 1757 the Society of Arts had been giving prizes for the best examples of furniture, carpets, ceramics, and other domestic and decorative artifacts. In 1837 the Art Union was formed to promote creativity by issuing subscriptions to a draw, similar to a lottery, wherein the prizes were works of art rather than cash. Top prizes were usually paintings, but after them came statues in marble and bronze or the new highly acclaimed "parian" ware or statuary porcelain (*see* Pl. 26), down to a lithographic print as the bottom prize.

Lithography is a method of printing using the reaction of grease versus water on a steel, paper, or stone surface, and it was invented by Alois Senefelder (1771–1834) in 1798. It was originally intended for printing music and calico, but its potential benefits to artists was quickly realized. By the 1830s lithography was widely used for all manner of artistic impressions, and an affordable print was among the growing number of "latest things" to own.

Following the successful 1849 Society of Arts Exhibition, another prominent figure in the Society, Henry Cole, suggested to the Prince Consort that a grander exhibition should be considered. Two years later the Crystal Palace was erected in Hyde Park to house "The Great Exhibition of Works of Industry of all Nations", which was to have more far-reaching effects than anyone could have foreseen. It spawned a dozen further international exhibitions all over the world in major cities in Australia, France, Italy, and America, and continued spasmodically until World War I. These exhibitions gave work to thousands of craftsmen, designers, and engineers, whose sole purpose was to create the best, most novel, most efficient, or the most outrageous in the four categories: Machinery, Manufacture, Raw Materials, and Sculpture & Fine Art.

One such example was the French exhibition. Having spent his exile in London, Napoleon III was impressed with the city's modernization and, in particular, the Great Exhibition. Sufficiently enthused, he mounted a similar concept in Paris in 1855. Thirty-four nations were represented, exhibiting in a specially built Palais de L'industrie in the Champs Elysees, which covered an area of 168,000sq m (200,930sq ft). It was an economic disaster, with less than a fifth of the costs recovered from ticket sales and booth rentals, but it marked the perceived necessity for other countries to emulate Britain in creating world showcase events as more countries joined in international trade. These were shortly to include Japan. Virtually isolated since the 17th century (*see* pp.190–7), Japan remained a romantic mystery well into the 1880s, but the first chink in the gates was made when American Commodore Matthew Perry began negotiations for a treaty between America and Japan on 14 July 1853. Having presented letters from US President Fillmore to the Emperor, he left to return a year later when, on 31 March 1854, the first treaty between the two countries was concluded, and ratified one year on. In the course of the next 20 years Japan was to become a powerful trading force, with enormous influence on fashion and culture in the West, and by the early 1860s Japanese goods were already being sold in Paris, London, and New York (*see* p.190). This meant unprecedented changes in Japanese life, with the abolition of the feudal system, the disbanding of the samurai, and a new emperor, whose reign was named the Meiji (light or bright government) era.

The Great Exhibition of Hyde Park attracted 14,000 exhibitors, approximately half British, showing over 100,000 objects, and six million people attended the show in the six months that it ran from its official opening by the Queen on 1 May to 1 October. Many of these visitors were from abroad, and to help those travellers from the Continent the South Eastern railway co-operated with the

▼ **30 Design for an interior by George Smith, English, 1827.** The pattern of this sideboard influenced furniture made for the masculine apartments and hallways of houses for the next 25 years. For example, two side tables in the Dining Room at Osborne House are taken directly from this design, particularly in the style of the backboard.

BALLOON-BACK CHAIRS

A balloon-back chair is the perfect example of where the shape of an object brings immediately to mind a certain period, as balloon-back equals Victorian. What precise part of the Victorian era can then be established by the shape of the balloon and its decoration. Generally, the simpler both these details are, the earlier the chair is likely to be. The shape evolved during the 1820s, when the late-Regency period was engulfed with a Rococo revival and both old and new French designs were highly popular. A sturdy, curvilinear, open-frame back to family dining chairs developed at this time, and from this grew the more delicate parlour chair.

Parlour chairs have curved cabriole-pattern front legs, outswept back legs, and balloon-shape backs. Production grew dramatically with the advent of machine manufacture, and carved decoration became more varied in pattern and quality after the introduction of wood-carving machines. At the same time, the parlour suite became fashionable – comprising a settee or chaise longue, two upholstered armchairs (one smaller than the other, traditionally for grandma and grandpa), and between four and eight single chairs. Sometimes the balloon backs were upholstered, and by the 1870s they had ceased to conform to the plain oval shape illustrated below in Plate 31.

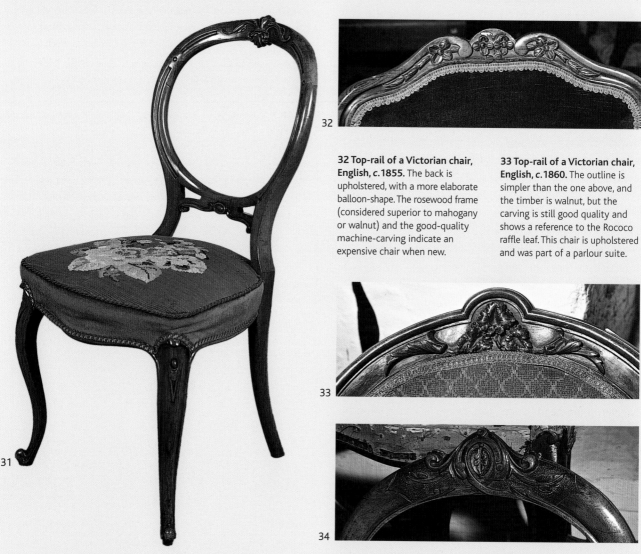

32 Top-rail of a Victorian chair, English, c.1855. The back is upholstered, with a more elaborate balloon-shape. The rosewood frame (considered superior to mahogany or walnut) and the good-quality machine-carving indicate an expensive chair when new.

33 Top-rail of a Victorian chair, English, c.1860. The outline is simpler than the one above, and the timber is walnut, but the carving is still good quality and shows a reference to the Rococo raffle leaf. This chair is upholstered and was part of a parlour suite.

31 Balloon-back chair, English, c.1855. This chair epitomizes Victorian furniture, and it remained popular for most of Victoria's reign. It is essentially a parlour chair, to be sat on quietly and without fidgeting. Its heavier counterpart, the dining chair, more usually had turned and tapering legs and thicker framework, to withstand the rigours of boisterous family mealtimes.

34 Top Rail of a Victorian balloon-back chair, English, c.1865, with a mahogany frame and good, rich colour. The carving is by no means poor, but it lacks the finer detail of the two chairs above. The background is matted or "pounced" to accentuate the design – an ancient technique achieved by machine during the last half of the 19th century.

Northern railway of France to provide a one-tide service per day, bringing passengers from Paris to London by rail and boat in 11 hours non-stop. Not bad for 1851!

Most astonishing is that the project came to fruition in under two years, with the building itself being designed and built in less than nine months. The man responsible was Joseph Paxton (1801–65), originally gardener to the Duke of Devonshire at Chatsworth House, who was later knighted. He had designed a fantastic glasshouse for his patron and applied the same technique for the exhibition. Against considerable scepticism the building defied all criticism, withstanding gales and hailstorms and remaining firm as troops with 8-ton wagons filled with cannonballs galloped up and down the aisles to test its resilience. Using 293,655 panes of glass, equating to 83,600 sq m (900,000 sq ft), held together with 40km (25 miles) of sash bars, 48km (30 miles) of iron frame for the roof alone, and 170 cubic metres (6,000 cubic feet) of timber, the Crystal Palace provided 92,144 sq m (991,857 sq ft) of exhibition space. Its highest point was 33m (108ft), tall enough to encompass the great trees in the park, and it was a fraction under 564m (1,851ft) long. It looked like a huge cathedral of glass. For the rights to sell refreshing drinks at the exhibition, the drinks company Schweppes paid £5,500 ($8,800). They actually sold £75,500 ($120,000) worth of drinks, so it was a good investment!

The benefits to the decorative arts trade all over the world were endless, with orders for the new screw mechanisms for music stools and "wind-up" dining tables, enormous vases of malachite, and wrought- and cast-iron fascias for municipal buildings giving an indication of the range and contrast of merchandise that was now available.

Osborne House

The retreat for the royal family on the Isle of Wight, Osborne House, was very much to the designs of Prince Albert. In collaboration with his chosen architect, Thomas Cubitt (1788–1855), Albert went along a strong Italian path, with references to the early Renaissance, when he started building in 1848. In contrast to his predecessor, George, Prince of Wales, who advocated – to the horror of his advisors – the use of gas for lighting, Prince Albert ensured the latest fireproofing methods were incorporated. But he did promote Cubitt's latest mass-production building methods, and had a Swiss Cottage prefabricated on the mainland and shipped in parts to Osborne. This miniature house had a working kitchen, and gardens for the children to grow vegetables.

ROCKING CHAIR

It was not until the late 1780s that "rocking chair" appeared in *The Oxford English Dictionary*, which suggests that while curved blades on cradles had been known for centuries, and added to existing chairs for almost as long, a chair made specifically for the purposes of rocking was comparatively late in the history of furniture. Rocking chairs from the mid-18th century will exist, as there has to be a period of general usage of something before its description enters a dictionary. Nevertheless it is from the 19th century that the variety of rocking chairs grew rapidly. The Swedish *gungstol* (rocking chair) looks to be the prototype for the Boston rockers made after the 1840s, and from then on the very name rocking chair is associated with America. Made in all manner of materials, from the green and bentwood chairs of the remote homesteads to the sophisticated laminates of the Thonet factory in Vienna (*see* p.169), cane, bamboo, iron, steel, and brass were all used. The chair shown below is a fine example of the latter and was made by R.W. Winfield & Co., of Birmingham, England around 1850. This particular concept is said to have been designed by Peter Cooper (1791–1883), who founded the Canton Iron Works in Baltimore, USA in 1829. Originally intended to be made, and most commonly found, in iron, it was produced by the English company in brass.

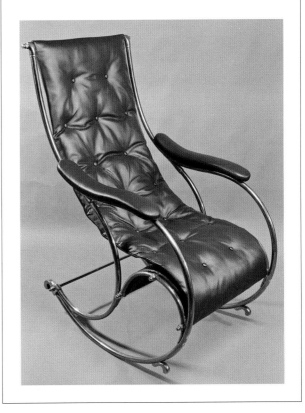

◄ **35 Card table with boulle-type decoration, "Franglaise", *c.*1850.** Similar carcases were made on both sides of the Channel, and decoration was added in both France and England, so it is difficult to be sure of the origin of such tables. The red part of the marquetry is not tortoiseshell but an early type of plastic.

▲ **36 Card table with boulle-type decoration, "Franglaise", *c.*1850,** showing the top open ready for a game. The fact that the top swivels to open dates it from the 19th century; even if the table were of the very best quality, there can be no question of its date.

Inside the main house, Albert designed the layout of the rooms, some so modern, critics say, as to be impractical, as well as items of furniture, including the extraordinary Raphaelesque billiard table. He was a great patron of fine art, both ancient and modern, and encouraged the then Director of the National Gallery to start buying 15th-century paintings when they were still totally out of fashion. He also patronized contemporary artists, such as Winterhalter and Landseer. The several rooms of Osborne House that are now open to the public display many absolutely typical Victorian interiors and a selection of Empire relics. The Durbar Room is a prime example, but of great interest in this context is the use of established late-Regency furniture, such as that designed and published by George Smith in 1827 (*see* Pl. 30).

There are charming aspects to this royal family, such as the fact that each of their children was given a garden at Osborne, with their own tools (still there, bearing their initials) – the progress of which was professionally appraised. For this work they were paid by the hour, taught to make bricks, and taught how to erect a tent. It was their parents' intent that the children should be sufficiently capable to survive, in whatever station in life

they found themselves. But my favourite anecdote concerns Albert's command of semaphore signalling, which he passed on to his gardeners. When you visit Osborne, as you surely must, stand and imagine Prince Albert perched on the great tower, flags in hand, indicating to the workers below precisely where to put that tree or this shrub. A little bit to the left… a little bit to the right… what a wonderful picture.

Patents and marks

With the proliferation of innovations, designs, materials, means of transport, and communication in every walk of life, it became necessary to bring some order to protect inventor and public alike from the plagiarist and the unwholesome. In 1847 a system of registering patents and marking goods accordingly was brought in that displayed the day, month, and year the design had been granted a patent (see Pl. 21). It was in the form of a diamond or kite shape, with a three-quarter circle at the apex within which a series of letters and numbers disclosed this information. It lasted in this pattern until 1883, when a simpler but less informative method was introduced in the form of a stamp that read "Regd. Patent", followed by a five- and later six-figure number. Sight of this mark on any object, usually furniture, glass, silver and other metalware, fabric, ceramics, iron, or steel, will add to its historical rather than commercial value, but it is always of extra interest. Mostly the stamp was applied to items made by machine.

Developments in furniture and interiors

By the mid-19th century the ancient town of Warwick had become recognized as a provincial centre of excellence in the production of fine furniture, with an accent on lifelike carving in high relief. The preferred timber was oak, and it is from this period that enormous sideboards emerged, with the lower part enclosed by panelled doors flanked by bowed ends below a super-structure of one, two, or even three shelves backed by mirrors or carved panels. The decoration took the form of realistic human and animal figures, and, strange though it may seem today, it was the height of fashion to have such pieces adorned with groups of dead game, birds, and a slaughtered stag's head in the dining room, particularly in hunting lodges.

By this time what was fashion for one could be fashion for all, and by the 1860s cheaper, mass-produced examples were available in major stores throughout Europe. However, the Warwick School of Carving was a leader in the movement against the pervasive machine, and its carving remained completely hand-done. Although other areas such as Newcastle and London were responsible for creating work of equal quality, the credit and the name stuck with Warwick. The name was specifically given to the type of carving that was created by the firms of William Cookes and James Morris Willcox, the main instigators, characters, and leaders in the field. Their work was so popular and much copied that "Warwick School of Carving" became a generic name for that style.

The style, which actually owed its popularity to the grandiose attitude of new captains of capitalism, swept across Europe, with machine copies as well as handmade originals being produced in France, Italy, Belgium (Flemish examples are among the most common), and America. This romantic medievalism melded with a toned-down Gothic taste and formed one of several sides

in the "Battle of the Styles", which was staged in the same countries. In the fashionable houses of New York, Detroit, and other rapidly expanding American cities, the new competed with the established Empire, Neo-classical, and *Tous-les-Louis*. A charming example of this can be found in D.S. Kennedy House, 41 Fifth Avenue, New York.

Generally speaking, the European houses of the mid-19th century were over-furnished, for in addition to the elaborate sideboard there would be other cupboards – both standing and hanging – huge overmantel mirrors, and dumbwaiters, all decorated with allegorical episodes from the age of chivalry combined with classical ornament and Rococo enrichments. Of course this was all prohibitively expensive but, thanks to the machine, no longer exclusive, and by the second half of the century it was being replicated at a cost affordable to a mass market worldwide.

In fashionable houses of the 1840s the drawing room was used to receive the series of callers it had become fashionable to expect; they would have left a visiting card (*carte de visite*) earlier in the day. Printers had a surprise upturn in business as suddenly every aspiring man and

▲ **37 Three-tier side table, English, c.1827.** An important and exuberant example of late-Regency furniture, the design for this table is drawn from a variety of international sources. The overall shape can be traced to the last publication of George Smith (*see* p.129), the turned and carved columns have an Irish feel to them, and the pierced side panels are a French detail.

woman needed a personal card. These were carried in card cases made of silver, ivory, tortoiseshell, papier-mâché, and lacquer, and were of two sizes – up to postcard size for ladies, and the equivalent to modern-day size for men. The latter were sometimes slightly curved to fit a waistcoat pocket. The lady of the house was responsible for the reception and dispensing of tea – with cakes – at the appropriate time. (Individual bread or cake plates appeared in common use after the 1850s.) Closer friends were taken into the morning room or even the boudoir. This means polite society was reverting to distinction in the area where one gave audience, as in Elizabethan days in England and the gentleman's levee in Europe of the early 18th century. However, there was no return to exposure through undraped windows, for the Victorians prized their privacy. Soft folds of muslin diffused the daylight and thick velvet curtains kept out prying eyes at night. This was a distinct change from a hundred years earlier, when wooden boards cut out and painted to resemble human or animal figures (called dummy-boards) were placed in front of an open fire to give passers-by the illusion of people in the room.

The drawing and morning rooms, and the boudoir, were still high-style "old French" in décor, consisting of wall panelling, fireplace, ceiling mouldings, and mirror frames, but were furnished with the latest styles of furniture. A low-seated upholstered chair with a high back, the top of which overhung each side, could be knelt upon using the back as an arm rest when family prayers were held. Known as a *Prie Dieu*, it became a standard item and was popular from the late 1830s throughout Europe and America. Some of the finest examples were made in Paris, and will usually bear a maker's stamp or label. The self-descriptive balloon-back chairs (*see* p.158) and the wide-seated armchairs with matching sofa all accommodated women's full skirts. Quartetto tables were still popular, together with the French *étagère* – a small table with several shelves. In the late 18th century English cabinet-makers had adopted the idea of a multi-shelved stand of square or rectangular form, essentially for use in the library or music room. The first record of such a piece being called a "whatnot" was in 1808. When combined with the *étagère*, the shape became varied and the supports were

LEADING MAKERS AND STAMPS

The last 40 years of the 19th century saw many leading makers throughout Europe follow the example of Messrs Gillow of Lancaster and stamp their furniture with their name, usually on the top front edge of a drawer or door. The existence of such a stamp will enhance the historical and commercial value of any piece, but once again it is important to remember that fake stamps exist. Make sure that the quality of the piece you are looking at merits the stamp it bears. Few, if any, companies put their names to poor goods.

There were more than a dozen prestigious manufactories in Britain, and even more in France, Italy, Germany, and Spain. An idea of the size of the industry is gleaned from the numbers employed, varying from 100–200 up to the 1,000 people who worked for Messrs Jackson & Graham from c. 1840–85, arguably London's most prestigious furniture suppliers. Bearing in mind that production was now universally aided by machines and mass production, it is possible to see the enormity of the output. The satinwood and ebonized chiffonier shown is not stamped but deserves to be, for it is of great quality. It would have been made by one of the leading makers, and shows a typical blend of Neoclassical decoration and innovative shapes – the turned spindle gallery became much used in the Aesthetic period.

▲ **38 Mahogany dressing table, American, *c.*1850**, an exemplary piece of Rococo-revival furniture by the most sought-after southern maker, Prudent Mallard, who worked in New Orleans shortly after arriving in the USA in 1829. This style epitomized southern taste in the great plantation houses, prior to the Civil War that caused so much of it to be destroyed.

▲ **39 Rosewood half-tester bed, American, *c.*1850.** The canopy, or tester, which here extends over no more than a third of the bed, was used in Medieval times. It was revived periodically though each successive century, but never more so than in the mid-1800s, particularly in Britain and the USA. This bed was made by the renowned cabinet-maker Charles Lee.

made curved, carved, turned, and twisted in every possible manner and the shelves decorated throughout with inlays and veneers. Some were kidney-shaped, some circular, some triangular, and some were graduated in pyramid form. After the 1860s the whatnot was often joined with another standard piece, such as a "Canterbury", to make a combination piece.

The term "Canterbury" is understood to describe a rectangular stand for magazines or sheet music, with three or four divisions on a box base with a drawer, with short legs and castors. But the name is also applied to a taller stand, the top of which has one end rectangular and the other semicircular, with a raised gallery all around. This was a dining-room piece to hold cutlery and plates. Both are first mentioned in the early 1800s, and the name is attributed to the bishop who first commissioned such a piece, but precisely which one has never been established – so it's a bit of an unknown factor for the moment.

Glass and pottery wares

Compared with the elaborate menus of the 18th century, the selection of food prepared for a household of ten was simple fare, but still might seem excessive to us today: a course of fish and/or soup, a remove (*see* pp.109–10) – either joint or poultry – and entrée with vegetables, a pudding or tart, and a dessert. However, the remains had to supply the next day's breakfast, lunch, and nursery and servants' dinners, and it was now standard practice for the main family meal on Sunday to provide for cold cuts and mince for much of the following week. In addition to brightening the room with inexpensive pottery plates and figures (*see* Pls. 20 and 21 in ch.4), the average family bought

◄ 40 Cotton album quilt, Baltimore, USA, 1847–9.
Album quilts were also known as presentation quilts, as they were often made to mark a special event or someone going away. They were pieced and appliquéd in panels, which were frequently done by different contributors and signed by each. They were much-treasured and rarely used, so their condition is usually good.

▼ 41 Civil War memorial quilt, American, c.1860. Solid-colour and printed calico cottons were pieced and appliquéd to create this emblematic quilt. Apart from its obvious charm, it is historically important because it has provenance and tells a poignant story: it was made by Mary Bell Shawvan, whose husband died while fighting with the Union Army in 1863, leaving her with six children and a Civil War widow's pension. Any family history is a valuable asset to an heirloom, so make sure all your treasures are recorded for future generations.

the latest coloured glass, made in England, Scotland, France, and Bohemia. Despite the evidence that glassmaking was a successful industry in Britain, it had considered itself under constant threat of insolvency due to the taxes imposed upon it by a succession of Excise Acts, particularly after 1745, and there is no doubt that abolition of the tax in 1845 gave a tremendous boost to the production of glass. Not only were fresh colours available, but novelty objects appeared to delight and amuse. Model sailing ships, walking sticks, rolling pins, animal models (usually pigs or swans), tobacco pipes, and top hats – as well as every type of tableware from bottles, flasks, and decanters to epergnes and paperweights – were made in Edinburgh, London, Nailsea near Bristol, Stourbridge, Birmingham, and Dudley. Those items that were purely novelty, being of no practical use, are known as "friggers" and were made, to begin with, by craftsmen very much in their own free time, but they became so popular that they were soon enveloped in the legitimate

glass industry. The more complicated pieces, such as models, fountains, and groups of birds, were placed under glass domes to protect them from dust. (These domes were also used to cover elaborate mantel clocks, and flower displays made of wool, wax, and seashells).

Coloured glass had been enjoyed for centuries, but it is the famous cobalt blue that collectors of 18th-century glass automatically associate with the era. It is best known as "Bristol Blue". Bristol had long been associated with blue glass due to the fine-quality cobalt imported there from Saxony during the 18th century, and its early establishment as a centre of glass production. Among the 50 or so factories the best known was that of Lazarus Jacobs and his son Isaac in their glass house in Temple Street, Bristol, where Lazarus was appointed "Glass Manufacturer to His Majesty" (George III). The company was active from c.1775 until the early 1800s. In truth, cobalt-blue glass was made in most major factories, which means positive attribution is extremely difficult, if at all really possible. The addition of copper oxide gives glass blue, green, and ruby hues, while manganese gives it an amethyst hue. Other materials can make yellows, pinks, and black, and by 1850 the entire palette of the spectrum could be created. It was found that layers of different-coloured glass could be applied to an object and the surface then cut away to reveal those layers with dramatic effect. Called overlay glass, this looked, and was, expensive, and before long a cheaper method using a translucent colour "wash" was introduced to be cut and engraved to give a similar effect. (Overlay glass is thought to have originated in Bohemia c.1800–10.)

In 1840 Elkington and Co. introduced their method of electro-plating, which revolutionized the domestic silver trade worldwide, and press-moulded glass was being made in Birmingham and Stourbridge by semi-skilled labour. This process is said to have been imported from America, where it was perfected by Deming Jarves in association with Hiram Dillaway. Jarves had founded the Boston and Sandwich Glass Company in 1825, probably the best-known of all American glassworks, and from 1827 onward several patents for the process were granted. The company flourished until 1887 and continually produced the best pressed glass in imitation of English and Irish cut glass. Competition was fierce from the many glassmaking centres throughout Europe, and cheaper production abroad gradually undermined sales of the superior product. When he opened his first general "antiques" store (unregistered) in the 1870s my grandfather, John, used to

▲ **42 Staffordshire pot lid, English, c.1850.** These shallow pots, made to hold hair grease, tooth paste, or savoury relishes, had decorated lids that have now become collectables. Commonly called "Prattware", after the main manufacturer J&F Pratt, the lids were printed with topical subjects by means of a complicated multi-coloured transfer process developed by J&F Pratt 1846–80.

◄ **43 Stoneware figure of a bird, English, late 19th century.** By the 1860s ceramic production in Britain was mostly mechanized, but, as in other decorative arts, this led to the growth of individual workshops and potteries. One such was run by the Martin brothers in Fulham and Southall, London, renowned for their outrageous birds with cynical expressions. No two were the same; each was signed.

buy direct from the Sandwich Glass Company to supplement his stock, and we still have a piece as a keepsake. Had it not been for the family connection it would have been thrown away years ago, because for a long time press-moulded glass, with its telltale ridged seams, was considered worthless. This is no longer the case today, although good examples can still be found at a reasonable price.

The developments in pottery production were evident at the lower end of the market in particular, with splash-decorated items on the one hand and finely transfer-printed surfaces on the other. The Pratt brothers of Fenton are attributed with introducing the method of multi-coloured printing in the mid-1840s, which became the standard decoration for all types of Staffordshire items but most particularly the lids of shallow jars made to contain food pastes and cosmetics. The scenes depicted on these pot lids covered every possible subject and became collectable in their own time. In the early 1900s they saw a strong revival that continued into the 1960s; thereafter their popularity and interest waned.

Undoubtedly the longest-surviving collectable of the 1840s is the Staffordshire "flat-back". None-too-accurately modelled figures of international heroes and villains, famous and notorious buildings, and any other commemorative subjects were brightly coloured in typically vibrant blues, greens, reds, and oranges, with black moustaches and eyebrows, and spots of gold for watch chains, buttons, and the odd item of jewellery. One fine, but now rare, example is that of Queen Victoria

standing between two red-jacketed military figures, one the King of Sardinia, the other Napoleon III. The group is entitled "The Allied Powers" and was made in 1854. It illustrates well the then-current interest in the personalities and events of the Crimean War.

The unique feature of these flat-backs is that, as the name implies, they were flat rather than rounded, and could be stood on any depth of shelf. Indeed, so popular were they that by the 1860s they were being replicated in many of the 57 hard-paste porcelain factories in Bavaria and shipped into England to supply the huge demand. By 1870 this source was the main supplier of the even cheaper "fairings" – the pennyworth prizes won at shows and bought as tourist souvenirs when travel for the masses became affordable by train.

Another reminder of my grandfather's first shop is a charming circular plate with a pierced border, decorated with pink lustre resist with its translucent mirror-like surface. In the centre is a transfer print showing a part of Tring High Street, under which is the legend "A Present

◄ **44 Collection of Tunbridge ware, English, c.1875–1900.** It had long been known that the water flowing through the ancient town of Tunbridge contained elements that coloured the local timber. Taking advantage of this, an industry developed making pictures as if in mosaic to be applied to a variety of treen and furniture in the form of a veneer (*see* pp.149–51).

from Tring". On the reverse of the plate is a small round mark in red that says "Made in Austria", which indicates that the plate was made after 1900 (*see* p.203).

In 1845 T.B. Jordan developed a steam-powered wood-carving machine (*see* p.152), which enabled one operative to produce several pieces of identical decoration at one time. In the same year the January issue of the *Art Union Magazine* reviewed most favourably the newly refined bisque (unglazed) porcelain being made by Messrs Copeland & Garrett. First known as statuary porcelain because of its fine surface resembling that of marble, and thus being ideal to make reduced-size models of famous ancient and modern sculptures, it soon became called parian ware, taking the name from the Aegean island Paros – where Roman and Greek marble was mined. Other leading potteries, such as Minton of Stoke, soon began to emulate Copeland, but both were superseded by Messrs Robinson & Leadbetter, also of Stoke, as the largest manufacturers of parian ware in the later 19th century. The quality of parian ware varied greatly toward the 1880s and production waned thereafter.

The popularity of American craftware

During the mid-19th century there was considerable interest in England in American quilts, coverlets, counterpanes, and bedspreads. The first two were used for warmth, the second two more for decoration. Still homemade with great pride and skill, these items have provided a fascinating insight into the ways of life in this period of American history.

From the days of the earliest settlers women and girls used salvaged fabrics to make covers. During the 17th century this quickly became a matter of pride in the skill with which the different pieces of cloth were placed together to create patterns. By the 1650s, according to the records of one Henry Landis, a Boston shopkeeper, more than 40 types of imported material could be purchased specifically for this purpose. Such wonderful names as "Black Turkey" tamet, tamy cheny, linsie woolsy, and red satinesco tufted Holland appear in his advertisements, but 100 years later most American quilts were made of various types of cotton, such as gingham, calico, dimity, and chintz. In 1793 a machine that separated the cotton seeds from the blossoms was invented by Eli Whitney, and that single invention was the foundation of the American textile industry. Bedcovers generally fall within three categories: the first is the wholecloth type, which has one sheet for the

◄ **45 Admiral Fitzroy barometer, English, c.1850.** Admiral Fitzroy (1805–65) was, among many things, a meteorologist, and in 1860 he published the first daily weather forecast in *The Times* newspaper. His barometers, which appeared in this form in the 1850s, contained observations and instructions to assist the user, and by the end of the century were produced cheaply for the mass-market.

front and another for the back; second is the appliqué type; and the third is the pieced, or "patchwork", type.

Bedcover pattern books showing designs for panels of needlework, which were available in Europe from the late 17th century, reached America via the East India trading ships and gave further inspirational sources to the already plentiful repertoire of designs, including scenes of daily life in the New World. Figures in domestic pursuits were juxtaposed with pomegranates, apples, and cherries growing from the same tree, and with exotic birds flying over somebody tending a garden with a watering can. Some patterns show small separate interior scenes that are so accurately detailed that they show us the types of furniture in use and the placement of household articles. Complicated flower arrangements compete with immaculate geometric patterns in gaining one's admiration for the ingenuity, skill, and patience of the creators of these masterpieces.

From the 1720s the American quilt was established as an art form, but it was not really until the early 20th century that it was recognized as such outside of that country. The discovery in 1856 of coal-tar colours, the first of which was mauve, gave rise to the synthetic colour range available to the later Victorians, but, as in the rest of the world, the rise of textile factories heralded the decline

▼ **46 Part of an ironstone dinner service, English, *c*.1820.** This is the prototype for the extensive services that became so popular during the 19th century, made increasingly in cheaper as well as good-quality materials. This example is in Davenport stone china, with printed pattern marks on the reverse. The Chinese-style decoration is printed and then coloured over.

of home-spun, hand-crafted artifacts in all but country areas. However, the art of cover-making in all its various forms still thrives in certain parts of the USA.

Many pieces are dated and signed, but equally many are not, so it is a knowledge of the materials used that enables dating, as the same patterns were often continued for generations out of love and affection for the originators. Space does not allow a full description of the several identifiable motifs that can reveal provenance, but the American Museum in Bath, England, has one of the finest collections outside the USA. Examples of American quilts are shown in Plates 40 and 41.

The pros and cons of mass production

It is not surprising that there should be a reaction to mass production from people of sensibility, such as the aforementioned Henry Cole (1808–82) and Owen Jones (1809–74), who supported the principles but not necessarily the style of Pugin, and who were to lay the foundations for the Arts and Crafts Movement that followed. Cole was a reformer who later became the first head of the South Kensington Museum (now the Victoria and Albert Museum), and Jones launched *The Journal of Design and Manufactures* in 1849. While they were not interior decorators as such, they advocated the putting together of sympathetic rather than themed carpets, wallpapers, curtains, furniture, and selected objects to create a tranquil and satisfying atmosphere. Their natural heir and pioneer of the Arts and Crafts Movement was William Morris (*see* p.186).

The formation of the Arts and Crafts Movement had already begun in the late 1850s. Within ten years the great names of individualism and reform would be well-established and revered among the fashionable classes. Although they strove for handmade idealism, it was inevitable that the decorative arts, given access to machinery and factory production, would react in the same way as modern *haute couture*. As soon as a prototype was spotted that could be copied commercially, it was. And in order to sell it, the name "art" was attached – so there was Art Wallpaper, Art Furniture, and even Art Linoleum. This much-derided flooring was invented in England by Frederick Walton in 1863 by mixing linseed oil, pine resin, and wood flour, and coating this onto a jute backing. (The name comes from the Latin *linum*, flax, and *oleum*, oil). Linoleum later became universally popular when Michael Nairn from Kirkcaldy in Scotland developed a means of inlaying patterns, which were ideal for Art Flooring.

THONET

The word Thonet is synonymous with the curved lines, light weight, and caned or plywood seat of the bentwood chair shown here (*see also* p.159); indeed, so much so that Thonet has become a generic term for the style. Michael Thonet (1796–1871) and his five sons started a factory in Vienna in c.1856. Thonet's innovation was the use of laminates of thin veneers pressed into formers while wet, and then allowed to dry. This was a procedure formerly only successfully used for ship building, but by 1871 it had made the firm of Thonet the largest furniture-manufacturers in the world. The advantage to Thonet's design was that there were no corners to get knocked. Damage to caning (as seen below) and its repair need not affect value, providing the work is done professionally.

THE NEW RENAISSANCE

1860–1910

Extremes in all walks of life were never greater than now. From the cosiness of clutter to the austerity of Japanese minimalism, from traditional means and materials to futuristic methods of communication and transport, and the emancipation of women, this was a phenomenal period.

◄ **1 Interior of 18 Stafford Terrace, London, purchased by Edward Linley Sambourne in 1874.** This epitomizes the eclectic taste of the late Victorians, who put together all the elements of their heritage: furniture from France and Italy, porcelain and pottery from China, Japan, and Europe, carpets and rugs from Turkey and India, bronzes from Germany, and prints and pictures from everywhere. Marvellous.

The identifying look of each period in the development of the decorative arts had, until the mid-19th century, been that of the upper and middle classes. These people were the trendsetters whose manner, dress, and personal possessions the lower orders emulated according to their means. However, by 1860 the enduring image that immediately says "Victorian" is more the interior of a middle-class drawing room or parlour than that of a stately home or a nobleman's portrait.

This change in influence may well have been due in part to the popularity of paintings, drawings, and prints depicting scenes of joyful family gatherings around the laden dining table or Christmas tree, or dramatic scenes of discovered infidelity, remorse, rejection, tragedy, and those "never darken these doors again" episodes in such accurately detailed settings that we know precisely what the average Victorian interior looked like.

Another reason for our strong recollections of the mid-Victorian period is the advent of photography. By the early 1860s there was a professional photographer in every town. In Wells Street in the town of Buckingham my great-great-uncle William Simmons had a studio where he took photographs of local people, which he printed on cards to be placed in family albums or used as *cartes de visite*. These became so popular that by the mid-decade 400 million a year were being produced

(nationwide that is, not just by my uncle). His retoucher and colourist (every photographer had one) was his niece, and as well as a number of his studies, I have her inks and brushes and the small balloon-back chair his sitters sat on. (A similar example of the chair is shown and discussed on page 158.)

By the 1860s representations of all fashionable styles in décor and artifacts were affordable and therefore present in most houses to impress visitors with the *savoir faire* of the family. Gothic was mixed with Old French, Medieval mixed with the formality of a revival of the Louis XVI style, and all were surrounded by fringes, tassels, geometric-pattern carpets, and floral wallpaper. Added to this was the heartening effect created by indoor plants, such as palms and the "cast iron" aspidistra, which thrived on oil-lamp fumes in dark corners. There was also a passion for goldfish in glass bowls. Paintings,

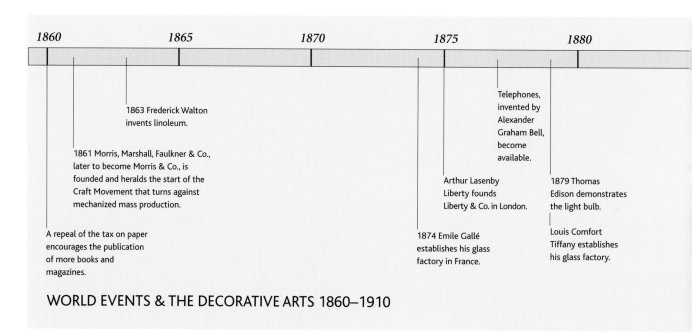

| 1860 | 1865 | 1870 | 1875 | 1880 |

1863 Frederick Walton invents linoleum.

1861 Morris, Marshall, Faulkner & Co., later to become Morris & Co., is founded and heralds the start of the Craft Movement that turns against mechanized mass production.

A repeal of the tax on paper encourages the publication of more books and magazines.

Telephones, invented by Alexander Graham Bell, become available.

Arthur Lasenby Liberty founds Liberty & Co. in London.

1874 Emile Gallé establishes his glass factory in France.

1879 Thomas Edison demonstrates the light bulb.

Louis Comfort Tiffany establishes his glass factory.

WORLD EVENTS & THE DECORATIVE ARTS 1860–1910

carvings, and metal castings of lilies of the valley and fern leaves abounded, and these became the two most popular decorative motifs applied to papier-mâché, small pieces of furniture, treen, and iron garden seats and tables from 1860 until the early 1900s.

The drawing rooms and sitting rooms were filled with chaise longues, settees, pouffes, easy chairs, and the newly introduced "conversation seat" – a three- or four-sided seat arrangement around a central backrest (as the sitters each faced a different direction it is difficult to understand how any conversation took place). To these a new "parlour suite" was added. This comprised a settee with deeply curving show-wood frame, two easy chairs with open arms – one slightly smaller than the other, latterly known as grandmother's and grandfather's respectively – and up to ten small balloon-back chairs, similar to dining chairs but less robust and with less upright backs.

Another addition to the well-to-do house was the smoking room, where male occupants retreated to enjoy pipes and cigars. This room was also well draped, dark in colour and atmosphere, and far from free of clutter. As well as the now obligatory souvenirs and knick-knacks from the British Empire, all types of smoking paraphernalia

▶ 2 Portrait of His Majesty King Edward VII, by Sir Samuel Luke Fildes, English, 1901. This dramatic and imperious pose belies the warm and kindly character of one of the best-loved monarchs in Britain's history. Edward was the eldest son of Queen Victoria and Prince Albert, and was acknowledged as a hard-working and diligent prince and king.

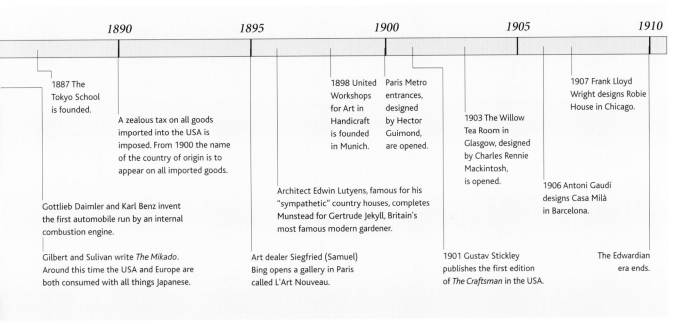

| 1890 | 1895 | 1900 | 1905 | 1910 |

1887 The Tokyo School is founded.

A zealous tax on all goods imported into the USA is imposed. From 1900 the name of the country of origin is to appear on all imported goods.

1898 United Workshops for Art in Handicraft is founded in Munich.

Paris Metro entrances, designed by Hector Guimond, are opened.

1903 The Willow Tea Room in Glasgow, designed by Charles Rennie Mackintosh, is opened.

1907 Frank Lloyd Wright designs Robie House in Chicago.

Architect Edwin Lutyens, famous for his "sympathetic" country houses, completes Munstead for Gertrude Jekyll, Britain's most famous modern gardener.

1906 Antoni Gaudí designs Casa Milà in Barcelona.

Gottlieb Daimler and Karl Benz invent the first automobile run by an internal combustion engine.

Gilbert and Sulivan write *The Mikado*. Around this time the USA and Europe are both consumed with all things Japanese.

Art dealer Siegfried (Samuel) Bing opens a gallery in Paris called L'Art Nouveau.

1901 Gustav Stickley publishes the first edition of *The Craftsman* in the USA.

The Edwardian era ends.

were introduced. These included a smokers' compendium, which usually took the form of a small cabinet containing a tobacco jar, pipe racks, cigar drawer, match case and strikers, tampers, and cutters. Smokers' tables with built-in ashtrays and match dispensers, Grecian-style model lamps filled with spirit with cotton wicks (which were the first "table lighters"), and a stand to hold the smoking caps completed the setting. The flat Turkish- (Ottoman Empire until 1922) type caps, embroidered and with a long tassel to one side, were worn to save the fashionable Macassar oil hair dressing from absorbing the smell of tobacco. Macassar, now in Indonesia, was said to be the source

for the ingredients for this hair dressing, which was one of the many products sold in Staffordshire shallow pots, the lids of which were decorated by the multi-coloured transfer printing developed by the Pratt brothers of Fenton (*see* p.166).

The white crochet slipcover over the back of an upholstered chair, the antimacassar, became particularly popular at this time as a decorative item as well as being necessary to protect the upholstery. But it was not invented by the Victorians: silk slips had been introduced in the 18th century to guard against the greasy make-up and powder so liberally applied by the Georgian gentry.

▲ **3** *Summer*, **an oil painting by John Atkinson Grimshaw, English, 1875.** By this time women's fashion had changed from wide, crinoline-supported skirts to the bustle, but still used wonderful vibrant fabrics. In this country home is further evidence of the fashion for eclecticism – particularly in the deliberately displayed antique Delft punch bowl and the new Japanese fans.

▶ **4 Detail of an interior print by Walter Crane, English, 1878**, for the cover of Clarence Cook's periodical *House Beautiful*. There is a mixture of old and new international items in the décor, and this picture shows the essence of the new Aesthetic Movement, as Crane was imbedded in the socialist ideals, theories, and practices of John Ruskin and William Morris.

In the dining room, the extending table with central pedestal supports was less popular than the alternative with legs around the edge, and by the 1860s existed only as an heirloom. The modern dining table had sturdy, turned, and sometimes reeded or faceted, tapering legs, and could be extended easily using the new winding mechanism that was introduced at the Great Exhibition in 1851. The chairs, usually matching, were also sturdy and comfortable, as main mealtimes, despite being attended by more family than guests, were still disciplined, regimented, and long affairs. Carving and serving was done at the sideboard, and so the fine white damask tablecloth, previously splashed and therefore removed for dessert, remained spotless throughout the meal. This gave additional splendour to the coloured and engraved glass that, for a short time, replaced the cut glass of the Regency and early Victorian periods (*see* pp.164–5). Fine, brightly coloured china and ironstone dinner services (*see* p.168) added to the mêlée of patterns, while posy holders with live flowers, and namecard holders of silver or enamel in front of each place setting provided the final touch.

One other piece of furniture that appeared early in the 19th century and featured strongly in Victorian-period houses throughout Europe and America was the large round table on a centre pedestal, known as a Loo table. It served as a useful dropping place for visitors' hats and gloves in the entrance hall, or as a conveniently sized table for informal family meals, but its essential function was to provide space enough for five or more people to play the card game of Loo. This is a trick-winning game that can be as harmless or intense as the company wishes, and it was introduced from France to England in the 1660s. Its name is an abbreviation of Lanterloo or Lenterlu, a word of no meaning but used in early nursery lullabies. By the 1860s Loo tables were no longer necessarily circular but shaped in undulating ovals or round-ended rectangles on a variety of solid and openwork pedestals, and were rarely used for playing Loo.

Any household able to afford this much comfort had at least four servants, and anyone earning a regular salary employed at least one. Agriculture and domestic service were the two main occupations at this time, but at the lower end of the wage scale people were often not far from the breadline. When the river Thames in London froze just before Christmas 1860, and remained solid until 19 January 1861, thousands of people who relied on the river for their living were laid off work and pauperism rose from over 96,000 to more than 135,000. Such a statistic is necessary to remind ourselves of the curious double standards of most Victorians: strong religious beliefs, high moral standards, and close-knit family establishment, and an ability to ignore the masses of starving poor in their midst. The Poor Laws of 1834, with their provisions for workhouses, helped, but not enough.

In 1860 Abraham Lincoln (1809–1865) became President of the United States of America, and in 1861 the American Civil War started. This was a tragic year for Queen Victoria too. Her mother died at the beginning of the year and her beloved Albert, only recently acknowledged as Prince Consort by the British, died of typhoid fever with complications on 14 December. The Queen was distraught to the extreme and went into mourning, from which she never really emerged. Black was the *de rigueur* colour in

◄ **5** *Shared Confidences*, **oil painting by Adrien Henri Tanoux, French, 1912.** By the end of the Edwardian period the tightly corseted "S" shape figure, with the monobosom and prominent backside, was losing favour. Instead a return to a Classical, simple look appeared, allowing fabric to follow the natural bodyline.

▲ **6 Thoresby Hall, Nottinghamshire, England, built 1864–75.** Designed by eminent architect Anthony Salvin, Thoresby shows a return to Elizabethan values in architecture, which ran through most of the 19th century. It was just under three hundred years since William Cecil, Lord Burghley, completed his great house at Stamford (*see* p.14), upon which Salvin based this design.

dress and jewellery, until Her Majesty went increasingly to Balmoral, Scotland, when tartan patterns began to appear in ribbons and trims, on boxes and caskets, and small items of treen. Balmoral, a 15th-century castle situated almost equidistant between Aberdeen, Inverness, and Dundee, had been bought by Her Majesty and Prince Albert in 1852, and was demolished and rebuilt for them by 1858. During the last 40 years of the 19th century Scotland became the strong commercial and artistic force it remained until well into the 20th century.

The repeal of a tax on paper in 1860 encouraged the publication of books and magazines advising on home management and "husbandry". Beautifully illustrated catalogues of goods from suppliers as diverse as iron founders, nurserymen, hatters, and potters were there for people who, even if they did not intend to buy, at least knew what was available. The ability to pick from such a variety accounts in no small degree for the lack of cohesion of style in the mid-Victorian house. But of all the bestselling books of advice from this period the one that comes to the mind of most people is the *Book of Household Management*, by Mrs Isabella Beeton, which was published in 1861 and sold 20,000 copies in its first 12 months. And well deserved too, for it is surely the most comprehensive book of rules, recipes, and guidance that anyone trying to run a household could have. It advocates good management as well as splendid recipes in such a way as to give us a great insight into the mind of the day, and much of the advice is still of use in the 21st century. It is well worth perusing today, and fascinating for such little snippets as "she who makes her husband and her children happy, who reclaims the one from vice and trains up the other to virtue, is a much greater character than ladies described in romances…".

Developments in Europe

While Britain was being lauded as the leader in the field of mass-producing decorative and domestic items, the rest of Europe was far from sitting back idle. In Austria, Michael Thonet (1796–1871) started experimenting with the craft of making furniture, particularly chairs, using solid or laminated wood that had been steamed or soaked in hot water to make it pliable (*see* p.169). Based on the 18th-century method of making Windsor chairs with wet or green timber, Thonet produced symmetrical, elegant and

WILLIAM MORRIS

Above all others, the name William Morris immediately springs to mind when Arts and Crafts, Art Nouveau, Art Wallpapers and Fabrics, and the Kelmscott Press are mentioned. And with some justification, for surely no one did more to revive the ancient crafts of dyeing, weaving, and printing, against the tide of mechanization and mass production.

Morris designed furniture and stained glass, gained recognition as a linguist (translating ancient Icelandic sagas into English) and as a poet, and founded the Society for the Protection of Ancient Buildings. Later in his life he took to printing and typography, and remained an ardent Socialist until his death at the relatively young age of 62. But it is probably for his designs of wallpaper and fabric that he is best remembered, for they are never far from sight in today's inteiors. For further details on Morris and the Arts and Crafts Movement, *see* page 186. Information can also be found at the William Morris Society in London (*see* p.251 for details). There is no question that Morris' prodigious talent in so many areas, and his unbridled enthusiasm, energy, and ability made him one of the most influential protagonists of his time, if not in history.

▲ **7 "Trellis" wallpaper by William Morris, English, 1862.** This is the first wallpaper he designed when living at the Red House in Kent. Morris drew the trellis and flowers, and fellow-artist Philip Webb drew the birds. Morris later studied birds and used them in a series of designs.

▲ **8 "Pimpernel" by William Morris, English, 1876.** This wallpaper pattern was used to decorate Morris' dining room at Kelmscott House, Hammersmith. Morris also used it in the billiard room of one of his greatest interiors, Wightwick Manor.

▶ **9 "Evenlode" by William Morris, English, 1883.** Named after a tributary of the river Thames, the design is derived from Persian and 17th-century fabrics. It required a complex process called indigo discharge, and 33 different printing blocks.

lightweight chairs, and founded a factory in 1842 in Vienna. His five sons joined the business and 30 years later the firm of Thonet Brothers was the largest furniture-making company in the world. The best-known model was catalogue number 14, which was developed in 1855 – a year later, under the name Gebruder Thonet, a patent was granted for the process.

Following this the Thonet Brothers developed mass-production techniques that enabled them to sell their chairs to every café and hotel in Europe. Later, sales went worldwide, and a showroom was opened in London. Another famous model was the Rocking Chair, which was made in a variety of patterns. This was adopted by leading makers in alternative materials, and a fine example of one made of brass and steel is shown on page 159.

The Thonet patents expired in 1869, and since then their methods and models have been much copied. However, the firm continues as an important force in the modern furniture industry.

Glass and ceramics

From the 1860s the glass industry continued to find ways of creating sparkle and lustre in otherwise sometimes sombre rooms, whether in the form of luxurious and deceptive-coloured glass paperweights or prismatic drops attached to tall vases. The latter were a development of the cut-crystal and -glass drops of the 18th century, which

were hung from the glass dishes on candlesticks and chandeliers, but the Victorian ones were longer. From the 1830s the drops, which are called "lustres", began to extend in straight-sided form, usually oval and faceted in section with one or two cut-glass "buttons" between the top and the vase. The vase, which had a narrow body below a flared rim, was really just a vehicle for these drops and

▲ 10 Oak court cupboard, English, c.1860, with 17th-century elements. The immediate guide to this being a pastiche is that it is so primitive. In the 16th and 17th centuries such a cupboard was expensive and therefore made with skill and precision; in the 19th-century-revival of such furniture it was wrongly assumed that to appear old furniture had to look rough.

◄ 11 Sideboard by William Cooke of Warwick, English, 1853. This is a perfect example of the Warwick School of Carving (see p.161). In an attempt to compete with machine-carving technology, excessive hand-carved decoration adorned massive furniture in the form of life-size game animals. The style soon was adopted in Europe and, ironically, made subsequently by machine.

19TH-CENTURY BRITISH CERAMICS MARKS

Printing detailed information of a factory and pattern on English ceramics did not start until the 19th century – any printed mark with the name of the factory, the pattern, and the material dates an item to after c.1810. The use of the word "Royal" in front of the factory name indicates a post-c.1850 date, and the incorporation of the Royal Arms means it's 19th-century or later. The name of the country-of-origin dates items to after 1891; the words "Made in", and then the country of origin, are 20th-century, as are "English Bone China" or "Bone China". Any printed mark with an 18th-century date alludes to the founding of the factory, not the date of the item. When a factory uses the same mark for a long period, it is the shape and decoration of the item that helps to date it.

◄ **12 Printed mark on English ironstone, c.1837–97.** The use of the garter frame is mid- to late-19th-century and the pattern is named "Indian Tree". With this knowledge it is possible to find the JM&S mark in any good ceramic marks book, listed as "John Meir & Son of Tunstall" within the dates above.

◄ **13 Printed mark of the Minton factory, used 1825–35.** This is a rare mark, recorded on the Earl of Shrewsbury's dinner service. Hidden in the "E" and "B" are the words "Stoke-on-Trent" (not visible in this illustration).

◄ **14 Impressed mark from the Worcester Factory, used 1865–80.** Worcester is an exception to the guides given above, as there are rare painted and printed examples of marks from the late 18th century. However, the factory mostly used symbols or initials until c.1800.

◄ **15 Printed mark from the factory of Francis Morley & Co., operative under this title 1845–58.** The use of the garter is an immediate guide to the date, further confirmed by the word "Royal" and the Royal Arms inside the garter. Although the name of the pattern is not given, the factory and place of origin are clear.

◄ **16 Printed mark from the factory of Turner, Goddard and Co., operative with several different marks 1867–74.** The factory's rather grand address was Royal Albert Pottery, Tunstall, Staffordshire. The inclusion of the Royal Arms indicates this piece was made after c.1850.

◄ **17 Printed mark from the Hammersley & Co. factory, operative from 1887.** The words "Made in England" identify this as 20th-century. This particular mark was not introduced until 1939, and has a slightly home-spun look that you might expect to find on tea-sets and kitchenware of the post-war years.

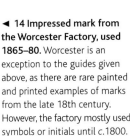

◄ **18 Printed mark from the Hammersley & Co factory, used after 1939.** This mark was used in several different versions until the factory merged and finally closed in the 1980s. It is an example of the diversity of marks often adopted by a factory at one time.

was not suitable to hold a candle after the 1860s. As the drops got longer they became triangular in section, which created prismatic displays on walls and ceilings as sunlight caught the glass through a window. The next effect was created by cutting a simple shape into the back corner edge of the drops, whose pattern was repeated in the reflective nature of the prism – thereby adding enormously to the light transmitted. The effect of these "lustres", when stood in front of a mirror over a fireplace or pier table, was dazzling, and they remained popular, although frowned upon by the cognoscenti, well into the 20th century.

▲ **19 Part of earthenware dinner service, English, late 1800s.** This bears the mark of one of the great names in Staffordshire pottery – Booths of Tunstal – a prodigious maker of dinner wares.

▼ **20 Rosewood centre table, Indian, c.1850,** an English-based design made by a local craftsman. The result is a charming mix of European elements (e.g. acanthus leaves) in unmistakably Indian style.

A great competitor for the English glass market was Bohemia, where huge amounts of fine-quality as well as junk glass were made specifically for export to Britain. Some lustre vases were so complex, large, and expensive that they were supplied with glass domes to protect them from dust – and from being dusted. Glass paperweights needed no such protection, but for over 60 years were just as highly prized and admired. They first appeared in the mid-1840s and the best at this time were made in France at the Baccarat, Clichy, and St Louis factories, but they were soon challenged by English and American glass-makers. The description of Tunbridge ware on page 134 mentions a bundle of different-coloured strips of wood being arranged so as to form a pattern, rather like a stick of Brighton-rock candy. The same format was true for glass paperweights: a bundle of different-coloured canes of glass were arranged to form groups of flower heads (called *millefiori*), or swirling ribbons, or formed into plants, reptiles, butterflies, baskets of fruit, or a mixture

through which the viewer could spy the treasure inside. These are called "overlay" paperweights and are associated with the St Louis factory, the usual colours being deep blue, emerald green, or, more rarely, apple green and pink. The rarest St Louis overlay colour is yellow, and in 1957 the only known example, formerly in the Maurice Lindon Collection, made £2,700 ($4,320) at auction. Wonderful paperweights are still being made in Britain, particularly Scotland and England, as well as in America and China, but it is unlikely that they or their antique forebears will reach those dizzy heights in the market in the foreseeable future. But who knows, now might be the time to buy.

In 1815 John Doulton (1793–1873) established a ceramics factory specializing in stoneware products – particularly water pipes and drains – at Vauxhall with John Watts (*d.*1853), and by 1818 it had moved to Lambeth, South London. It had been discovered that the repetitive outbreaks of cholera in the city and elsewhere were due to poor sanitation rather than air pollution, and Doulton was hugely successful in supplying nearly a quarter of the sewage pipes for the new London drains. In the 1860s he collaborated with the Lambeth School of Art to produce salt-glazed stoneware, and eventually acquired premises for students to work away from factory surroundings and the restrictions on imaginative thinking that they created. Unusually, the students were allowed to sign their work and were free to experiment with designs and materials. Famous artists, such as Hannah Barlow (1851–1916) and George Tinworth (1814–1913), were invited to decorate some pieces, examples of which are highly collectable today. By proving that terracotta was a sound and decorative building material the commercial side of the Doulton empire flourished, and so funded the art side.

The business passed to John Doulton's son, Henry (1826–97), who was knighted by Queen Victoria in 1887 for his services to the pottery industry. At the time of his death, over 400 modellers were working under the Doulton name, producing a wide range of high-quality decorative objects that were readily bought by enthusiasts all over the world. There was no Doulton "style" as such, and yet a Doulton vase or bowl is instantly recognizable, and the joy for us today is that each piece bears marks that

aptly named "scrambled", and enclosed by a sphere of clear glass at the end. This sphere magnified the ends of the glass canes to the extent that they appeared to fill the glass ball, enabling the viewer to see the minute detail in each subject. This was particularly significant in the Baccarat *millefiori* weights, where one of the flower heads might include the initials of the maker – usually B, F, or J, although whose these stand for no one knows – or, more importantly, the year when the weight was made. The years 1846 to 1849 were incorporated into the design, the most common being 1848 and the rarest 1849. A further enhancement was a coating of white and then coloured glass, which was cut away to create "windows" in the ball can tell us where it was made, who modelled it, who decorated it, and when. In 1901 King Edward VII (*see* p.205) conferred upon the company the double honour of a Royal Warrant and the specific right to use the Royal title. The company has been Royal Doulton ever since, a well-earned recognition for what was, at the time, the largest single ceramics company in the world.

With the fashion for iron hearths, firebaskets, and grates to be inset with ceramic tiles it was natural that these would be made by Doulton, and the flowing lines of Art Nouveau and Japanese styles (*see* pp.190–9) were ideal for portrayal within the rather sombre framework of the polished black fireplace.

The extremes of new-found freedom of expression in ceramics could not be better illustrated than in the work of the Martin Brothers. True eccentrics, Wallace Robert, Edwin, Charles, and Walter began operations in Fulham, London in 1873 before moving to Southall, London, where they stayed until the firm closed in 1923. They are best known for their extraordinary figures of birds

(*see* Pl. 43 in ch.5) and vessels applied with whimsical creatures and designs made exclusively of salt-glaze stoneware. Edwin and Walter had worked for a while at the Doulton studios, and, when established with a family business, maintained the habit of signing each and every piece they made until the company's cessation in 1923.

Clocks

In an earlier chapter we looked at the development of clocks and how a preliminary glance could tell us what approximate period one would come from, judging from its general shape and movement (*see* p.82). It was noted that the longcase clock went out of production towards the 1830s, hence its latter-day name, the "grandfather" clock. But there are two types of clock that are typically associated with the 19th century, each of which was made in a great variety of styles. One is the wall clock, the other the travelling or "carriage" clock. Wall clocks were not new in the 19th century, for timepieces mounted on inside walls without the fear of being knocked or jolted, or on

◄ **22 Mahogany and inlaid armchair, English, *c.*1895–1910.** The combination of a mish-mash of elements from the 18th century typifies this revival period. The cabriole legs in pre-1770s style are too weak to be from that original period, and the arms have a boxwood line inlay that, like the vase-shaped back panel within the George II-style frame, just didn't happen originally.

▲ **23 Details of the mahogany and inlaid chair back, shown left.** The differences between this marquetry panel and an 18th-century original may be subtle, but the inclusion of a lack-lustre imitation-ivory is positive proof of its period. This was a development of the first man-made plastic, shown at the 1862 Great International Exhibition in London by the inventor Alexander Parkes.

exterior walls, with faces large enough to be seen by the community at large, had been in use since the early 18th century. (These are often referred to as "Act of Parliament Clocks", after the tax on clocks and timepieces was imposed *c.*1797/8.) But the elegant, simple, Neoclassical-frame model, as shown in Plate 34, was not introduced into homes in Europe until the early 1800s. This model was developed in Vienna and, to begin with, was marked by a single driving weight. The accuracy of these Vienna clocks, particularly the "regulator" model, and their tasteful appearance assured them of the success they quickly achieved. By the 1830s the Biedermeier style (*see* pp.144–5) had lent itself to the case, and, with its pedimented top and simply constructed case, it soon became mass-produced and over-sold. However, the idea of varying the style of the case soon caught on and, when springs became mass-produced toward the end of the century, millions of simple and circular-framed wall clocks with enamel dials were being produced throughout Europe and America. The first of these had a small case below the dial with a glass panel in it so that viewers could see the pendulum. This type, known as a "drop dial", was made in all manner of timbers, sometimes inlaid with mother-of-pearl (after 1830), and sometimes lacquered onto wood or papier-mâché (*see* p.151).

One of the reasons that longcase clocks went out of fashion was the huge production of cheap wall and shelf clocks made in Germany and America after the 1840s,

▲ **24 Machine-carved mahogany adjustable music seat, English, c.1880.** The development of the metal screw thread enabled adjustable seats such as this to defy weight distribution. The shaping, turning, and carving were all multi-produced; the result, no doubt taken seriously at the time, seems almost comical in appearance today.

▶ **25 Gilt-metal and faux malachite *garniture de cheminée*, French, c.1850–1900.** The popular revival style in the last half of the 1800s spawned the manufacture of sets in a variety of materials and range of prices. The best were of ormolu (gilded bronze), with fine marble, onyx, or malachite, and a leading clock maker's movement; the cheapest were of spelter and paint on metal or wood, with a factory-made barrel movement.

which virtually eclipsed the production of the superior but more expensive models from France and England. The American clock, with its spring-driven eight-day movement and sturdy spruce-wood case that was stained to look like the more costly mahogany, was a decorative and reliable addition to the lower- and middle-class home. As it usually had a glass panel below the dial with a transfer-printed topographical scene of America on the reverse, it gave the impression of international *savoir faire*.

Carriage clocks date from the late 18th century. These small rectangular clocks were often supplied with a case to protect them, and on luxury models a repeat mechanism was added that, when operated by a lever, allowed an approximate time to be estimated by the chiming bell(s).

The first definitive record we have is of one made for Napoleon I in 1798 when he was on his Egyptian campaign. It was made by the Swiss-born watchmaker Abraham-Louis Breguet (1747–1823), and Napoleon was so delighted with it that he ordered that each of his generals should have one. By the end of the 18th century Breguet was specializing in self-winding watches and had developed a mechanism to compensate for the jarring of his travelling clocks while they were moving around. Until 1791 he signed his work "Breguet a Paris" but found he was being copied, and so thereafter his signature is hidden. The carriage clock was at the height of its popularity from around 1850 up until the outbreak of World War I in 1914. Most were made in Paris and ranged in quality and price from the plain-case, simple timepiece to the multi-belled *petite sonnerie* and *grande sonnerie* movements, which had cases decorated with enamel panels on porcelain or *cloisonné*, and frames that copied Classical columns or faux bamboo. The *petite sonnerie* has the option of striking the quarter-hours and a two-phase lever enabling silence, and the *grande sonnerie* can be set to strike the hour and the quarter, just the hour on the hour, or be silenced. There are other combinations too. Usually these levers are under the case, and the repeat press button on top of the case may be the only indication of a superior movement – except its elaborate decoration.

During the last half of the 19th century there was a great interest in the three- or five-piece mantel set, comprising at best a pair of candlesticks, a pair of urns or vases, and a clock. These were mostly made in Europe and might be of: cheap pottery; expensive porcelain; gilded, silvered, or bronzed spelter; imitation marble and alabaster; cast and gilded brass; bronze; or ormolu. Wherever the cases were made, the movements for the clocks were mostly produced in France and, while many of the gilt-metal ones might be mistaken for 18th-century originals, a quick glance at the model and its quality and the movement itself will soon disclose its provenance.

The Arts and Crafts Movement

The Great Exhibition of 1851 had been intended to "present a true test and living picture of the point of development at which the whole of mankind has arrived". Rather more importantly to the British, it was to show that they led the world in manufacture and were about to lead the world in commercial expansion. In all of that and more the exhibition was a success, and the ever-growing middle classes enjoyed such comforts as never before. However, William Morris, generally regarded as the founder of the Arts and Crafts Movement, considered

▲ **26 Illustration from the *Art Journal Catalogue of the International Exhibition*, London, 1862.** These locks and keys show a Renaissance revival with Gothic overtones, emanating from central Europe in the mid-1800s. While Bramah, Yale, and Chubb invented new types of lock, it was the remit of German locksmiths to create the most intricate, ornate mechanisms.

it to be "tons and tons of unutterable rubbish", and here was the beginnings of a split even greater than that between the gentle designs of Thomas Sheraton and the relatively outrageous designs of the high-style Regency 50 years before. Now the situation of man versus machine arose, which is simple enough to understand and catalogue, but was made complex by a technology without a suitable style from which it could fully capitalize. New machinery was being used to make old-fashioned furniture; something different was needed and it came, slowly, from the very source that intended to undermine machine production, the Arts and Crafts Movement, which decried the use of machine production in favour of handmade items in the true craft tradition.

Arts and Crafts furniture was constructed in medieval form. It was made from the finest materials and to the purest lines, and its very being was linked to ideals of reform and purity. What irony, then, that by the end of the century the fashion intended to undermine mechanization of the crafts should be adopted as ideal for mass production.

William Morris (1834–96) was a highly educated craftsman, designer, writer, painter, typographer, reformer, and wealthy socialist. He might have taken holy orders but

events turned him to the decorative arts, where he concentrated on the more secular aspects of Medievalism as opposed to the ecclesiastical elements of Pugin's Gothic. Forecasting the advent of the machine as being responsible for the demise of handcraft, he and his group of talented intellectual contemporaries failed to see the potential benefits of mechanization and its inevitable success. Nevertheless, they created and passed down to us a period and design style of such forceful purity that it began to influence European taste in the 1860s and continued to do so well into the 20th century. Concerned with clarity of line and purpose, Morris designed furniture with such finely cut joints as to obviate the use of glue, returning to the ancient method of mortice and tenon joints (*see* p.23). This fitted well with the early form of art adopted by his associates, the Pre-Raphaelite painters, and was to create a compatible atmosphere for his future wallpaper and fabric designs. In 1861 Morris formed a company, with Charles Faulkner and P.P. Marshall as co-directors and Philip Webb, Ford Maddox Brown, Dante Gabriel Rosetti, and Sir Edward Coley Burne-Jones as co-founders. The company was named Morris, Marshall, Faulkner and Co., and was described by the participants as comprising

► **27 Liberty's smokers' cabinet, English, c.1900.** Elements of Art Nouveau and Arts and Crafts were combined in this cabinet, which would have been a commercial success for Liberty's, then the smartest shop in London. Smoking was not considered a problem at that time, and men had a range of different pipes, cheroots, tobaccos, cigarettes, matches, spills, and tapers filling cabinets such as this.

▲ **28 Brass-mounted oak hall stool, English, c.1890.** This style is associated with Messrs James Shoolbred & Co., a company that adopted a sophisticated aesthetic look with strong references to earlier Regency interpretations of Greek and Roman antiquity, usually enriched with brass mounts. Shoolbred was among the largest furniture retailers in London, and created the city's first department store in Tottenham Court Road.

◄ **29 Brass-mounted oak hall stand, attributed to James Shoolbred & Co., English, c.1890.** There are less historical elements than in the stool above, but the bracket feet are 18th-century and the brass finials Egypto-Roman in style. The mouldings, tramline reeding, and turnings are machined.

"Fine Art Craftsmen in Painting, Carving, Furniture, and Metals". Among their first recognized successes were windows of stained glass, which earned them prize medals in the World's International Exhibition in London in 1862. For this exhibition the Crystal Palace was recycled into use, but the fair was generally considered a poor follow-up to the 1851 Great Exhibition, with fewer exhibitors, fewer attendees, and without the driving and guiding force of Prince Albert. But out of it came at least one new machine, that is, one to be shown to an international public audience for the first time – the domestic sewing machine.

In 1865 Morris' company was reorganized and renamed Morris & Co., and its style, under the title Early English Gothic or Early English, began to attract general attention. This was encouraged by the publication in 1868 of *Hints on Household Taste* by Charles Lock Eastlake (1793–1865), which strongly advocated the "sophisticated primitive" look of Morris' designs. This followed the periodical magazine *The Cabinet Makers' Monthly Journal of Design*, which started in 1860 and also favoured the early style, and *Gothic Forms Applied to Furniture*, published in 1867 by Bruce Talbot (1827–81), the Glasgow-trained architect and designer. Talbot's furniture designs went even further than Morris', delving into the square shapes of the 13th century and employing painted surfaces. The combination of this early-style furniture and Pre-Raphaelite art, when applied to it, created extraordinary objects that were never available to those outside the William Morris coterie but are nevertheless important, as they epitomize the "look" and the ambience

▲ **30 Rosewood acorn-case wall clock, by Forestville Manufacturing Co., Bristol, Connecticut, USA, *c.*1850**, an early example of ogee-moulded rectangular case clocks imported from the USA in the late 19th century. A cheap brass movement made in 1838 by Noble Jerome widened their appeal.

of the Movement. The best examples may be seen at the Victoria and Albert Museum in Kensington, London.

The general feeling of the Arts and Crafts Movement and its anti-complacency stance spread throughout Britain, with centres in Birmingham, Lancaster, Edinburgh, and Glasgow. In Europe, where itinerant British craftsmen travelled and settled, Belgium, France, Spain, Germany, Austria, Hungary, and Scandinavia all took up the style – as did the North Americans. In the USA it found a warm welcome among the Quaker communities, where the simplistic forms of Shaker furniture linked labour and sacrament – a belief held by John Ruskin (1819–1900) – and in the rapidly growing major cities in the north, where certain wealthy industrialists were keen to show their patronage of something different in architecture and interior decoration.

The Elizabethan renaissance

On page 177 is a picture of Thoresby Hall, Nottinghamshire, now a hotel, which was completed in the 1870s by leading architect and renovator Anthony Salvin (1799–1881) for the third Earl of Manvers. Often referred to as Salvin's masterpiece, it shows the then current Elizabethan renaissance in a more easily recognizable form than that of the Arts and Crafts Movement. Clearly there is a relationship with the skyline of this building and that of the true Elizabethan palace, Burghley House at Stamford, Lincolnshire (*see* Pl. 3 in ch.1). This close adherence to the original in certain schools of architecture was also required in much of their furnishings, and it is from this time, early in the second half of the 19th century, that we see the reconstruction and redecoration of many earlier household items. In market areas of many major cities in Britain, and to a lesser extent in Western Europe, early furniture could be found in pieces, dismembered and marked for sale to be rebuilt in a different format to suit the requirements of the new "Elizabethan" house. Because of its original pegged and joined construction it was easy enough to take apart an old coffer, buffet, or bed – the panels and frames of which were ideal for making up hall benches with lift-up-lid box bases, which rarely, if ever, existed originally. Cupboards with leaded-light glass doors – which definitely never existed

◄ **31 Green glass bowl with white-painted decoration, American or Bohemian, *c.*1880.** This type of decoration traditionally is attributed to Mary Gregory, a decorator at the Boston and Sandwich Glass Co., but she did not paint children, only pastoral views. Current opinion is that children were a Bohemian subject, later copied by other factories in the USA.

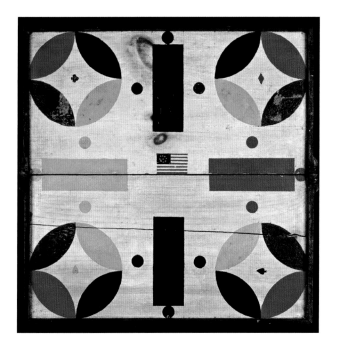

◄ ◄ **32 Painted folding Parcheesi gameboard, American, c.1870.** Parcheesi is described as the "Royal Game of India", and is for up to four people. It is played with pawns and spinners or dice, and the winner is the one to get four pawns home first, home in this case being the American flag.

◄ **33 Carved and painted whirligig figure, American, c.1910.** Whirligigs are wind-driven novelties that have been part of American folk-art for two hundred years. The harder the wind blows the faster the figure moves, and it is believed that the vibrations caused will drive away moles. This one is a "Dandy" advertising figure from Indiana.

previously – and court cupboards (*see* p.179), which certainly did exist but which at this time were rare to find, were also popular.

This category of altered pieces presents a problem today in that even the 19th-century pastiche has had 150 years of use and wear and, being made out of some old and originally carved timbers, it can be very difficult to recognize it as a hybrid. There are no golden rules in such cases but there are things to look for. Firstly, always bear in mind that any furniture carved when new, from whatever period, was expensive at the time and therefore will be above average in quality. When old pieces were reformed some new parts were necessary and it is these that are most likely to reveal the pastiche. Despite having some old sections of carving in front of them to copy, restorers all too often assumed that old means crude and primitive. This is not true. Crude and primitive means unsophisticated, and fine Elizabethan furniture was anything but that. So look for uncharacteristic bits of poor workmanship. Another guide is that oak is particularly difficult to make look old. It repels stain and can only take a surface colour, so where new wood is present the edges will have worn and will disclose a pale surface beneath the dark varnish. Finally just stand back and look at the piece and see if it looks comfortable. A little practice looking at the best examples in museums will help to attune your eye.

Curiously, such pastiche pieces now have a value as furnishing items in their own right, being a stage more interesting than the "new" reproduction "Elizabethan" or "Tudoresque" furniture that was made in the 1920s and 1930s. While the Arts and Crafts Movement was making some impact in the USA, this reconstruction of early furniture did not. It was not long, though, before original but plain pieces of the Chippendale and Sheraton periods were being taken into workshops and carved and inlaid to improve their status and their price, and this certainly did affect the American market in the early 20th century.

Wallpaper designs

During the last 40 years of the 19th century, wallpaper became an integral part of interior design and decoration. Most houses retained the dado – the lower decorated part of an interior wall – and its rail. Developments in production enabled the dado to be covered with heavy embossed paper simulating raised panelling below more embossed paper made to look like Spanish leather with all-over foliate patterns. When painted, the dado was usually brown, dark red, or green, and the woodwork for the rail, doors, doorframes, and picture rail were often grained to simulate mahogany or pitch pine. Plain rather than raised pattern paper was focused on by William Morris, while the inventive mind of Frederick Walton (*see* p.169) played around with the concept of making a type of linoleum for wall-hangings. In 1877 Walton achieved his goal and marketed "Lincrusta-Walton". He took the brand name from two Latin words – *linum* (flax) and *crusta* (hard shell).

In 1883 an employee of Walton, one Thomas Palmer, went to Walton with an improved version of Lincrusta using a cotton and pulp base but, seeing it as a potential competitor, Walton rejected it. Three years later Palmer left Walton to develop his own product, which he called "Anaglypta". Like Walton, Palmer looked to the classics for a name and chose the Greek *ana* (raised) and *glyptos* (engraving) to describe raised engraving, as in a cameo. He showed it at the 1887 Royal Jubilee Exhibition in Manchester, where its flexibility, lightness of weight, and comparative low cost were immediately recognized by the decorating trade, and at the Paris Exhibition Universelle in 1900 Anaglypta was awarded two gold medals. In the 20th century the two companies merged, and they are still leaders in the fine wall-coverings market.

The wallpapers designed by Morris contrasted with the geometric Gothic patterns of Pugin in their display of formalized and stylized scrolling sinuous flowers, exemplified by the "Daisy" pattern that he produced in 1862. This was the forerunner of a series with a similar theme, which was equally suitable for printing onto fabric. The now-famous "Pomegranate", "Trellis", and "Acanthus" patterns were immediately popular among the avant-garde decorators of the time, and are still immensely popular today (*see* p.178). There are several recognizable motifs of the Morris school, including the scrolling tendrils terminating in heart shapes or formalized tulip heads associated with C.F. Voysey (1857–1941), and the hand-beaten effect on metal panels of pewter, brass, and copper, which became part of furniture decoration during the 1870s (*see* p.195). This same effect could be achieved on silver and glass. The hammered look was created by engraving with a wheel that had a semi-circular edge, and when used in conjunction with several layers of different coloured glass the end result was stunning.

The Japanese influence

In Europe the designs of William Godwin (1833–86) and Christopher Dresser (1834–1904) were creating another aspect to new design that was in turn influenced by the appearance of Japanese goods on the open market.

After more than 200 years of near-isolation, it was going to be a while after the ratification in 1855 of the 1854 treaty between Japan and America (*see* p.157) before the benefits of world trade were realized and accepted by the Japanese, certainly by the older generation. But in 1862 a limited number of items were displayed at the International Exhibition in London. The British agent for

◄ **34 Mahogany-case wall clock, Austrian, c.1840.** This is a fine and early example of what is known as a Viennese Regulator, of which copies were cheaply mass-produced after the 1860s. Made by the eminent makers Elsner and Petrovits, this exemplifies the severe architectural case, large pendulum, and nonstriking movement.

► **35 Mahogany and tile fire surround, English, c.1875.** This is archetypal of the Aesthetic Movement at its best: severe architectural lines are lightened by the emblematic and narrative tiles. These tiles were made by W.B. Simpson & Sons, still a leading specialist tile-making company today, and the surround is believed to have been designed by the artist and illustrator Walter Crane.

◄ **37 Ebony and burr-veneered davenport desk, English, c.1880.** The davenport desk appeared at the end of the 18th century and remained popular thereafter. Here the dramatic use of contrasting timbers with incised and gilt highlights is typical of the style and quality of Messrs Holland & Sons. It was usual for this company to stamp their work on the top edge of a drawer or door.

▼ **38 Ebonized and ivory inlaid cabinet-on-stand, Italian, late 19th century.** The European cabinet emanated from Italy, and it is not surprising that even a revival piece from there will have an extra touch of style. Here bone as well as ivory is cut in marquetry and engraved on the door panels with ancient figures. Although it comprises two separate pieces, it is still as one in style and appearance.

▼ **36 Tripod Table with fabric top, English, c.1885.** This is a modest but attractive ebonized beech-and-gilt decorated occasional table in the style of Holland & Sons, but it is not of their quality. The original fabric would have had a deep fringe to the edge.

▲ **39 Inro, Ojime, and Netsuke, Japanese, c.1875–1900.** The Inro is a purse to take small personal items, held together by two silk cords and kept closed by a small bead called an Ojime. The Inro is suspended from a wide Japanese belt called an Ubi, and the Netsuke (pronounced "netskee") is placed at the end of the cords to stop the Inro falling through.

▼ **40 Pair of Imari porcelain jars and covers, Japanese, c.1890.** The name Imari is that of the port through which porcelain made in Arita was shipped to other parts of Japan and to the West. These jars are of ribbed form with shishi finials and typical distinctive shades of brick-red and blue.

these was the firm of Farmer and Rogers, whose store was in Regent Street, London. The manager responsible was Arthur Lasenby Liberty (1857–1931), who opened his own, now world-famous, shop, Liberty's, also in Regent Street, in 1875. From here he sold furniture from Egypt and Africa and objects from Japan, and in addition commissioned decorative household items to be made in what he called his "Cymric" and "Tudric" styles. In a combination of Medieval and Celtic styles, lamps, carriage clocks (*see* p.185), and ornaments were made with a hand-beaten silver or pewter finish; Cymric was silver and Tudric was copper. His chief designer was Archibald Knox (1864–1933). Liberty's style was so popular throughout Europe and America that in Italy, Europe's best-informed country at the time, it was named "Stile Liberty". At the same time, during the last quarter of the 19th century, a "Modernist" style was evolving, taking elements from the ideals of the Arts and Crafts Movement and making the look more formal and compatible with machine production. Christopher Dresser anticipated the style, and his insistence of linking design and functionality led to him and Godwin being held accountable for much of its considerable success. It was this "Aesthetic" movement, as it became known, that was to blend so successfully with Japanese taste. In addition to the rapid increase in imports of the genuine article, English and American manufacturers of ceramics, metalware, glass, silver, and

▶ **41 Imari porcelain charger, Japanese, c.1890.** With its asymmetrical arrangement of fans, book pages, and flowers set against a black background enriched with gold, this is less typical of Imari than the pair of vases above. The scenes are all emblematic or narrative, reflecting Japanese culture.

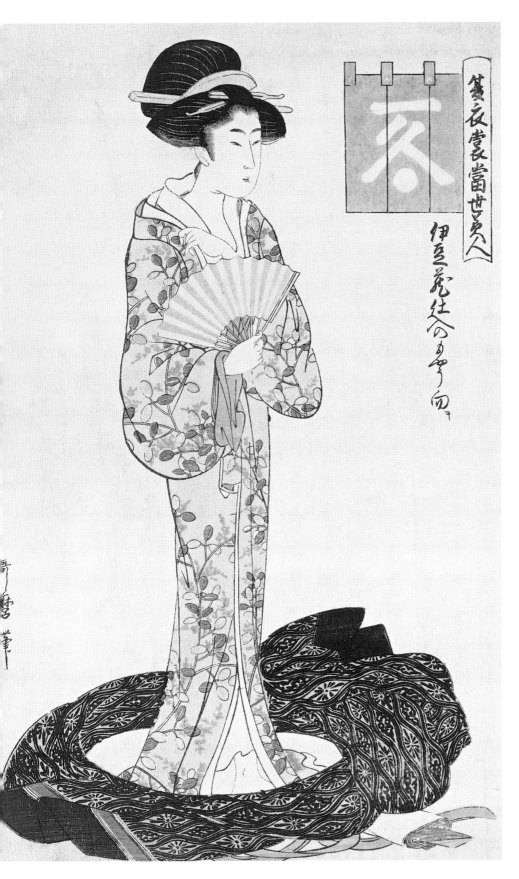

◄ **43 Four silver and lacquer Komei panels, English and Japanese, 1872–6.** On one of the three doors of the cabinet the geometric panels are so placed as to form an overall Egyptian shape, set within veneers of mahogany, satinwood, and ebony stringing. The scenes are a variety of emblematic and narrative subjects.

► **44 Mahogany and satinwood cabinet, English, 1876.** This is of the quality of Messrs Jackson & Graham; the door locks were made by Chubb & Son. The Egyptian-revival style was favoured by Bruce Talbert, who worked with Jackson & Graham. The cabinet was built to display the Japanese Komei panels of silver and lacquer with gold appliqué of which J&G had an exhibition in May of 1876.

◄ **45 Capitol top and Komei panel, English and Japanese, 1872–6.** The satinwood and mahogany formalized leaf pattern shows the Egyptian-revival taste used with effect in contrast to the Komei panel. Of further historical interest are the hinges, stamped Cope & Collinson, which confirm the date.

plate were producing all things "japonaise", with motifs such as fans and butterflies, geishas and sunshades, and screens – as well as panels of undulating foliate patterns or landscape scenes with Mount Fuji in the background being applied to both Western and Oriental shapes. Such motifs were enamelled, painted, cut, engraved, printed, or carved, depending on the object. By the end of the century it seemed as if no aspect of fashionable life in Europe or the USA was untouched by "Japonaiserie", for any up-to-date lady had at least one kimono-type gown of fine silk and several dresses with wide kimono-cut sleeves. Large and irregular embroideries of peonies, japonica, or branches of flowering cherry were applied by hand or machine, according to cost, and for entertainment people attended and learned by heart the music and lyrics of *The Mikado*, written by Gilbert and Sullivan in 1885.

By the mid-1870s the asymmetry of Japanese furniture had also caught the Western imagination, and vast quantities were being imported, made of bamboo, cane,

and lacquer. The demand seemed insatiable, particularly in England and the USA, and by the early 1880s imitation and real bamboo furniture was being made in both those countries. Again according to cost, the frame was of fake, standard, or fine-quality bamboo, and the top and shelves were of genuine lacquer and rattan, or embossed and printed paper in imitation. Following an exhibition in Paris at the Galerie Georges Petit in 1883 there was a revival of interest in Japanese prints, whose influence was to be unmistakably present in the work of countless artists during the next 30 years. Gaugin, Van Gogh, Toulouse-Lautrec, Manet, Monet, Renoir, and Whistler are just a few of the great painters whose masterpieces can be enjoyed from yet another perspective in the light of the works of Japanese artists Hiroshige, Hokusai, and Utamaro (*see* Pl. 42).

These Japonaise items are different indeed from the paraphernalia that cluttered every late-Victorian sitting room. Bronzes, swords and sword guards, and carved ivory

THE "PLANISHED" EFFECT

From time to time a particular surface treatment is introduced that catches the imagination of manufacturers and is adopted by makers of all branches of the decorative arts, with greater success in some fields than others. A good example is the hand-beaten "planished" background effect that became so popular during the height of the Arts and Crafts and Art Nouveau Movements, and which emanates from the hammer marks on hand-wrought metalwares and mounts.

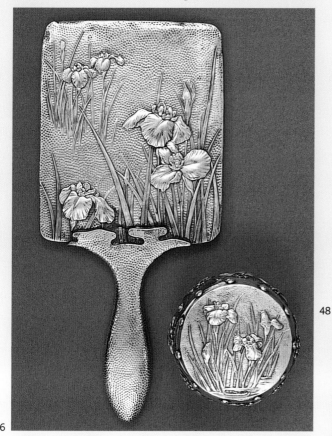

46

48

49

47

46 Part of a dressing-table set, English, 1896. This mirror and powder pot formed as a drum show a Japanese influence on the Art Nouveau style. The wistful portrayal of plants in water that seems to move due to the planished (hand-beaten) effect, was adapted for various materials throughout Europe by the end of the century.

47 Cased or overlay glass vase, French, c.1895, by the Daum Brothers (*see* p.198). Layers (cases) of clear, amber, and dark-green glass are cut away to create a flower on a hand-beaten surface.

48 Oak bookstand with applied copper plates, English, c.1885. Extended upright ends became a common feature in Art Nouveau furniture, as did the application of mass-produced copper panels with tendrils and heart-shaped leaves on a "hand-beaten" background, in the manner of Charles Voysey.

49 Illustration from the *Art Journal Catalogue of the International Exhibition*, London, 1862. This exhibition gave Westerners one of the first glimpses of Japanese goods (porcelains, bronzes, enamels and lacquer, ivory carvings, costumes, and wallpaper), the latter influencing Art Wallpaper.

figures, known as *netsuke* or *okimono* were all popular. A *netsuke* is a large button or toggle worn to prevent the little box of medicines (*inro*) carried on a loop through the wide belt on Japanese costume from slipping out of position (the belt is called an *obi*). *Okimono* are decorative ornaments, the best of which are carved in unbelievably realistic detail to represent characters from Japanese life. The subjects include samurai warriors, *bijin* (beautiful ladies), peasants, and fishermen. *Netsuke* may be made from ivory, wood, bone, walrus tusk, or lacquer. So, too, may *okimono*, but the best are of ivory or sometimes a combination including elements of wood and lacquer, and these were made in what is called the Tokyo School. (The Tokyo School of Art was founded in 1887 by Ishikawa Komei, *see* Pls. 43–5.) It retained the traditional skills of Japanese artistic culture while acknowledging

▲ **50 Bamboo and faux-lacquer table, Japanese, late 19th century.** The asymmetry of this is as beguiling now as when new, and was much copied in the USA and England. The shelves are covered with paper embossed to simulate leather, and the top is printed and varnished to have the appearance of lacquer.

▼ **51 Japonaiserie sideboard, English, c.1867–70.** This piece by Edward William Godwin, a leading exponent of the strict Japanese disciplines of design, is made of ebonized mahogany with silver-plated mounts and panels of paper embossed to look like leather. It is one of eight known to have been made by William Watt & Co. from an original intended for Godwin's use.

Western art and schooling. The term Tokyo School is generally used to describe Japanese ivory carving of the highest quality presented in a manner that would appeal to the Western market.) A small tablet of red lacquer is often found implanted on the underside of the base of *okimono* carvings into which a signature has been engraved; alternatively signatures are simply engraved onto the body of the piece. However, any signature has to tie in with the work itself, and expert opinion in this rarefied field is an absolute must before acquiring an expensive example, as 20th-century copies abound.

The emergence of Art Nouveau

A further Japanese exhibition was held in 1893 at the Galerie Durand-Ruel, Paris, but the most significant was probably the *Exposition Historique de l'Art de la Gravure au Japon*, held at the Galerie Bing in 1886. It was significant because it drew attention to Siegfried (Samuel) Bing (1838-1905), a German-born art dealer and guru who had imported Oriental crafts to Paris since the late 1870s. In 1895 he opened his gallery, which is now famous for its name: L'Art Nouveau. It was situated at 22 Rue de Provence, Paris, France, and it was here that Louis Comfort Tiffany had his first public exhibition of his glass. A wealthy and important figure in the *monde moderne*, Bing suggested to Tiffany that French artists of Bing's choosing should present to Tiffany paintings that could be transposed onto stained glass. It was a revolutionary idea that made both men even more wealthy, and gave worldwide exposure to the new form, which incorporated Celtic, Viking, Japanese, and Islamic art. It fed from the Arts and Crafts Movement as well as from Aestheticism and could be produced in every area of art – from architecture to jewellery. Louis Comfort Tiffany (1848–1904) was the son of Charles Lewis Tiffany (1812–1902), founder of the New York jewellery store Tiffany & Co. – which he opened in 1837.

Louis Comfort Tiffany was multi-talented and an accomplished artist, exhibiting at several prestigious shows, but in 1875 he began experimenting with glass manufacture and in 1878 established his own factory. A year later he founded a design studio, which later became the Tiffany Studios. Churches across the USA contain Tiffany's stained-glass windows, monuments, and chapels,

▲ **52 Silver and inlaid ivory jar and cover, Japanese, *c.*1875–1900.** The silver is decorated with enamel around the ivory panels, which are set with carved amber and mother of pearl. This technique is attributed to the artist Shibayama, whose name, due to the popularity of his work, has become the generic term used to describe all such decoration, good or bad.

► **53 Silver hair brushes and mirror, Japanese, *c.*1900.** These European objects were made for export to the West until 1939. The decoration is embossed prunus to the backs and engraved bamboo on the handles.

and in his family mansion on 72nd Street and Madison Avenue, New York, he built the first piece of American Art Nouveau – a huge fireplace with its chimney made to replicate a tree. But it is surely for his stained-glass lampshades that he is best remembered – coupled with the fabulous gemstones the store still provides to its wealthy clients. Production of the lamps began in 1893, quickly taking advantage of electricity rather than kerosene, enabling all-enclosing shades and directional light. In 1894 Tiffany registered the trademark "Favrile" for a new iridescent glass, derived from *fabrile*, which means "belonging to the craft". Tiffany's designer and manager, Arthur Nash, an English expert glassmaker, suggested the name and they melted 20 dollar gold pieces in the meld to create the new glass. Even when new, Tiffany lamps cost the equivalent of around $20,000 (£12,500), so it is no wonder that they have always been highly prized. However, they have also been much copied.

In the area of Art Nouveau glass there are three other main names whose positive identification with a piece will increase its value and guarantee the finest quality: Emile Gallé (1846–1904), Antonin Daum (1864–1930), and René Lalique (1860–1945). Emile Gallé and Antonin Daum had glass factories in Nancy, eastern France, and produced works of art in the, then modern, Art Nouveau style. Both started in the mid-1870s, but it was not until 1887 that Antonin and his brother, Auguste, turned to art glass production. They both used overlay or cased glass and a technique called *marqueterie-sur-verre*. This describes the method of taking a preformed motif in glass, such as a leaf or petal, and pressing it into the body of a main piece while it is still hot. But here the similarity between the two companies ends. The Daum factory seemed to lack the fineness of the Gallé work but it developed its own character and its own following of collectors. Daum pieces bear the engraved name "Daum", or "Daum Brothers", alongside the cross of Lorraine. Emille Gallé is most famous for his acid-etched cameo glass, so called because it resembles the cameos cut from stones and shells, wherein the artist uses the natural layers of stone or shell to create three-dimensional images. Gallé invariably signed his work, and after his death in 1904 the factory

continued this tradition until it closed with the outbreak of World War I in 1914. However, these post-1904 pieces have a small star next to the name Gallé. If only identifying glass by René Lalique were as uncomplicated. There are known to be 16 different marks of his name used during his lifetime. These included the letter "R" before the Lalique. After his death in 1945 the "R" was dropped but, in common with his predecessors, fakes and copies abound, so before buying a major piece by any of these three great makers, some expert advice is essential.

From Paris, Art Nouveau spread throughout Europe, known as *Secession* in Austria, *Jugendstil* in Germany, *Modernismo* in Spain, and *Stile Liberty* in Italy. A look around any of the major cities of these countries will reveal heavy commitment to the style in both private and public buildings. Hotels in Vienna, embassies in Brussels, the Paris Metro, restaurants virtually everywhere, and tea rooms in Glasgow were kitted out in the style. It seems in fact that, for once, England, and more particularly London, was almost reticent in following the newest style to those extremes, and certainly it never had anything to compare with the

► 54 Illustration from a McCall's sewing pattern, American, 1905. By this time women's underwear was so popular that dresses and even coats were made of lingerie material. No doubt Amelia Bloomer, the Can-Can dancers, and female participation in tennis, cycling, golf, and other sports contributed to this.

▲ **55 Bronze figure of a girl with ball, French, early 20th century.** Girls' hair at this time was parted in the centre, waved, and, if not cut too short, bunched either side. The inclusion of another material in this figure (in this case the ivory ball) was a foretaste of the combination bronze-and-ivory figures of the 1920s, most popularly made by Ferdinand Priess.

▲ **56 Bronze portrait bust on marble column, English, c.1910.** As princess and queen, Victoria Mary of Teck (Queen Mary, George V's consort) adopted the curled-fringe hairstyle introduced by Queen Alexandra when she was Princess of Wales. Some fashionable women wore them into the 1920s, but many wore false curls attached to a wire frame.

extraordinary buildings of the Catalan architect Antoni Gaudí (1852–1926). His mansion for Josep Battlo at 43 Passeig de Gracia, Barcelona, and La Pedrera apartments at 92 in the same street are among his finest secular work, while his Sagrada Família church remains an unfinished symphony.

Developments in the USA

One Westerner who furthered the Japanese culture from a different angle was the delightfully named Lafcadio Hearn (1850–1926). Hearn worked as a newspaper reporter in Cincinnati, Ohio and New Orleans. His career as a journalist eventually took him to Japan, where he settled in 1890, married a Japanese woman, and took citizenship and a Japanese name. If he was not the first,

he was certainly an early American to do so. His descriptive and explanatory writings of Japan and its tranquil culture, pleasing customs, and lasting values captivated the West, especially in his published collection of lectures, *Japan: An Attempt at Interpretation*, (1904).

Strong though the Art Nouveau influence was in the USA, the florid carved furniture and kerosene-lamp-lit clutter of the mid-19th century lingered on longer and more steadfastly than it did in middle England, particularly in more rural areas. The core background was the *Tous-les-Louis* style, but in upper-class homes each room adopted its own character and was furnished accordingly. For example, the hall was plain, the library dignified, and the drawing room lively. Or so recorded

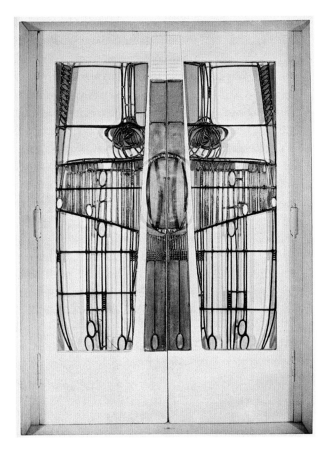

◄ **57 Pair of stained-glass doors, Glasgow, Scotland, 1904.** Probably the most quoted example of Art Nouveau design, this pair of doors was created by Charles Rennie Mackintosh for the Room de Luxe of the Willow Tea Rooms, owned and run by his patron, Miss Katherine Cranston.

► **58 Bronze door handle, plate, and lockbox, American, 1895.** The historically inspired pierced designs on the plate, when combined with embossed flower buds and the enamel inlaid handle in what is called Prairie Style, help to date this item. This piece is from the Guaranty Trust Building, Buffalo, New York.

the American architect A.J. Downing (1815–52) in his *Cottage Residences* in 1842. By the 1870s each room was fashionably decorated and filled with different styles, so an Elizabethan hall led into a Gothic library or an Empire drawing room. From about 1815 German immigrant craftsmen introduced the Biedermeier style and a version of the Renaissance arrived from Italy.

Among the most important makers in the flamboyant French curvilinear style was the German-born John Henry Belter (1804–63). He opened a shop in New York in 1844 and developed a technique for manufacturing laminated bentwood, using the rather exotic rosewood for the top "show" layer. Great swirls and curves formed the balloon backs for chairs and settees, table supports, and bed-heads and ends. This style was much imitated, necessarily often using inferior materials and construction. From the mid-19th century most large towns had a cabinet-maker employing from 40 to 100 workers, of whom only a handful were highly skilled, as much of the production was repetitive machine work once the prototype had been developed. Poor quality opened the door to Modernism in America in just the same way as it

had in England, considerably encouraged in 1872 by the publication of an American edition of *Hints on Household Taste in Furniture, Upholstery and Other Details* by Charles Lock Eastlake, the English architect and protagonist of the Aesthetic movement. As in England, this developed with the fascination of "Japonaiserie" and the development of Art Nouveau. (It was Eastlake who promoted the revival of the rectangular drop-end sofa, first used extensively in the 17th century at Knole Park in Kent.)

The person accredited with creating the first truly American furniture was Gustav Stickley (1858–1942). He had been totally enamoured by the ideals and designs of William Morris and Ruskin, and, when he published the first edition of *The Craftsman* in October 1901, Stickley dedicated it to Morris. (The second edition was dedicated to Ruskin.)

Stickley advocated that his furniture should encourage craftsmanship in its construction, and reflect the nature and way of life of the American people, and so designed it to be trustworthy, orderly, functional, and, above all, agreeable. He was also an architect of considerable talent, and the architectural elements of his furniture were sufficiently strong as to be a clearly visible influence in the work of the iconic American architect Frank Lloyd Wright (1867–1959).

In the 1880s Stickley, along with his two brothers Albert and Charles, founded the Stickley Brothers furniture company in Binghampton, New York, and in 1898 founded the United Crafts group. A falling-out between the brothers left Gustav on his own, but the remaining Stickley company was bought by Alfred and Ameni Audi in 1976 and now employs 650 craftsmen who continue the tradition of fine furniture.

One feature of Gustav Stickley's furniture was the occasional incorporation of matt-glazed tiles by the potter William H. Grueby (1867–1925), whose vases and other products Stickley advertised in his magazine. Having visited the World's Columbian Exposition held in Chicago in 1893, Grueby was totally smitten by the shapes, colours, and glazes of the ceramics he saw at the French exhibit there. Five years later Grueby had established his own matt glaze, and in 1900 he exhibited at the Universal Exposition in Paris, receiving two gold medals. By 1905 Grueby was showing at Tiffany in New York and a limited line of Grueby vase lamps, topped with Tiffany shades, was introduced. These have always been highly sought-after and so there are many inferior copies on the market. As an indication of the interest they still provoke, a genuine Tiffany/Grueby lamp was sold in June 1999 for $286,000 (£178,750).

Toward the turn of the century

During the final 20 years of the 19th century it was becoming increasingly hard to find that peaceful landscape of the Elizabethan world of 300 years earlier, as urbanization pushed further and further into quiet pastures. So much of Europe was a cloud of industrial smoke in countries separated by waterways constantly alive with shipping. But the people were very much the same: the rich were still ruling with arrogance, pomposity, and disdain. As an example, had Amelia Jenks Bloomer (1818–94), the American campaigner for more freedom for women, co-opted some wealthy, fashionable women of high social standing to popularize her bifurcated-skirt concept (forever after known as the "bloomer") in 1849, women might not have had to wait until the end of the century to be rid of faint-inducing corsets and stays. The pecking order of a feudal system and the degradation of craft into industry so despised by the wealthy reformers

VICTORIAN TILES

VICTORIAN TILES

Tiles have become as synonymous with Victorian interiors as the balloon-back chair (*see* p.158). In the home they were used as flooring, wall-coverings, insets in furniture for chair backs and in tabletops, trays, jardinières, hallstands, and as surrounds for kitchen and bathroom fittings, and they were constantly on view set into the surrounds of fireplaces. In municipal buildings, public baths, and conveniences tiles were everywhere, and they were used to create lustrous surfaces in the newly built underground train stations.

Decorative floor tiles had been made in Britain since the Middle Ages, and, although production never ceased, tiles went through periods of varying popularity. A high point was the second half of the 19th century, when mass production enabled their commercial use, as described above, and in particular the last twenty years of that century, when the individual artists of the Arts and Crafts, Aesthetic, and Art Nouveau Movements produced some of the most stylistically important designs in (relatively) modern times. The glazed tile pictured below is one such late-19th-century example, in a distinctive Arts-and-Crafts style.

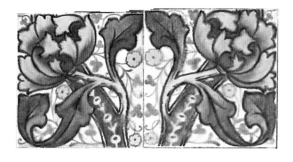

were maintained by them through their very ignorance of what it was like to be poor, and their lack of perception of true equality, for all their socialist ideals.

Britain had gained an empire, and from its farthest reaches and its strangest cultures the British filled their houses with objects reflecting their need to be acknowledged as cultured, well-travelled, sophisticated, and all the other desirable traits they did not have. Just like the Elizabethan barons, the wealthy Victorian captains of industry and commerce had hunting lodges where stuffed animal trophies were hung, hallways where arms and armour were displayed – in many Victorian grand houses it was fake – and huge numbers of staff. Progress in all walks of life – from travel, communication, visual and oral recording, and medicine to welfare and education – had not improved sensibility across the board, so there was no particular look for identification; it was a period when some aspect of anything and everything novel was expected to be in everyone's home. People felt deprived without the new, and so a consumer society was supplied with items cheaper and cheaper until they were affordable by all. We look at antiques of this period now with some respect because they represent a part of our past, but forget how lowly they were considered between, and just after, two world wars, when the true value of so much junk was clinically assessed and thrown into a pit at the bottom of the garden. We may be aghast at such waste and recall anecdotes of great aunt throwing away the rare Worcester vase or the fabulous iron bedstead. While obviously there were occasions when mistakes were made through ignorance and dislike of the items, they were rare. Unless it had been a gift from a grateful employer, it is unlikely that great aunt ever had the Worcester specimen, which would have been too expensive to buy and too valuable to keep; more likely the case that she owned a Bavarian or Japanese copy. When a Tiffany lamp is sold for an astronomical sum at auction there goes the cry, "I had one like that and threw it away", or words to that effect. Unlikely.

The majority of Tiffany's best lamps went straight into museums or private collections, and the rest were priced well above the means of ordinary people. What was thrown away was the cheap, mass-produced copy using ordinary coloured glass (no 20-dollar gold pieces mixed in it) and spelter (an inexpensive, impure zinc alloy introduced in the mid-19th century) metalwork, which could be treated to simulate bronze. So 1890 to 1910 is a complex period, difficult to define chronologically and rather tragic in the light of the horrors of war and disease that were soon to follow.

Nevertheless, it was a period packed full of detail that enables us to give dates and provenance to a whole range of items. Of the mass-produced types of glass from America, Britain, Italy, and Bohemia (the new Czech Republic), what proliferated was a cheap pinky-red glass known as "Cranberry" glass. It was used for every known item of table and decorative ware, and is usually finished with a crinkled edge, either of the same colour or clear. Soon other colours were included, such as amber, blue, green, and amethyst. Also added to this novelty was the application of painted scenes, usually in white. The most popular subjects were children at play in a garden setting, their faces in profile. Throughout the 20th century this decoration has been called "Mary Gregory" – named after, according to my grandmother, a kindly lady who created

► **59 Pair of silver two-branch candelabra, German, c.1905.** The flowing lines of the bases and realistic forms of the iris relate closely to those on the silver pieces on p.195, which illustrates the widespread influence of Japanese style and design throughout Europe in the late 19th and early 20th centuries.

◄ **60 Table lamp with stained-glass shade, American, c. 1900.** This lamp is marked "Tiffany Studios", which will date it to after 1895, when Tiffany started to use its own special glass. Many lamps by Tiffany were copied using spelter (see p.202) for the base and cheap glass. The finest Tiffany lamps went no further than private collections or museums, so are rare.

At first a new fashionable motif, this was ideal for mass production as it could be machined onto great lengths of timber that could then be cut as needed, with its decoration already applied. This was most common after the 1880s. A good example of this decoration can be seen on the cross-rails of the hall stand shown in Plate 29.

A renowned English furniture company, Messrs Holland and Son, took this type of formal decoration a stage further by ebonizing the main body of a piece and gilding the incised lines (see Pl. 37). At first applied only to expensive furniture, it was soon copied on mass-produced items, where it could transform a mundane piece into an attractive item. The table in Plate 36 is a good example. The company also popularized the use of inlay bands of burr-cut timbers, such as maple and walnut, in various widths, made even more pronounced with inset line borders of boxwood. The Davenport desk in Plate 37 is a fine example and shows the style that was highly popular in the USA during, and after, the 1890s.

In 1890 a tariff on goods imported into the USA was established to protect agriculture and "infant" industries such as tin-plate manufacturing. The tax was over-zealous, being as high as 48 percent, and was met with strong opposition as it made so many domestic articles too expensive. Its chief proponent was a Republican congressman, William McKinley (1843–1901), who was later to become the 25th President of the United States from 1897 until his assassination in 1901, and the tax has commonly been called the McKinley Tariff ever since. Of chief concern to us is that one of the results of the tariff was the obligatory application of the country of origin on all imported manufactured goods, so when the name of the country of origin appears on any item, that item will have been made after 1890. Soon after, but not before 1900, the words "Made In" and then the country's name appeared, which provides another dating clue.

The extremes of fluidity and the stylized foliate form of Art Nouveau were followed less enthusiastically in England than elsewhere in Europe, but Scotland, and more particularly Glasgow, made up for the shortfall on the English side of the Channel. The most significant and distinctive creator in this field was Charles Rennie

such idyllic childhood artifices in the Boston and Sandwich Glass Company (see p.165). Years later my illusion was shattered when I was informed that there was no such person. However, recent research has proved that there was, and she did work for the Sandwich Company. She did paint glass but did not paint children, just animals and landscapes. The children apparently were all done in various parts of Europe; so Grandma was half right. "Mary Gregory" glass has been collected on and off for a hundred years. The rarest colour is said to be amethyst. It was after the introduction of Cranberry glass that the range of colours expanded to include creamy, milky opalescence, multi-colours that looked like a bag of candies had been squashed and moulded, and silicate or "slag" glass with its oily iridescence.

One telltale sign of furniture made in the post-Aesthetic period is the incised parallel lines on drawer fronts and panels, friezes, and uprights. The lines, which were usually in groups of three or four, are not "stopped" before the end of the timber but "run off" at the ends.

Mackintosh (1868–1928) – architect, artist, and designer, especially of furniture, whose work was appreciated abroad far more than in his homeland during his lifetime. His designs reflected something of the uprightness of Scottish culture in his use of tapering, vertical lines, combined with a sense of Japanese tranquillity. His most famous extant work is in the Willow Tea Rooms in Sauchiehall Street, Glasgow, which, in collaboration with his colleague George Walton (1867–1933), he designed and furnished for Miss Kate Cranston, the owner and proprietor of a successful tea-room empire.

Many of the buildings in Glasgow are a fine monument to the Art Nouveau style and the period of 1880 to 1920, and the close links with the architectural ironwork in

Munich, Vienna, and Barcelona are clearly visible. Probably the best-known examples of such ironwork are the entrances to the Paris Metro, designed by Hector Guimard (1867–1942), which opened in 1900. Such designs could be used to create fashionable metalware on a much smaller scale too – for example in jewellery, which by this time had also gone through a renaissance of a more traditional nature (*see* p.207).

For more than 50 years Birmingham, England had been the centre for the mass-production of small single-bar brooches with filigree and set with pearls, sapphires, rubies, or even tiny diamonds. These became a traditional gift from a groom to his bride and were produced in their millions for domestic and export markets. During the second part of the 19th century, and for a while afterwards, the more affluent middle-class man could afford a handsome watch chain at a modest price, to string across the front of his waistcoat. This might have a swivel mounted with a seal of cornelian or bloodstone to hang

▼ **61 Room set in the Folkwang Museum, Hagen, Germany, 1902.**
The furniture was designed by Henry van de Velde, a Belgian who is described as the chief theoretician of Art Nouveau and a disciple of William Morris. There is now a foundation in his name in Weimar, Germany.

◀ **62 Pottery vase with three-colour daffodil, American, c.1905.** This is a William H. Grueby vase decorated by Ruth Erickson. At the peak of his career Grueby collaborated with Tiffany, supplying lamp bases for Tiffany's shades. Cheap mass-production imitations caused Grueby to go bankrupt in 1909, and finally close in 1920.

▶ **63 Royal Doulton salt-glaze stoneware vase, English, c.1885.** The formality of the borders and style of the panels is very Aesthetic compared to the freedom of the Art Nouveau vase, shown left. This was decorated by Florence Barlow who painted birds and flowers, while her famous sister, Hannah, painted horses and other animals.

from the centre. As most were made of 9ct gold they remain of no great commercial interest, but provide us with a decoration to be worn when appropriate as a reminder of our ancestors. Early in the Victorian period the love of flowers led to a revival in the "language" of them in much the same way, but less sophisticatedly, as the Elizabethans had done 300 years earlier. Like the bar brooches, millions of little pendants were made in Birmingham, formed as forget-me-nots to indicate true love in turquoise or pale aquamarine ("something blue"), set with rubies for passion, or set with seed pearls for purity or in reference to Venus, as they both came from the sea. But an important innovation towards the end of the century was the manufacture of what is known as "costume" jewellery. *Haute couture* dresses could be copied quite simply, but to set them off a piece or two of jewellery in the style of Boucheron, Cartier, Tiffany, or Garrards was needed. By the beginning of the 20th century a huge industry had grown in Europe, where labour costs were still low, producing masses of finely made copies using base metals washed with a silver or gold finish and coloured glass for the gems. These items are well worth collecting for enjoyment today, as so much was produced that prices remain low.

A new century and a new king

On 22 January 1901, Queen Victoria died at her beloved Osborne House on the Isle of Wight. She was buried in the Mausoleum, Frogmore, Windsor on 4 February, following a two-day Lying-in-State in the Albert Memorial Chapel. It was an end to a remarkable reign and was marked, like the Jubilees in her lifetime, by the production of a host of commemorative objects, ranging from respectful to the tasteless, in all manner of materials. Victoria had presided over the growth and establishment of the British Empire, and most of the items alluded to the greater incidents in the course of her 64 years as Head of State. In this context Victoria had witnessed some of the greatest social and economic changes for the potential improvement of her citizens in the history of the Western world. But whether the typewriter, the telephone, the camera, or the motorcar actually helped those in need as much as they might is a matter of opinion. Had she lived a few years more, Her Majesty might well have been amused at the sight of Orville and Wilbur Wright flying overhead, following their first manned flight on 13 December 1903 at Kitty Hawk, North Carolina, USA.

Queen Victoria was succeeded by her son, Edward. He was crowned king and pronounced Edward VII at Westminster on 9 August 1901. He saw a united South Africa as the outcome of the Boer War, and the establishment of the power of women in 20th-century society. He was, according to all records, the most diligent of men in matters of state and personal affairs.

While the King was living up to this accolade, the average English interior was getting in an even bigger muddle, for the revivals of earlier styles started to infiltrate the already overcrowded rooms. The old French Rococo style for furniture, which had never really disappeared completely, became weaker in substance. It now had thinner legs and uprights, while retaining all the fussy scrolls and encrustations, but was more elaborate in form. Sideboard cabinets, which were unique to this period, had glazed and solid wood doors below superstructures with mirrors and fanciful shelf arrangements. Alternatively recognized as the *Belle Epoque* ("beautiful era") style, it was the antithesis of the simplistic Aesthetic movement, but it was sufficiently popular among the masses because it looked expensive but could be made and sold cheaply. It spawned a revival of the somewhat plainer Georgian look, and so began an interest in mid-to late-18th-century furniture.

This started in the early 1900s with the period and designs associated with Thomas Chippendale. Soon the demand was greater than the supply.

It is important to bear in mind that the majority of English furniture made between 1740 and 1775 was curvilinear but plain – that is, uncarved. It was this majority that did not satisfy the requirements of the early 20th-century collector, in either Britain or the USA. (There was no demand outside those two countries for antique English furniture as yet.) And so it was during the Edwardian era that piles of perfectly genuine 18th-century English furniture went into workshops all over Britain, as plain as the day it was made, to emerge a little later carved as if by Grinling Gibbons, let alone by Mr Chippendale. Today this seriously affects the value, so experience is necessary to identify such pieces. As with the reconstructed oak of the post-1850s, after the best part of 100 years' use the subtle differences are not easily spotted by the untrained eye. A major clue is whether or not the carving stands proud of the outline of the surface. When a piece of furniture was made to be carved in the 18th century, the person forming the part to be carved allowed enough excess timber for the carver to create his designs as if they had been applied. Carving was an expensive luxury and it had to look expensive. It must not, could not, meld into the general shape of the piece; that was not the object. But the 19th-century improver had no such additional timber to work on, so had to carve into the outline already created in the 18th century. This means that when viewed in profile the carving disappears.

Within a few years the Neo-classical lines of furniture made to the designs of Thomas Sheraton during the last quarter of the 18th century also came into favour. Here there was no carved element; instead the (best) original pieces were inlaid with panels of marquetry (which had in all forms become fashionable again), while naturally the great majority was plain. The same process of embellishing was applied. In this case the surfaces to tables, bureau desks, sideboards, chests, and chair backs were inset with brightly stained Neo-classical-style oval and circular paterae containing shell patterns and flowers within borders of boxwood stringing. Also inlaid were

◄ **64 Mahogany cupboard, British, c.1905.** There are several classic Art Nouveau influences here, in the overall shape, the Tudoresque metal handle, and the stylized flower inlay of harewood, boxwood, and mother-of-pearl. Such a blend suggests a date just after, rather than before, the turn of the century.

EGYPTIAN REVIVAL (c.1870–1925)

In the 25 years either side of 1900, when the fashionable world was influenced by the Arts and Crafts, Aesthetic, and Art Nouveau Movements, there was an Egyptian Revival that filtered through into all three styles, as well as remaining in evidence in its own right. This revival sprang from the opening of the Suez Canal in 1869. In December 1871 Giuseppe Verdi's opera *Aida* was performed in Cairo, and "Egyptomania" began.

It can be seen in architecture in Europe, Britain, and the USA, particularly in Chicago and New York, but its widest appeal was with jewellers, especially those accustomed to working in the Art Nouveau style. Leading exponents such as Lalique, Tiffany, the Czech artist Alphons Mucha, and Philippe Wolfers were copied internationally when they used new semi-precious materials including moonstone, amethyst, citrine, and peridot, as well as lapis-lazuli, pearl (both freshwater and Baroque, as seen below), ivory, tortoiseshell, and horn. Copper, silver, and gold were also used, often combined with complex enamelling techniques such as *basse-taille* (designs engraved on the metal showing through the translucent enamel), and *plique-a-jour* (background metal removed from the enamel after firing). The brooch below, with garnets and abalone, dates from the 1920s, when a further revival of interest in all things Egyptian was prompted by the discovery of Tutankhamun's tomb in 1922.

▲ **65 Cut-glass two-branch candelabra, English, c.1870.** These imposing lustre lights were made in various forms from the 1830s and, generally speaking, the more complex they are the later the date. While cheaper models were imported, the best and heaviest quality ones continued to be made in Britain.

festoons and garlands of husks, double and triple lines to every edge, and a spandrel of fan pattern in every corner. There are ways to determine whether or not this was done originally or at a later date, but the simplest guide to this type of dubious improvement is whether the item is of sufficient importance to merit such expensive treatment in the first place.

Furniture was by no means the only category of domestic or decorative item to be revived. From the Sheraton and Adam period the work of the artist Angelica Kauffman (1741–1807) was reappraised. It epitomized the rather romantic view of Classicism that dominated that part of the 18th century, and which appealed likewise to the Edwardians. Kauffman was born in Switzerland and came to live in London, where she stayed until 1781. She married Antonio Zucchi (1726–95), a Venetian artist, and together they worked on allegorical and historical subjects,

▼ **66 Writing desk inlaid with pewter, American, early 1900s.**
Designed by Harvey Ellis and created by Gustav Stickley, this desk epitomizes the strictest adherence to Art Nouveau ideals in furniture, with references to contemporary European decoration but a distinctly American approach. This is one of only three so far recorded.

▲ **67 Walnut Renaissance-revival chair, Italian, c.1890**, sometimes referred to as a Savonarola chair, after a Dominican friar attributed with its original design. Similar chairs were known in England during the 16th century. It was one of the most popular revival pieces, and examples are common, but the 16th-century original ones are extremely rare.

as well as portraiture. They created frescos for interiors designed by Robert Adam. So talented was Kauffman that she was admitted to the Royal Academy, the only woman in England to be granted that honour. So, in a partially retrospective period what better subject to emulate and bring back to life than a beautiful artist (Angelica Kauffman was extremely attractive) and her scenes of mythical history? Nymphs, maidens, satyrs, and cherubs were depicted in woodland or architectural settings and transfer-printed onto expensive hard-paste porcelain and cheap pottery plates, vases, jugs, and basins. Each picture was carefully signed "A. Kauffman" (*see* p.213). But here's the rub: Angelica Kauffman did not paint scenes on porcelain or pottery and her signature never appeared as shown. Even so, the best examples are often on really fine porcelain and, when accompanied by top-quality gilding and border decoration, they can still be desirable to a collector.

Good and busy gentleman as he was, it is doubtful King Edward had time or cause to notice the dramatic changes in the attitudes of those with country estates, or those wishing to acquire them. Unless the estate was vast, it was unlikely to be as profitable as it had been 50 years previously; the

import of cheap American corn in the 1880s was but one contributory factor to the depression in the economy. Old, established families traditionally existed on the rent from their farms, and while by 1900 these had started to rise, they were still too low to maintain the high standard of living the squires had come to take for granted. By the end of the 19th century the "country house", particularly, as depicted by contemporary writers such as John Buchan and P.G. Wodehouse, had become the aspiration of many a city dwelling merchant or factor in coal, gold, or linoleum, and with the market depressed there were plenty available.

Coincidentally, in the late 1890s a young businessman, Edward Hudson (1854–1936), started a magazine called *Country Life*. Apart from appropriate articles to intrigue the city readers, it showed photographs in estate agents' advertisements of the plethora of idyllic country houses. The weekend house parties became legendary and, as it was now possible to travel rapidly by train, and soon by motorcar, were attended by a growing number of guests.

However, there were changes below the surface that would mean such grand events would become less frequent and less grand as households shrank in numbers. Staff were all-important, but wages were rising. Death Duties, introduced in 1894, were beginning to bite, and Income Tax was creeping up. One service industry after another sprang up to compensate for fewer staff: commercial laundries, confectioners, and grocers delivered their wares using motorized vans, and staff quarters were given over to garages for cars. Electricity for lighting meant less dirt from oil and gas lamps and no need for wicks to be trimmed and reservoirs to be filled. Central heating meant fewer fires to be tended, and more bathrooms eased the maids' workload of ewers of water delivered to every room. If the estate was large enough the outlying farms could be sold, otherwise the main houses started to fall into disrepair. So the houses in *Country Life* needed careful viewing and then a simple choice could be made: buy an old house and have it sympathetically restored, or buy new.

It was at this time that the architect Sir Edwin Lutyens (1869–1944) became recognized for his extraordinary sensitivity in creating houses that blended with the countryside yet suited a modern lifestyle. They were careful amalgams of old bricks and treated oak beams, whose colours were soft and corners gentle. If old bricks were not available then new ones were made in scale with the house and new-cut oak was made grey rather than harsh black. The style was of an indeterminate earlier age, with deep tiled roofs over gabled walls, the tall chimneys set to peek out from the countryside as if snuggled in there since time immemorial.

Among Lutyens' more prestigious works are the Cenotaph in Westminster, London and the British Embassy in Washington, but it is for his country houses that he remains best remembered. During the 1890s he was commissioned to build the house "Munstead Wood" (completed in 1896) for Gertrude Jekyll (1843–1932), Britain's most famous gardener in modern history. Following this, Lutyens and Jekyll collaborated on more than

one hundred house-and-garden schemes in a style so distinctive that it bears their names. Lutyens planted established climbing plants as soon as possible after any house was completed, complementing Jekyll's revolutionary look for the gardens, a look that is still popular today.

Here again there were contributory factors: in common with in-house staff, the number of gardeners was reduced and it became fashionable for the lady of the house to take more than a visual interest in the upkeep of the grounds. Owners took to tending their gardens, along with any house guests who wished to be invited back, and the sight of an aristocrat pruning the roses was considered more normal than eccentric. But the formality of the Victorian potentates' gardens could not be maintained without several dozen pairs of hands – for example, Lord Rothschild employed 60 gardeners at Tring Park – and Gertrude Jekyll's concepts changed the fashion to fit. Hers was the natural look of established random planting of indigenous flowers, shrubs, and trees that has remained the basic manageable format ever since. Except that to keep her "small" garden of 15 acres (6 hectares) looking natural, orderly, but unmanicured she employed 14 gardeners!

▶ 68 Illustration from the *Art Journal Catalogue of the International Exhibition*, London, 1862. This shows the boundless imagination of glassmakers in the 19th century: a table in exact replication of a wooden one, and a table "fountain" epergne with arms to carry shell-type baskets. The base is formed as a desert island to take an arrangement of exotic fruits.

The furniture and *objets* in the Aesthetic and Art Nouveau styles fitted the interiors of Lutyens houses perfectly. The long Medieval-style hinges on doors, the planished (hand-beaten) surfaces of metalware, and the Celtic matt-glazed pottery created a permanent, established atmosphere in houses that were warm around the large inglenook fire in winter and cool in summer.

This was a particularly good period for potters who acknowledged the advantages of technical manufacture and applied them, where appropriate, to their studio-type production. Two names synonymous with the "Art Pottery" of the time are William de Morgan (1839–1917)

▼ **69 Pair of rosewood and leather-covered side chairs, Portuguese, 19th century.** The cessation of furniture made in the Rococo style was less dramatic in the rest of Europe than in England, and many styles continued to be made or revived on the Continent over a longer period, making recognition of date from shape more difficult.

and William Moorcroft (1872–1946). Both men were sufficiently distinctive and successful to be copied extensively and have their names applied, often carelessly, to their style rather than more strictly to their wares. De Morgan was a disciple of William Morris, and used designs inspired by him to be decorated with lustre glazes over colours derived from the earlier *Hispano-Moresque* wares (*see* p.45). He is best known for his tiles and earlier work, when he established a pottery with Morris at Merton Abbey in London, in 1882. He later ran a studio workshop from 1888 to 1907 in Fulham, London.

Lustre is a metallic or iridescent surface to pottery that is created by the application of metal oxide to the glaze before a firing. Although an ancient technique, it was most common in the 19th century on the mass-produced Staffordshire figures of dogs, jugs, bowls, and plates in the pinky copper colour that is known as "copper lustre".

▲ **70 Mahogany chest-of-drawers, Dutch, early 19th century.**
A revival of marquetry, particularly in the Netherlands, meant many earlier plain pieces were later decorated. The veneers are thinner than those of the 18th century – visible where there is damage; otherwise careful study of the design is needed to be accurate as to date.

De Morgan used the extensive range of lustre colours available, including dark red and purple, as well as metal finishes of gold and silver.

Moorcroft was a Staffordshire artist and potter who was inspired by the later Art Nouveau movement, and his work is characterized by his lifelong use of plant motifs depicted in deep, vibrant colours. In 1898 he joined the firm of James Macintyre & Co., working as a designer and also running the Art Pottery department. Here, at the age of 24, he designed his first piece of "Moorcroft" pottery. By 1913 he had been financed by the Liberty family and had set up his own pottery, W. Moorcroft Ltd., at Cobridge in Staffordshire. Having been awarded a series of gold medals W. Moorcroft Ltd. was appointed Potters to Her Majesty The Queen in 1928.

By the end of the Edwardian period there were many styles of interior decoration, dress, taste, and fashion that can accurately be described as "Edwardian". Furniture and *objets* in every quality and made in every known country were represented and proudly displayed in front rooms, living rooms, and morning rooms. There was connoisseurship and great interest in the genuine antique as well as the furnishing reproduction, and items from former major trading nations such as Spain, Portugal, Italy, and Holland were held in high esteem. In many an American mansion of the 1920s there stood, on marble floors, inlaid chests from Holland, tables from China and Japan, chairs from Portugal, and *varguenos* (cabinets on stands) from Spain (*see* Pls. 68, 69, and 70).

The age of the "Great American Collector" (the American equivalent to the acquisitive English noblemen of the 17th and 18th century) was about to begin. At the same time, the totally revolutionary Art Deco style could be seen in Hollywood movies, with its stark dramatic interiors that were toned down for the modest new houses of the 1920s and '30s.

On page 182 there is an illustration of a chair made of satin birch, machine-carved and absolutely without fault in its proportion, elegance, and quality. It is an example of the revival of the Neo-classical taste of the late 18th century, but is not precisely like anything produced at that date and can therefore be recognized as a fine example of

◀ **71 Walnut *vargueno* on carved and turned stand, Spanish, 17th to 20th century.** *Vargueno* is a 19th-century name for this type of fall-front, writing-desk-cabinet, which was popular in Spain for over four hundred years. Early examples are rare, and most date from the early 1900s, particularly in the Spanish-influenced parts of the USA.

its period (1890). It has an extra delicacy that almost says "don't sit on me", and it is perfectly balanced. One look can tell you all of that. Equally unmistakably Edwardian is the chair illustrated on page 183. But here you can see the poor designer befuddled by popular demand for too many ingredients. The general look is of a Queen Anne or George I chair *c*.1710–25, but the frame is far too thin to be of that period. There is a combination of designs that would never have occurred before the late 19th century: the cabriole legs in the style of the first half of the 18th century are in fact far too thin for that period and terminate with no feet to speak of; the centre panel to the back is part Adam, part George I in outline but pierced and carved and inlaid, representing Rococo and

Neo-classical influences with a Sheraton type of decoration. Looking closely at the inlay one can see engraved boxwood within stringing of the same wood, but with the addition of lines of an ivory-coloured composition, which was introduced in the 1890s. Great example though this is, it borrows too much from too many sources to have quite the character of the chair on page 182. However, this type of furniture, of which a great many examples were made, should not be dismissed, especially when it is of the quality and condition of this chair.

Within three generations prior to 1910, the people of Western Europe and the USA had seen huge developments in every sphere of life. Virtually every household item was mass-produced and affordable to the majority. But it was far from a large majority; there had been little progress in solving the problem of the vast numbers of poor, whose existence was shifting from employment on the land to working in factories. In four years time the Great War was to see their numbers reduced by the summary deaths of millions of young men, poor and rich alike, whose inheritance of houses and their contents, grand or humble, simply disappeared after they were demolished, sold, or taken in lieu of taxes. Thereafter, in peacetime, there was not much left to invent or develop for use and comfort in the home. However, there was already furniture, glass and metalware, ceramics, and fabrics for every occasion and purpose, so the only thing to change dramatically was the design. This certainly occurred in ways as distinctive as those in any period that has been covered in the preceding chapters, and still continues today.

▲ **72 Elmwood altar table, Chinese, mid-19th century.** This illustrates the difficulty of dating items by a rustic or sophisticated appearance. Here the rectangular-top table, joined and pegged with stretchers in primitive form, and with a patina like it has been in a barn forever, is actually 200 years younger than the one shown below. Nevertheless it is still wonderful.

► **73 Trestle-leg side table, Chinese, mid-17th century.** This elegant table made of *huanghuali*, a well-figured hardwood, has a dished or "ice-plate"-bordered top and pierced ends carved with stylized animals. Such sophisticated furniture was ahead of the West, and is highly desirable today.

CLEAR EVIDENCE

There are times when the reasoning behind establishing the date of something is quite complex, as it may rely on several different aspects and circumstances. Elizabethan oak furniture that was dismantled and reconstructed in the 19th century is a good example, and an illustration of such a piece is shown on page 179. Does the form of the item fit any known Elizabethan model? Is it sufficiently important and of good enough quality to have been made in the Elizabethan period? Is the oxidization of the timber compatible with 150 or 350 years of wear? Does the decoration marry up with the earlier period and is it of fine enough quality? (It was a common 19th-century misconception that to make anything look old it had to look primitive, so often the reconstructed pieces have poor-quality decoration.) All these questions have to be taken into account to establish whether a piece is original or not, and the problem is made more difficult because even the later piece will now have had 150 years' wear, giving it some convincing signs of age.

However, there are other instances where the information is actually written down for us. Such a case is the plate illustrated right. At first glance it shows all the style and decoration of an 18th-century hard-paste porcelain "cabinet" piece – an item intended for display only rather than use. It is lavishly decorated with matt and burnished gold, around and over a rich red border, encircling a painted panel showing a romantic scene of nymphs and a cherub, also in the late-18th-century manner. However, close inspection, especially with a magnifying glass, will disclose that the panel is a transfer print and that there is a name (which may sometimes be written in script in the style of a hand-written autograph). These two things are all the proof that is needed of a later origin. Irrespective of any identifying marks on the back of the plate, multi-coloured machine-made transfers did not exist until the 19th century, and Angelica Kauffman is not recorded as ever decorating porcelain or putting her name to it, and certainly never in a modern typeface, as shown here. She was a prolific and highly talented Swiss-born artist who lived and worked in London from 1766–81. She was a founder member of the Royal Academy, and worked with her husband, Antonio Zucchi, for Robert Adam – creating frescos of mythical and idyllic scenes. She was sought-after for her portraiture from the early age of 12, when she painted the Bishop of Como, Italy. She was also a gifted musician and strikingly beautiful.

▲ **74 Hard-paste porcelain plate, Bavaria, c.1910.** Display or "cabinet" pieces from Meissen and Sèvres were popular during the late 18th century, and again one hundred years later. In the Rococo-revival period they were made in varying degrees of quality, determinable on close inspection.

▲ **75 Detail of the plate above**, showing the easily recognizable cheap transfer print, and the modern typeface "signature" of the artist Angelica Kauffman, who died in 1807 – just about 100 years before this plate was made!

ANTIQUES ANALYSIS

This practical section gives a good idea of exactly what this book is all about – the identification and dating of period items by their shape, material, and decoration.

CAKE BASKETS

The earliest known example is dated 1597, and throughout the 17th century their construction suggests that they were not rarities but popular items on a rich man's table, though sadly few have survived. They were ideal for showcasing the latest decorative styles and so can be dated quite accurately on sight, as confirmed by the hallmarks (or method of manufacture if silver plate). By the 1730s a centrally fixed handle (soon after pivoted to swing down on either side) became the standard form. The main body was usually pierced and chased, and had finely cast borders; the central, plain area was often engraved with a coat-of-arms. The most elaborate examples are from the Rococo period, c.1720–70 (see below), while those made c.1775–1800 perfectly express the Classical style (see top right). During this time the advent of machine presses, the use of wirework, and the development of Sheffield Plate meant cheaper production was possible, and by 1800 only the very finest were made totally by hand. Cake baskets reflected the Rococo revival of the 1820s (see bottom right), and mass production was boosted by the launch of electro-plating in 1840.

GEORGE II SILVER CAKE BASKET ENGLISH 1755

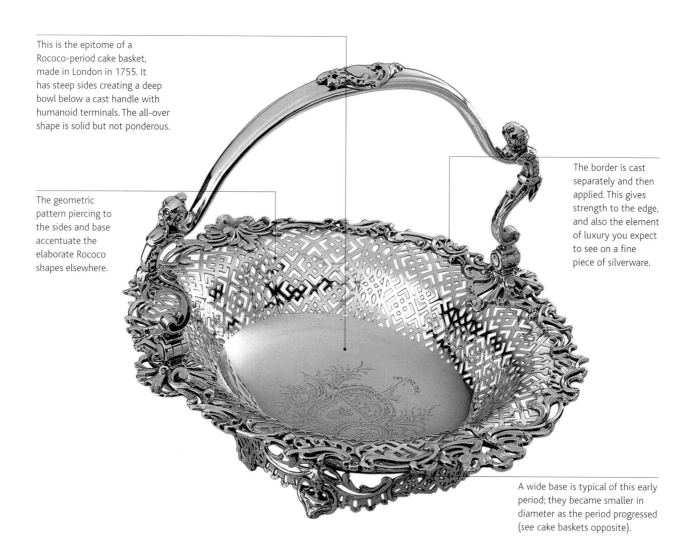

This is the epitome of a Rococo-period cake basket, made in London in 1755. It has steep sides creating a deep bowl below a cast handle with humanoid terminals. The all-over shape is solid but not ponderous.

The geometric pattern piercing to the sides and base accentuate the elaborate Rococo shapes elsewhere.

The border is cast separately and then applied. This gives strength to the edge, and also the element of luxury you expect to see on a fine piece of silverware.

A wide base is typical of this early period; they became smaller in diameter as the period progressed (see cake baskets opposite).

GEORGE III SHEFFIELD-PLATE PIERCED CAKE BASKET ENGLISH C.1785

The piercing is a good example of the type easily executed by machine; it is repeated on the foot to create continuity.

The plain oval shape, with pierced bands and paterae joined by bright-cut engraved swags, tells us that the date must be post-1775.

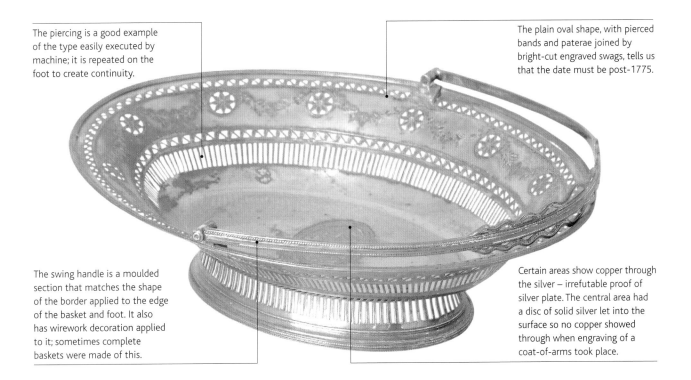

The swing handle is a moulded section that matches the shape of the border applied to the edge of the basket and foot. It also has wirework decoration applied to it; sometimes complete baskets were made of this.

Certain areas show copper through the silver – irrefutable proof of silver plate. The central area had a disc of solid silver let into the surface so no copper showed through when engraving of a coat-of-arms took place.

SILVER CAKE BASKET ENGLISH 1838

The flamboyance of the Rococo-style decoration may raise the question of why this may not be 18th-century in date. The reason is that the form is wrong for the earlier period: the bowl is too shallow, and the foot is too small.

This handle is too thin and thus too weak for appearance and use in the rumbustious Rococo period of the 18th century. As it is without doubt original to the piece, this adds further confirmation of its 1830s date.

After assessing date from general shape, then consider the complexity of the design. There are too many "C" scrolls facing the same way, and the flower baskets are proportionately too large, for this piece to be 18th-century.

Vast numbers of silver baskets were made in a similar pattern throughout the 19th century and, after 1840, in electro-plate versions.

TOILET MIRRORS (OR DRESSING-TABLE MIRRORS)

Toilet mirrors, with a compartment supporting two uprights to take an adjustable swing mirror, were introduced at the very end of the 17th century and were in general fashionable use by the 1720s. Their form and decoration was at first elaborate and luxurious, with the base often made in the manner of a miniature writing bureau with perhaps two tiers of drawers, and finished in walnut veneers or lacquer in the Chinoiserie style. However, by *c.*1730 a call for more affordable models arose, and the type shown below became the most popular – made well into the 1760s. They are known as "box-base" toilet mirrors and were required to take cosmetics. Sometimes a subtle shaping to the frame will indicate a more precise date, as will the use of Virginia walnut (before the mid 1740s) or good mahogany on later models. The "ogee" (double-curved) bracket feet and the projecting lower part to the drawers are good indicators of the pre-1770s. The next period is clearly defined (*see* top right). Toilet mirrors were little affected by the more exotic Regency designs, remaining much the same until the 1830s, when a variety of designs appeared (*see* bottom right).

MAHOGANY DRESSING-TABLE MIRROR ENGLISH *c.*1750

This toilet mirror has a plain rectangular frame with a slightly rounded surface, indicating a date of *c.*1750 or later. Until this period the frame had a moulded frame, usually of "ogee" (double-curved) shape.

Original 18th-century glass plates will not be perfect, and although not obligatory, it is always good to see a bevelled edge.

Quality models of this type will usually have a border moulded with a quarter round section set into the edge. This is known as "caddy" moulding, and was less used after the 1770s.

The rectangular box base, containing one, two, or three drawers, was the standard model from the 1730s for nearly 50 years. The projecting lower part disappeared around the mid-1760s.

HEPPLEWHITE-STYLE MAHOGANY DRESSING-TABLE MIRROR ENGLISH C.1775

The caddy moulding on the edge has been replaced with an inset stringing of boxwood. After 1800 ebony or ebonized inlay became popular.

The vase or shield shape of this mirror immediately tells us that its date will be from the last quarter of the 18th century, and the little "ogee" bracket feet suggest it would be prior to 1790, allowing for a transition period on smaller domestic items.

The serpentine bow front to the drawer compartment confirms a Classical influence, but could date into the early 19th century.

The application of turned buttons, or paterae, became popular during the 1770s; they might be of wood, ivory, or, later, ebony, as well as gilt metal.

MAHOGANY DRESSING-TABLE MIRROR ENGLISH C.1830

The curved and moulded frame supports are Classical in origin, but were not much used on toilet mirrors until after 1830.

The use of highly figured "flame-cut" mahogany veneers became popular after c.1830, when new machinery enabled the timber to be cut thinner than ever before, and therefore they became more widely affordable.

Turned-wood, flat "bun" feet complete the picture of this predecessor to the many varieties of toilet mirrors that were to follow during the Victorian period.

It is the form of the box base, with its semicircular moulded and concealed drawer front flanked by two columns, that gives us the first indications of this mirror dating from the early 1830s.

TEA CADDIES

The word caddy is a derivation of *kati*, the Malay word for a weight of just over one pound, used in England to describe the cannisters in which tea was imported. By the 1720s the caddy was established as decorative and necessary in the serving of tea, providing another item to be made by craftsmen in silver, wood, ceramics, and, later, other metals, papier mâché, glass, enamels, tortoiseshell, mother-of-pearl, ivory, curled paper, and leather, with many decorations. But it is the basic shape that is the main guide to the date. By the 1720s the Rococo-decorated baluster shape became most popular, in circular, rectangular, or square section (*see* below). A simple rectangular box was the standard mid-18th-century tea caddy, often with two or three compartments to take silver or wooden containers. After the 1770s the Neoclassical influence is clearly visible in the oval and round straight-sided boxes (*see* top right), adaptable to all materials and decoration. After Nelson's death in 1805 the sarcophagus shape became popular, followed by a number of styles during the Victorian period. Rosewood was the most desirable timber for the outer case (*see* bottom right).

SILVER TEA CADDY ENGLISH 1764

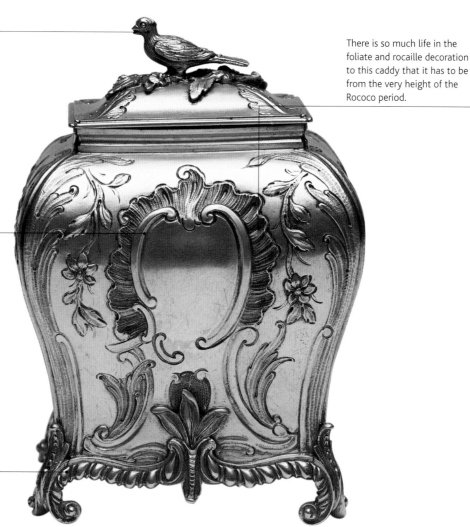

The cast finial of a little bird sitting on a leafy branch adds the final touch of luxury, completing the transformation of a domestic item into a work of art to delight participants in the ceremony known as "the tea table" during the last half of the 18th century.

There is so much life in the foliate and rocaille decoration to this caddy that it has to be from the very height of the Rococo period.

The asymmetrical "C" scrolls create a natural cartouche for the owner's coat-of-arms, if required. Although the space looks just as fabulous blank, many coats-of-arms have been removed at a later date, which, if carelessly done, may be detrimental to the value.

Additional impact is given to the inverted scrolling feet by the swirling gadroon border, which links them and the applied foliage to the corner of each foot.

HAREWOOD TEA CADDY ENGLISH C.1790

Marquetry was revived approximately 100 years after it was first popular, but with a subtle difference in the later version: the blackened lines of the detailing are etched on rather than being cut through as they were in the 17th century.

The spray of flowers is unmistakably late-18th-century, for while it is lifelike it is symmetrical and tied with a carefully arranged ribbon. Combined with the oval inset panel to the top, the whole effect is of total balance and lightness.

The classic straight-sided oval tea caddy, especially popular during the last 20 years of the 18th century. It was often considered a handsome gift when new and complete with contents.

The main veneer is harewood, another name for sycamore or maple, dyed with iron oxide to create a bright green colour. Imagine the enchantment caused by the spray of marquetry flowers set in a green field (now faded).

ROSEWOOD TEA CADDY ENGLISH C.1830

The imposing bulk, waisted outline, and finely figured rosewood veneer immediately point this caddy to the late-Regency, William IV period, c.1830.

Two tea containers, usually for Fine Green and Bohea tea; these boxes sometimes have lids engraved or inlaid with the initials "F", "FG" or "B". There is also space for a set of teaspoons and two further covered glass jars.

This turned quarter-section moulding became fashionable on English furniture during the early 1820s and continued so for about 30 years.

At one time thought to be for blending two types of tea, the glass bowl, a popular optional extra from the late 18th century, has been proven by contemporary invoices to have been for sugar.

DECANTERS

From the 1750s to 1770s there were two main types of flint-glass decanter: shouldered, with a body that tapered in below the shoulder, and no shoulder, with a body tapering out to the base (*see* below). After the 1770s several other shapes were introduced, decorated by cutting, engraving, enamelling, and gilding, and, in Ireland, by blowing hot metal into moulds. Two or more rings encircling the neck then came into more general use, and there was a greater variety in the design of stoppers. The vertical disc type, or "lozenge" (*see* below), and the horizontal "mushroom" (*see* top right) were the most common (a multi-faceted conical stopper had been popular on the early shouldered decanters). By the mid-19th century a new shape had appeared – the pillar and globe, or "onion" shape (*see* bottom right). In 1833 John Gold of Birmingham developed a machine to grind, cut, smooth, and polish several decanters at a time, thus bringing mass production into every stage of the process. Ships' decanters, with wide, heavy bases, were introduced in the late 1700s and are still considered best for aerating wine. Square spirit decanters were popular during the late Victorian and Edwardian eras.

MAGNUM TAPERING DECANTER ENGLISH 1770

This shape of decanter should have a vertical stopper like this. Note both neck and stopper are ground to fit, a process not introduced until after 1745 but considered normal practice by the 1770s.

The simple lines of this magnum decanter epitomize the elegance of the 1770s and the rest of the 18th century, during which time this shape continued to be popular.

Note the early form of everted lip, which became larger as the 18th turned into the 19th century, as shown in the picture at the top of page 223.

The body is often gilded, faceted, cut, and engraved in the classical manner. The fashionable swags and festoons executed by bright-cutting on silver could be replicated by cutting on glass.

PILLAR-CUT DECANTER ENGLISH C.1820

The wide and thick everted lip is indicative of decanters from the early 19th century.

The shoulder is step-cut to the neck – a decoration fashionable after the turn of the century.

The body is pillar-cut below the shoulder, another style of decoration that became popular in the early 1800s.

The general outline of the decanter, combined with the thickness of the glass, makes it unquestionably from the later Regency period, c.1820.

SHAFT-AND-GLOBE DECANTER ENGLISH C.1850

This shaft and globe or "onion" shape of decanter must date around, or subsequent to, the 1850s – the earliest date that decanters appeared in this form.

The hollow, balloon-shape stopper was not new in the 19th century, but it became popular for use in this type of decanter at that time.

The neck is facet-cut in a similar manner to an 18th-century drinking glass but, when used on this shape of decanter and in contrast to the lower-body engraving, it has to be c.1850.

The globe is finely engraved with vine leaves and bunches of grapes in a free, random manner. This is in contrast with the formality of the neck, and gives more than a passing nod to the emerging Arts and Crafts designs.

SPOON HANDLES

Silver spoons from the 18th century onwards probably represent the best and most affordable items for starting an antiques collection. Aside from hallmarks (which provide the most history, with information on the spoon and the person responsible for its manufacture), the shape of the handle will give the first indications of how old a spoon is likely to be. The outline that developed early in the 18th century is shown below. This is the Hanoverian pattern, *c.*1710–60, recognized by the upturn at the end of the handle. It was superseded by the Old English pattern, *c.*1760–1820,

which is of the same outline but the end turns down. Around 1800 an alternative emerged with a flattened end, known as the Fiddle pattern, and a shoulder appeared at the junction of the bowl (*see* top right). Elongated versions of this were popular in Europe, Scotland, and America. In the early 1800s an hourglass shape was introduced to take elaborate cast and chased decoration (*see* bottom right); this was called the King's pattern and was quickly followed by the similar Queen's pattern. A galaxy of handle shapes from the Victorian period have been in production ever since.

SERVING SPOON WITH HANOVERIAN PATTERN HANDLE ENGLISH 1740

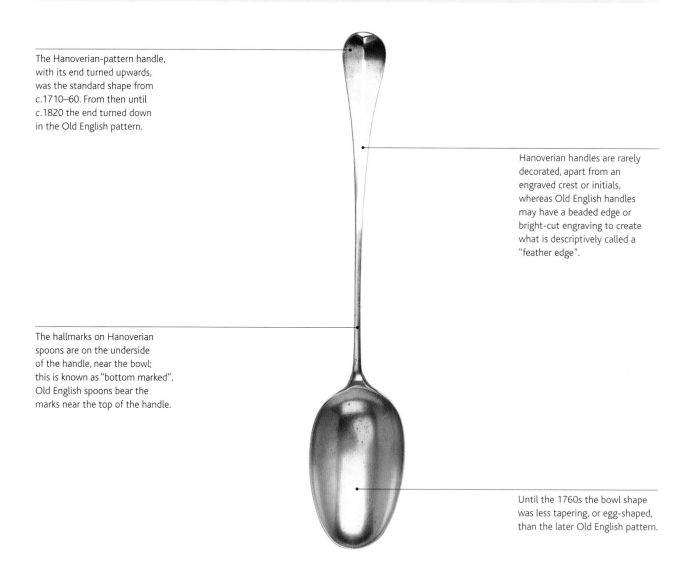

The Hanoverian-pattern handle, with its end turned upwards, was the standard shape from *c.*1710–60. From then until *c.*1820 the end turned down in the Old English pattern.

Hanoverian handles are rarely decorated, apart from an engraved crest or initials, whereas Old English handles may have a beaded edge or bright-cut engraving to create what is descriptively called a "feather edge".

The hallmarks on Hanoverian spoons are on the underside of the handle, near the bowl; this is known as "bottom marked". Old English spoons bear the marks near the top of the handle.

Until the 1760s the bowl shape was less tapering, or egg-shaped, than the later Old English pattern.

TODDY LADLE ENGLISH C.1825

The end of the handle is flattened into the Fiddle pattern, which came into general use around 1800 and thereafter. Elongated versions were popular in Europe, Scotland, and the USA.

Fiddle-pattern handles were subject to a variety of decorations. A simple line border is called a Fiddle and Thread, and when a shell is moulded within the rounded top it is known as a Fiddle, Thread, and Shell pattern.

Shoulders appeared at the junction of bowl and handle some time before the turn of the century on Old English handles, but were not in general use until combined with the Fiddle pattern after 1800, as here.

This ladle bowl typifies the shape used in the newly introduced large canteens for several different sizes of spoon, from the largest, used to serve soup, through sugar (with a pierced bowl), sauce, and cream spoons, to the smallest, used for salt.

WILLIAM IV KING'S-PATTERN SPOON ENGLISH 1830–37

This is the perfect King's-pattern handle, with its hourglass outline and a shell at the top flanked by two "C" scrolls. This pattern did not appear until after 1800.

The stem of the handle has a thread edge or border, which was also used on the Fiddle-pattern handle (*see* above).

By the 1820s, and thereafter, this King's-pattern handle may have the hallmarks struck centrally on the underside.

This spoon was part of a large canteen that contained items made specifically for a wide range of uses. The reverse taper of the bowl, being wider at the tip, indicates it was intended as a serving spoon.

POLE SCREENS

Pole screens were necessary early in the 18th century to shield people's faces from the fire when heavy make-up was worn to disguise the scars from diseases such as smallpox; it was thick and often consisted of wax and white lead, which was highly toxic, especially when warmed. So a large screen or "banner" was required, normally rectangular. At the same time there was interest in needlework and embroidery, especially floral arrangements (*see* below). The stands for banners prior to the 1770s were similar to the tripod bases for tables of the period, with curving legs

and a turned column to hold the pole. Many pole-screen bases were altered into more desirable small tables by removing the pole and replacing it with a suitable top. By the 1780s the ravages of plagues had lessened and so heat from a fire was no longer life-threatening. Smaller banners became fashionable and followed the vase or shield shape of the Neoclassical period (*see* top right). After 1820 banner frames became more elaborate, and the bases again followed those of tables. A brass pole was often used, particularly with a stand made of fashionable rosewood (*see* bottom right).

MAHOGANY GEORGE II WALNUT POLE SCREEN ENGLISH C.1750

The large rectangular screen, or "banner", and the shape of the tripod base clearly indicate a date of 1720–60. As the timber here is walnut, *c.*1750 is most likely, as confirmed by the details of the decoration to the stem.

The majority of pole-screen banners up to the mid-18th century were used to display panels of needlework with foliate arrangements that were copied from numerous books illustrating the design.

The tripod legs are joined directly to the main stem rather than being fixed to a three-sided platform, as shown on page 227, which was an earlier form and is another indication of the mid-18th-century date of this piece.

The turned cup below a tapering and reeded column is a combination of features popular from *c.*1745.

GEORGE III SATINWOOD POLE SCREEN ENGLISH C.1785

The advent of the shield or vase shape, which epitomized the last quarter of the 18th century, was an ideal design for the fashionably smaller banners required for pole screens at the time, and confirms a date of post 1775.

The banner designs were no longer restricted to floral displays, and were often of silk embroidery or panels cut from expensive fabric.

Rather than a tripod, here the base is circular, probably weighted with a ring of lead inserted underneath for stability. Its form precisely replicates the silver candlestick shown on page 100, which was made c.1785.

The timbers used were most popularly satinwood and mahogany, which were sometimes enriched with painted swags and festoons. More rarely, carved wood, gesso, and gilt were used.

ROSEWOOD POLE SCREEN ENGLISH C.1825

The combination of the elaborate banner frame and the triform base make this unmistakably late Regency, c.1820–30 or soon thereafter, particularly when made in rosewood, as here.

The brass pole was introduced during the late Regency period and is acknowledged as a mark of quality.

After c.1810 the banner design would most likely be from the wide range of subjects available in Berlin Embroidery (see p.147).

The swept triform base with scroll bracket feet, the lobed collar supporting a Classical column below the acanthus-carved baluster, and the tapering stem are all typical of the period c.1830.

CHESTS-ON-STANDS AND CHESTS-ON-CHESTS (TALLBOYS)

The chest-on-stand is associated with the late 1600s and the chest-on-chest from the early 1700s (both derived from the enclosed cabinet-on-stand imported from the Continent a century earlier). The stands were open (*see* below), with one or more drawers above six legs, often turned with cups and bun shapes or in a spiral pattern and joined with stretchers. By 1700 the base with drawers had become more popular, and remained so. There are features common to both, such as the cushion-moulded drawer in the cornice, which, in a chest-on-chest, will point to an early date. (It disappeared

soon after 1700 on all but provincial items.) Quality and decoration indicate the original cost and affect today's value. Corners to the top, and sometimes the base, were cut at an angle (canted) and fluted in architectural style on expensive examples until the 1780s, when a squarer look was required. At the same time the feet changed from a plain square bracket (*see* top right) or a double curved "ogee" to a sweeping splay or "French" foot (*see* bottom right). Until the 1760s the difference in size between the set-in top and the base was quite evident, and marked by a well-moulded edge.

WILLIAM AND MARY WALNUT CHEST-ON-STAND ENGLISH C.1690

This chest-on-stand displays so much character that it has to be from the William and Mary period, c.1690. The careful placing of wildly figured walnut veneers onto pine carcase timber and the construction of the drawers (*see* Dovetailing, p.26) confirm this.

Various patterns of pendant handles, which were attached with wire split-pins, were fashionable into the early 18th century.

The fantastical, deep, moulded cornice, which looks more like a hat, sits over a cushion-moulded "secret" drawer. The rest of the drawers are surrounded by a double-reeded beading, which is fixed to the carcase, as it should be in an original piece of this date.

The base has turned legs, and stretchers supporting its three drawers. The shaped outline of the apron is emphasized by a cock-beaded edge – a strip of wood applied when wet and fixed with nails.

WILLIAM AND MARY ELM TALLBOY ENGLISH EARLY 18TH CENTURY

The cushion-moulded drawer combined with the chest base on this elm tallboy suggests an early-18th-century date. This is confirmed by the use of a double-reeded beading around the drawers – another feature that was soon to go out of fashion.

The pendant handles, which are original, are further confirmation of an early-18th-century date. Even if they were replacements, they are nevertheless of the correct type for this period.

Square bracket feet, with the double-curved "ogee" pattern as an elaborate alternative, were popular during the first 75 years of the 18th century, succeeding the turned bun feet of the 17th century.

The top is markedly smaller than the base, which creates the same proportional look as the chest-on-stand on p.228. This sizing was to change as the century progressed, as can be seen in the chest-on-chest pictured below.

GEORGE III MAHOGANY TALLBOY ENGLISH C.1785

A George III-period mahogany tallboy showing the moderate lines of the 1780s. The cornice is simpler and the difference in size between top and base is less marked than in the other two chests pictured above and opposite.

Just beneath the cornice it was fashionable to apply a crossbanding of satinwood to replace various earlier architectural devices, such as dentil mouldings or fret decoration. This is an indication of fine quality and expense when new.

These two-pin drop handles are in the French taste, being formal and rectangular. Alternatively they might have been curved in the "swan neck" pattern. The drawers are surrounded by a single "cock" bead – a slip of wood attached to the drawer, not the carcase.

These feet are so elegant they look too weak to support such a large piece, but they have survived. The fashion for this splay or "French"-pattern foot continued during the period, influenced by the published works of George Hepplewhite and Thomas Sheraton (*see* pp.107–8), *c.*1775–1815.

SALT CELLARS

The first individual salt cellars, or "salts", appeared in Europe in the late 1600s. Dished, or sunken, with a moulded border (*see* below), they were known as trencher salts as they were placed close to the large platters (trenchers) that held a portion of food. Trencher salts, made in silver as well as other metals and ceramics, remained popular until a bowl (bun) type on three legs superseded them (*see* top right). This style was ideal to take all forms of Rococo decoration and there was no limit to the variety after *c*.1730. As salt will damage the surface of silver, it became common to apply a plating of gold on the insides of even quite plain examples. Then developments in the glass industry meant small glass liners (usually blue) could be dropped into the salt cellar instead. These liners became a feature from 1775 to 1800 (*see* bottom right). At the time, mass production of Classical-style salts in Sheffield Plate as well as silver meant most people could afford them. They were stamped, pierced, engraved, and made of sheet silver, plate, and wirework in oval, round, vase, boat, and bucket shapes before the Rococo revival in the 1820s brought an even greater variety.

GEORGE II SILVER TRENCHER SALT ENGLISH C.1720

The marks, which at this period were struck by hand, will be on the underside of the well and may be visible from above, although this does not affect the value.

The shape is enough to tell us that, subject to confirmation by the hallmarks, this trencher salt is likely to date from the first half of the 18th century. Copied by Chinese potters, it was also adopted by brass- and pewter-makers.

Unless made before 1697 or after 1720, this type of trencher salt will be made of Britannia Standard silver (a higher grade than Sterling), which was obligatory during that period.

The deep moulded apron border always sweeps outward, and is most often of octagonal form.

SILVER BUN SALT ON PAD FEET ENGLISH 1735

An early bun-type salt, raised on three little legs with pad feet. This basic shape remained popular from the early 1730s until the last quarter of the 18th century. It was revived in the 20th century to be miniaturized in presentation cases.

The interiors of bun salts (and later styles) were often plated with gold, which, unlike silver, is impervious to salt. After the 1750s glass liners, usually blue, were available as an alternative.

The design of the legs may be used as an approximate date guide: as the century progressed this early squat shape became elongated into a cabriole or double "C" scroll, with feet formed as hooves, shells, or a claw and ball.

The lack of elaborate decoration is not a guide to date. Although those from the 1730s tend to be plain, salts were made according to cost and therefore the wealth of the individual purchaser.

SILVER SALT CELLAR DUTCH EARLY 19TH CENTURY

The beaded edge to the rim and handles was common throughout Europe, but there are regional differences in the interpretation of the piercing. This fan-shaped piercing is distinctly Continental as it is more pointed than the English version.

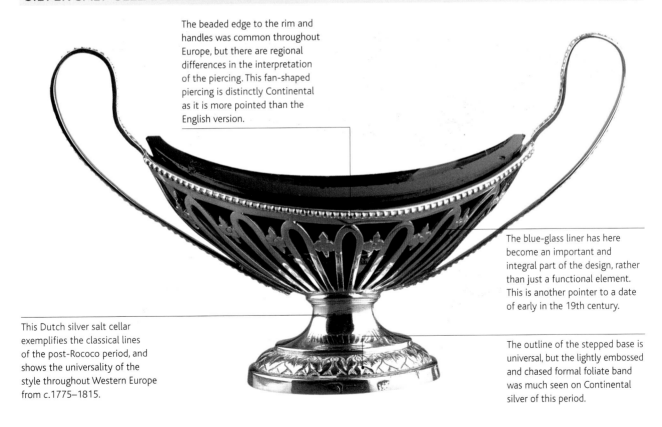

The blue-glass liner has here become an important and integral part of the design, rather than just a functional element. This is another pointer to a date of early in the 19th century.

This Dutch silver salt cellar exemplifies the classical lines of the post-Rococo period, and shows the universality of the style throughout Western Europe from c.1775–1815.

The outline of the stepped base is universal, but the lightly embossed and chased formal foliate band was much seen on Continental silver of this period.

SOFA TABLES

The sofa table appeared during the last quarter of the 18th century, when the classic form of sofa and daybed became popular. A table was devised that would draw over the end of the sofa to allow the reclining occupant to read or to pen a languorous note. The earliest sofa tables look like the one pictured below. Their disadvantage was that they were unstable, even with a high stretcher (just visible below the drawer line). So on later models a bar or stretcher was added lower down (as seen in the picture at the top of p.233), thus solving the problem but making the original purpose of the table obsolete. After the turn of the century the designs for the end supports and legs became more elaborate and by 1810 a centre column was introduced as an alternative design, which remained popular well into the Victorian era. As long as the leaves are on the end of the rectangular top it is still known as a sofa table today, irrespective of its support. When the leaves are on the long sides of the rectangular top it is called a Pembroke tea table or, if it dates from after c.1800, a pedestal breakfast table.

SHERATON ROSEWOOD SOFA TABLE ENGLISH C.1790

Better-quality sofa tables tend to be decorated with inlaid stringing of boxwood and crossbanding of fashionable exotic timbers, such as rosewood and satinwood. The more complex the decoration, the later the date of the table.

It was usual to have two drawers to the frieze (see Glossary p.240) on one side and false drawers on the other; but various options were used, sometimes with four short drawers, or alternate real and false drawers on each side.

The original early sofa tables, c.1790, had open-frame supports to enable them to be pulled over the end of the sofa or daybed.

The plain standard ends and graceful swept legs shown here are typical of the earliest designs for a sofa table.

The plain square toe castors were most fashionable during the last quarter of the 18th century; after that time the lion's-paw shape became a favourite alternative. After 1815 scrolls and acanthus-leaf motifs were also used.

MAHOGANY SOFA TABLE ENGLISH C.1820

A different drawer configuration might suggest northern county origins – two small drawers flanking a long one had been popular on bureaus and chests during the 18th century.

The leaves are supported by two hinged flaps, commonly known as lopers, which are more clearly seen to the left of the table on p.232.

The central stretcher immediately indicates a later model, particularly when combined with the elaborate scroll legs and cast-brass castors. The inlay of brass rather than boxwood stringing also indicates a date that is post 1815.

The use of finely figured veneers and deep crossbanding, in this case rosewood and satinwood, indicates high quality.

GEORGE IV ROSEWOOD SOFA TABLE SCOTTISH C.1825

The spiral gadroon edge, which was also much used on silver, is a revival of a pre-1780s border decoration from c.1820. It was popular in Scotland, as was the panelled frieze that camouflaged the drawers. Sometimes the central entablature was part of a wider drawer.

The central column, quatrefoil platform, and splay legs each with a high scroll knee indicate a date of c.1810 or later. There are innumerable variations on this theme that continued into the 1860s.

The column comprises a squat baluster, deeply carved with stylized acanthus leaves, below a tapering column that is heavily fluted; this combination, plus the quite graceful style of the legs, gives us a date of between c.1820 and c.1835.

TEAPOTS

Silver and porcelain teapots came into general use in the early 18th century. Pear shapes of circular and octagonal section, balusters, and plain round "bullet" pots (*see* below) were later joined by square, rectangular, and plain cylindrical patterns. These straight-sided pots were often faceted into elaborate ovals or serpentine section, lightly decorated with "bright-cut" engraving. The classical style of the post-1770s (*see* top right) facilitated fashionable shapes being produced at affordable prices through the simpler lines required, but in the early 1800s a squashed baluster below a multi-stepped lid (*see* bottom right) came into prominence and remained so until the 1920s.

In the 1890s teapots were often decorated with lobing, referred to as "Queen Anne" style. The advent of Sheffield Plate during the last quarter of the 18th century augmented the supply of less expensive tea wares, which continued with the development of electro-plating in 1840. This enabled cheaper metals than copper to be used as a base metal, while potters were producing cheap earthenware. After the 1860s straight-sided pots came back into fashion.

SILVER TEAPOT SCOTTISH C.1739

The chasing to the lid and shoulder is of the Rococo style. As this is chasing (which is done with the use of a hammer) rather than engraving, it will be visible on the inner surface.

The silver handle, insulated with ivory inserts, is a strong indication of Scottish manufacture as it was not until the 19th century that English handles were made in this way. Throughout the 18th century English handles to all pots containing hot liquid were normally made of wood, sometimes ivory, or metal covered in fine-woven cane.

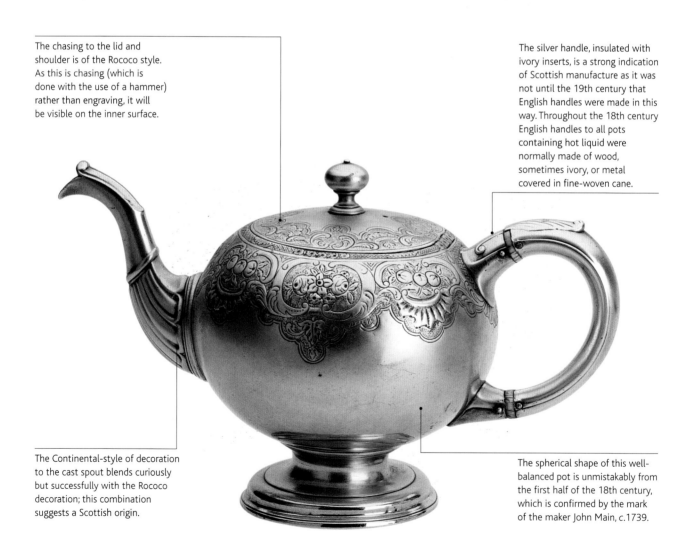

The Continental-style of decoration to the cast spout blends curiously but successfully with the Rococo decoration; this combination suggests a Scottish origin.

The spherical shape of this well-balanced pot is unmistakably from the first half of the 18th century, which is confirmed by the mark of the maker John Main, *c*.1739.

HESTER BATEMAN TEAPOT ENGLISH 1780

Wooden handles of this period are traditionally shaped for comfort rather more than for a balanced look. Because of the disparity in the reaction to heat of metal and wood, these handles often wore loose, and at times had to be replaced.

By the 1780s the finial was either of wood or ivory and was detachable by means of the central retaining pin being threaded to take a small, square-shaped nut inside the lid.

The simple, classic, oval lines of this straight-sided pot of the 1780s exemplify the designs that enabled cheaper yet fashionable manufacture in silver and Sheffield Plate.

Here the pure classic lines of the *cartouche* and the coat-of-arms are totally compatible with the date of *c*.1780.

DERBY TEAPOT ENGLISH C.1810

The sweeping graduated tiers to the lid are reminiscent of an earlier 18th-century style but are more boldly drawn, and in this form do not appear until after 1800.

This English china teapot is instantly recognizable as being after 1800 by its squat baluster form, which was replicated in silver at the same time. This pot was made in Derby *c*.1810, but the shape and style remained popular into the 20th century in many materials.

Placed in its original stand, this pot has four ball feet and lobing to the lower part of the spout, both of which became popular after the turn of the century.

It is interesting to see the extent that the potters copied the silversmiths in the details, even replicating the handle form on a silver pot – down to the little studs that connect a wooden handle to the silver sleeves.

CARTOUCHES

Of the several meanings that exist of the word "cartouche", it is the one describing an ornate frame that concerns us here. Cartouches were used traditionally to surround armorial bearings (coats-of-arms), and as their style changed dramatically at certain times in history they can provide valuable information as to when the decoration was applied, and whether it was contemporary to the piece or added later (the original bearing having been erased).

Armorial bearings were sculpted in stone, carved in wood, enamelled on porcelain, and engraved on metal, but it was only on metal that they could be erased and replaced at a later date. This is particularly important to consider for items made of silver and gold, as not only is a later engraving something of a minus point in value – depending on the historical circumstances – it also means that a certain amount of the body metal has been lost to this process of erasure.

Prior to the 19th century there were three main types of cartouche, each with many variations, examples of which are shown here.

SILVER TANKARD ENGLISH C.1680

At this time the cartouche took the form of a stylized arrangement of plumes or scrolling leaves.

17th-century coats-of-arms on silver were presented on a plain shield, very much in the shape of the protective shield of armour on which they would originally have been displayed.

The plumage was symmetrical, and tied at the bottom of the shield. This armorial bearing and its cartouche are absolutely right to be contemporary with this late-17th century tankard.

GEORGE II SILVER SALVER ENGLISH 1744

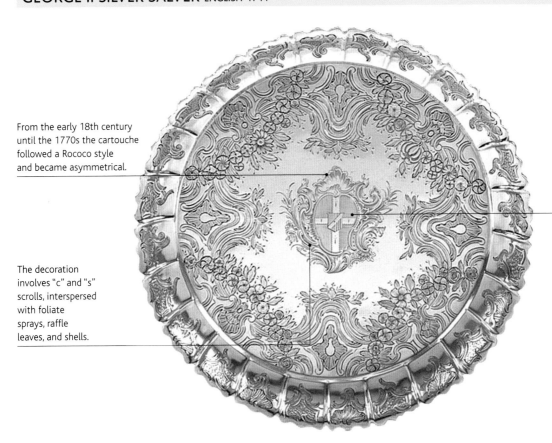

From the early 18th century until the 1770s the cartouche followed a Rococo style and became asymmetrical.

The shape of the shield has lost all connection with anything protective, and has taken on the shape demanded by current fashion. This armorial bearing and its cartouche are absolutely right for this Rococo-period salver.

The decoration involves "c" and "s" scrolls, interspersed with foliate sprays, raffle leaves, and shells.

GEORGE III SILVER TEAPOT ENGLISH C.1785

The straight-sided body, shape of the wood handle, and finial are so similar to the teapot on page 235 as to tell us that this should be of the same date and possibly maker. The hallmarks confirm this, but the decoration belies it and must, therefore, have been engraved later.

The crest shows a dove rising, on a chapeau; the latter indicates a peer or Scots laird who is a territorial baron. Lesser mortals were allowed a wreath of twisted silk, on which their crest could appear to stand.

The geometric banding to the top is typical late-Victorian/Edwardian, and was not used earlier in this form. The lower band of bright-cut crescents were used in the late 18th century, but the other way up.

The cartouche resembles a strap, belt, or garter, which indicates a 19th-century design. Such an oval frame did not appear earlier in this form. The foliate swags and pendants are impressionistic and lack the realism of 18th-century patterns.

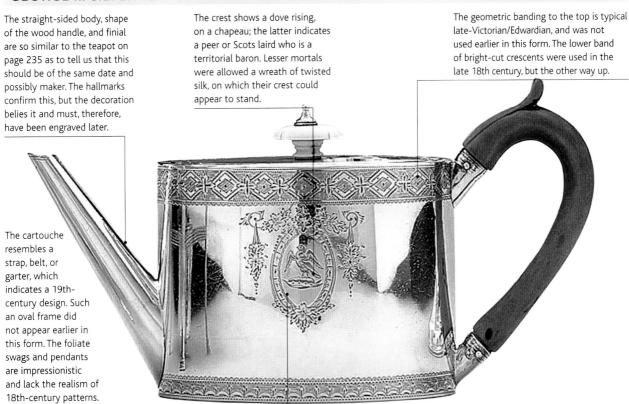

GLOSSARY

acanthus Decorative leaf motif used to adorn a wide variety of objects.

acroterion Corner bracket on architecture and furniture.

Adam style Neoclassical style, first introduced into Britain by the Scottish architect/ designer Robert Adam, typified by Classical motifs such as palmettes and festoons.

Aesthetic Movement Decorative arts movement with a strong Japanese influence, which flourished in Europe and the USA from c.1860s to the late 1880s.

agateware Pottery resembling the marbled effect of agate, made in Staffordshire in the 18th century by mixing together clays of various colours.

air-twist stem On drinking glasses and other glassware, a stem decorated with spiral filaments of hollow glass.

alla certosina Type of decoration using inlays of bone and ivory.

alloy Amalgam of two or more metals; in silver, the base metals added for strength.

ambulante Small portable pieces of French furniture.

amphora Two-handled jar used originally in Classical antiquity.

annealing Process for restoring the malleability of silver or other metals made brittle by hammering. The metal is heated until red-hot and then immersed in cold water.

anthemion Stylized ornament derived from Classical architecture, based on the honeysuckle flower.

Apostle spoon Silver spoon with a finial moulded in the form of one of the 12 Apostles; particularly popular in the 16th and 17th centuries.

applied decoration Ornamental motifs made separately from the main body and attached to it to provide decoration.

applied work Wire, moulding, or cast pieces made separately and soldered onto the main body of a piece, to ornament or strengthen it.

appliqué In textiles, applying small patches of fabric to a base fabric to make a design.

apron Concealing skirt of wood running beneath the seat-rail of chairs and sofas or between the drawers and legs of case furniture and dressers-on-stands.

arcading Series of decorative linked arches derived from architecture.

arcanist One who knows the formula (arcanum) for making hard-paste porcelain.

architrave Moulded framework; in Classical architecture, the lowest part of an entablature.

argyll Vessel resembling a small coffeepot, designed for keeping gravy warm.

Arita An important centre for Japanese porcelain production, and the name of one distinctive type of porcelain made in the area.

armada chest Chest for storing valuables from the 16th century; usually has metal bandings and an elaborate lock.

armoire French tall cupboard with one or two doors.

armorial An engraved design showing a crest or coat-of-arms.

Art Deco Style characterized by geometric forms and bright, bold colours, popular from c.1918 to 1940. The name is taken from the 1925 *Exposition des Arts Décoratifs et Industriels Modernes* in Paris.

Art Nouveau Movement and style of decoration characterized by sinuous curves and flowing lines, asymmetry, and flower and leaf motifs, prevalent from the 1890s to c.1910.

Arts & Crafts Movement A late-19th-century artistic movement led by William Morris, which advocated a return to Medieval standards of craftsmanship and simplicity of design.

assay Testing metal to establish its purity.

astragal A convex moulding, usually of wood, used for glazing bars on a cabinet.

automata A term covering a wide variety of mechanical toys with moving parts, popular during the 18th and 19th centuries.

aventurine From the Italian for "chance"; decoration of flecked metallic particles.

bachelor's chest Chest-of-drawers with a hinged top that can be supported on lopers and opens to form a larger surface.

backboard The wood (often unpolished) used to infill the back of furniture made to stand or hang against a wall.

backstool A rudimentary form of chair made in the 16th century.

ball and claw Popular style for feet on chairs etc., depicting a taloned bird or animal footclasping a ball.

ball foot Orb-shaped style used for the feet of chests of drawers.

baluster Vase-shaped form with a bulbous base, narrow waist and slightly flared neck. Commonly used on silverwares, ceramics and stems of drinking glasses.

balustroid A taller, lighter form of baluster.

banding Strips of veneer laid around the edge of drawer fronts and the tops of tables and case furniture.

barley twist Spiral-turned pillars popular on chairs and tables in the late 17th century.

Baroque Extravagant and heavily ornate style of architecture, furniture, and decoration that originated in 17th-century Italy. Characterized by abundant use of cupids, cornucopia, and similar decorative motifs set in curvaceous designs.

Baroque pearl Irregularly shaped pearl.

Basaltes Unglazed black stoneware, developed by Wedgwood.

basket weave Low-relief motif simulating woven twigs or reeds.

bat printing Printing decoration made using glutinous bats (sheets), popular in the early 19th century in Staffordshire.

beading Decorative border of tiny compact beads, either cast and applied or embossed.

Belle Epoque ("Beautiful Period") Term describing the lavish, ornate styles in fashion from the late 19th century to World War I.

bentwood Solid or laminated wood steamed and bent into a curvilinear shape. The process was developed by Michael Thonet in the early 19th century.

bergère French-style armchair with wood frame and upholstered sides.

Berlin ironwork Black ironwork jewellery made during the Franco-Prussian war (1813–15) in exchange for gold jewellery surrendered for the war effort.

Berlin woolwork Amateur embroidery using coloured wools on a canvas grid.

berrettino Grey-blue tin-glazed ground used on 16th-century Italian maiolica; first introduced in Faenza c.1520.

bevel Decorative angled edge of a mirror.

bezel Ring, usually brass, securing the glass dial cover on a clock or watch. Also refers to the groove or inner rim of a cover, for example on coffeepots.

bianco di Faenza Type of maiolica, developed in mid-16th-century Italy, covered in a thick, milky-white glaze. It is usually cursorily decorated in a restricted palette of ochre, yellow, and blue with figures, flowers, or coats-of-arms.

Biedermeier A bourgeois style that influenced all the decorative arts in Germany c.1825-40; the glass is characterized by the quality and range of its colours.

birdcage support Hinged mechanism with small posts supporting two platforms, used on the top of a pedestal support to allow tripod tables to swivel.

biscuit Unglazed porcelain, fired only once.

blackware Iron-rich type of ancient Chinese pottery.

bleu celeste A sky-blue enamel ground colour developed in the Vincennes factory in 1752 and particularly associated with Sèvres and Vincennes porcelain.

blue-dash charger A delftware dish decorated with a border of blue brush strokes.

bobbin Type of turning in the shape of a bobbin or reel found on the legs of 17th-century furniture.

bocage Encrustations of flowers, grass and moss generally used to decorate the supporting plinths of ceramic figures.

body The material from which a piece of pottery or porcelain is made (the word paste is also used for porcelain).

bombé Bulbous curving shape favoured particularly in Continental Europe for commodes and other types of case furniture.

bone ash Powder derived from burnt, ground animal bone that was added to porcelain in England in the mid-18th century.

bone china Porcelain made by the addition of large quantities of bone ash.

bonheur de jour Lady's small writing-cabinet-on-stand, popular in the 18th and 19th centuries.

booge The sloping sides of a plate or dish.

Boulle (Buhl) marquetry Inlaid tortoiseshell or horn with metal (usually brass), developed in late-17th-century France by designer André Charles Boulle.

bow front Convex form on chests of drawers from the late 18th century.

bracket clock A type of spring-driven clock, designed to stand on a surface.

bracket foot An 18th-century flat, shaped foot that extends diagonally from the floor to the carcase on the front and sides of case furniture.

break fronts Furniture with a prominent central section, commonly seen on large bookcases and sideboards.

bright-cut decoration Type of engraving whereby the metal surface is cut, creating facets that reflect the light.

Bristol blue Generic description for rich blue glass, coloured using cobalt oxide.

Brittannia metal Electro-plated pewter used as a metal substitute for silver.

Britannia standard Higher standard of British silver used between 1697 and 1720; contains 95.8 percent pure silver.

brodérie perse French term for cut-out floral and bird motifs in printed cottons and chintzes sewn onto plain quilts.

broken pediment A pediment, or triangular superstructure, in which the central apex is absent and often filled with a carved motif, common on bureau bookcases, bookcases, etc.

brownware Salt-glazed brown stoneware, especially that made in England in Nottingham, Derby, and elsewhere .

brushing slide Retractable wooden board, found beneath the top and above the drawers of chests.

bun foot Similar to a ball foot but more squashed, common on late 17th-century case furniture.

burnishing Method of polishing metals by rubbing the surface with a hard, smooth tool, such as agate, to create a lustre.

cabinet wares Cups, saucers, and plates made for display rather than use.

cabochon Gemstone (often heavily flawed) with an uncut but highly polished surface.

cabriole leg A furniture leg in the shape of an elongated "S".

caddy spoon Spoon for taking a measure of tea from a caddy.

caillouté Term derived from the French word for "pebble", meaning gilding applied in a series of dotted patterns.

cameo Hardstone, coral, lava, or shell carved to show a relief design (usually a bust or head in profile) against a contrasting coloured background.

cameo glass Wares made by combining two or more layers of differently coloured glass which was carved to make a design in relief.

campana vase Vase shape derived from ancient prototypes resembling an inverted bell.

canapé Type of French settee with padded back and seat, open arms, and often elaborately decorated frame.

candelabrum Candlestick with arms and nozzles for two or more candles.

canes Rods of glass drawn out by the glass blower to a required thickness for use as decoration.

caneware Stoneware of pale buff colour, fashionable in the late 18th and early 19th century.

canted corner A chamfered or bevelled corner used as a decorative feature on 18th-century case furniture.

Canton porcelain Elaborately decorated and gilded Chinese wares produced in the Canton (Guangzhou) district for export to the West.

capricci Fantasy scenes, often appearing on marquetry furniture.

carat Measurement of gold; one carat equals 200mg.

carcase Basic structure of a piece of furniture; often forms foundation for veneering.

carriage clock A small portable clock with a carrying handle.

cartel clock Type of ornate, spring-driven wall-hung clock, produced mainly in France during the 18th century.

cartouche Decorative shield, normally engraved, embossed, or cast, and generally containing an inscription or coat-of-arms.

carver 19th-century term for an elbow dining-chair.

caryatid A female figure of Ancient Greek origin used as an architectural support; they sometimes form the supports on a cabinet base.

case furniture Furniture intended as a receptacle, such as a chest-of-drawers.

cased glass Pieces made of two or more layers of coloured decoration sandwiched between two layers of clear glass.

caster Vessel with a pierced cover, for sprinkling salt, sugar, or ground pepper.

casting Process for making metal objects or their components, whereby molten metal is poured into a mould and then soldered to other parts.

celadon Semi-opaque glaze, usually of greenish colour, applied to Chinese stoneware.

cellaret Container used from the 18th century onward for storing and cooling wine, sometimes in a sideboard.

chaise-longue Upholstered chair with an elongated seat to support the legs in a horizontal position.

chamberstick Utilitarian candlestick with a short stem and saucer-like base.

champlevé ("raised field") Type of enamelling set into grooves or recesses cut in a metal surface.

charger Large circular or oval dish or plate, often richly decorated.

chasing Method of decorating silver using hammers and punches to push metal into a relief pattern; metal is displaced not removed.

chesterfield Deep-buttoned, upholstered settee.

chest-on-chest Tall chest-of-drawers, mounted on another similar, slightly larger chest; also known as a tallboy.

chest-on-stand Tall chest-of-drawers on a stand; also known as a highboy.

cheval mirror Tall, freestanding mirror supported by a four-legged base.

chevron Linked zigzag motif.

chiffonier Side cabinet with cupboards and drawers below and one or more low shelves above.

china clay A fine white clay also known as kaolin, which is mixed with petuntse to form true hard-paste porcelain.

Chinoiserie Oriental-style fixtures and scenes used to decorate many different types of object.

chocolate cup Large cup with two handles, a cover, and a saucer.

claw-and-ball foot Foot modelled as a ball gripped by an animal's claw or bird's talon.

claw setting Type of jewellery setting in which the gemstone is secured by projecting prongs.

cleated ends The tops of trestle and refectory tables made from long planks were often secured at each end by a strip of wood with the grain at a right angle to the top.

cloisonné Enamel fired into compartments (*cloisons*) formed by metal wires.

cobalt blue Mineral used to create blue-and-white decoration.

cock beading Curved strip of moulding often applied to finish edges of drawers.

commode French term for a chest-of-drawers. Also refers to a piece of furniture concealing a chamber-pot.

console table A table made to stand against a wall between windows, usually with no back support.

cornice The projecting moulding at the top of tall pieces of furniture.

crabstock Spouts and handles modelled as knotted trees and branches, a popular form in the 18th century.

crackle/crazing Fine network of cracks seen in certain types of glazed surfaces, sometimes used as a deliberate decorative effect, or as a result of ageing.

creamware Creamy-white earthenware.

credence table Type of small table originally used for storing food before serving or tasting; now refers to a semi-circular table with a hinged top.

credenza A long side-cabinet with glazed or solid doors.

crest Heraldic device surmounting a coat-of-arms.

cresting Carved decoration found on the highest part of a piece of furniture.

crewelwork Embroidery using crewel, a fine two-ply yarn; often used to decorate curtains and bed-hangings in Britain and North America.

crinoline stretcher A curved stretcher commonly found on early types of Windsor chairs.

crocket Stylized, protruding carved leaf or flower motif of architectural origin, commonly seen on Gothic-style furniture

cross-banding A veneered edge at right angles to the main veneer.

cruet A frame for holding casters and bottles containing condiments.

Cup and cover Bulbous form of carved decoration resembling an acorn, found on Elizabethan and early-17th-century furniture

cut-card decoration Flat shapes of applied silver used as decoration and for reinforcement.

cutting Decoration, either polished or matt, created by offering the piece to a stone wheel at varying angles.

davenport A small writing desk with a sloped top above a case of drawers.

delftware Tin-glazed earthenware from England or the Low Countries.

dentils Small rectangular blocks inspired by Ancient architecture, used to form cornices and mouldings.

Deutsche blumen Naturalistically painted flowers derived from prints used as a popular decorative motif on 18th-century pottery and porcelain.

diamond-point engraving Line-drawing on a glass surface using a diamond or metal point; designs comprising a series of dots rather than lines using this type of tool are called stipple engraving.

die-stamping Method of pressing sheet silver between solid dies with complementary patterns to create or decorate an item.

dish ring Used to protect the table surface from damage caused by hot plates.

distressed A term used to describe an object that has been artificially aged.

dovetails Spreading wedge-shaped tenons that interlock in shaped mortises to form a joint.

drop handle Tear-drop-shaped handle commonly seen on late-17th/early-18th-century furniture.

drop leaf A table with hinged flaps that can be raised when required.

drum table A circular-topped table with a frieze containing drawers and supported by a central pedestal.

dummy drawer A false drawer-front that looks like a drawer.

ebonized Stained black in imitation of ebony.

electro-plating Method of using an electric current to coat one metal with another (usually silver over an alloy).

embossing method of creating relief ornament on metal by hammering or punching from the reverse.

***Empire* style** French style inspired by the civilization of ancient Rome and celebrating the empire of Napoleon I, c.1804–15. It typically features such motifs as palmettes, winged lions, and sphinxes. The second *Empire* style refers to the revival of Neoclassicism during the reign of Napoleon III (1852–70).

enamel Colours made from glass which fuse with the glaze during firing.

encoignure The French term for a corner cupboard.

Enghalskrug Type of narrow-necked jug with a bulbous body popular in Germany and Holland from the mid-17th to the mid-18th century.

engraving Decorative patterns cut into the surface of silver using a sharp tool; metal is actually removed.

entablature Horizontal beam that surmounts architectural columns. Divided into the cornice (top), frieze (middle), and architrave (bottom).

epergne Centrepiece consisting of a central bowl and several small detachable bowls to display and serve fruit and sweetmeats.

escritoire Fall-fronted writing desk with a fitted interior.

escutcheon Brass plate surrounding a keyhole.

étagère Two- or three-tiered table intended for displaying objects or serving food.

Etruscan style Style characterized by the use of red, black, and white and motifs such as lions, griffins, and sphinxes; popular in the late 18th and 19th centuries following the rediscovery of Ancient Etruscan sites and artifacts.

faceted Decorative surface cut into sharp-edged planes in a criss-cross pattern to reflect the light.

façon de venise Glassware imitating Venetian styles.

faïence Tin-glazed earthenware from France.

fall front The hinged flap of a writing desk that pulls down to make a writing surface.

famille rose Chinese porcelain decorated with a distinctive palette of opaque enamels.

fauteuil A French or French-style upholstered armchair.

faux bois French term meaning wood painted to resemble a more exotic timber.

featherbanding Strips of veneer around the edge of a surface, cut diagonally to the main veneer.

Federal style American version of the Neoclassical style, popular *c.*1789 to *c.*1830.

fêtes galantes Open-air scenes of aristocratic amusement that were a favourite theme of French Rococo painters.

fielded panel A raised panel bordered by a bevelled edge.

figuring The pattern made by the grain of wood.

finial Decorative turned knob.

flame figuring A veneer cut to enhance the grain of the wood and resembling flames.

flange Collar or rim applied to an object to strengthen it or for attaching it to another object.

flatback Ceramic portrait figures with flat, undecorated backs, designed to stand against a wall or on a mantelpiece.

flat-chasing Chasing on a flat silver surface, leaving an impression of the punched pattern on the back.

flatware Any flat or shallow tableware, such as plates or cutlery.

fluting Pattern of concave grooves repeated in vertical, parallel lines.

fretwork Carved geometric decoration that may be pierced or blind and is used as a border, or to form a gallery.

frieze A band of horizontal carved or painted decoration or horizontal band of wood; may run along the top of a bookcase under the cornice, or beneath the top of a table.

gadrooning Border composed of a succession of alternating lobes and flutes, usually curved.

galletto rosso Decorative ceramic pattern of red-and-gold Chinese cockerels, devised at the Italian factory of Doccia.

garniture A set of three or more vases of matching and complementary form intended to stand on a mantelpiece or on the top of a cabinet.

gauge Thickness of a metal sheet or the diameter of a wire.

gesso A plaster-like substance used as a substitute for carved wood, or as a base for painted or gilded decoration.

gilding Process of applying a gold finish to a silver or electro-plated object.

girandole A type of elaborate candelabrum or a sconce with a mirror behind, made to hang on the wall.

glaze Glassy coating applied onto the biscuit body of pottery and porcelain and fired to make it non-porous.

Gothic Decoration in the style of Gothic architecture, featuring such motifs as pinnacles, crockets, and trefoils. The style was revived from the 1820s in Europe and from the 1840s in North America.

graining Painting an inexpensive wood, such as pine or beech, to simulate a more expensive timber, such as mahogany.

Greek-key design A geometric decorative motif from Ancient Greek architecture.

ground Background area of a single colour onto which further enamelled decoration or gilding may be applied.

guéridon A small French table, usually in the form of a column or pedestal with a tray top, to hold a candlestick.

guilloche Decorative motif inspired by Classical antiquity, formed from a continuous figure-of-eight pattern.

hallmark The marks stamped on silver or gold objects when passed at assay (the test for quality).

hard-paste porcelain Porcelain made using the ancient Chinese combination of kaolin and petuntse.

harlequin Chairs of similar design but not a proper set; a piece of furniture with a mechanism that when activated pops open to reveal hidden fittings.

hausmaler Term used to describe an independent painter of German porcelain blanks (most often with reference to Meissen).

highboy American term for a chest-on-stand.

hollow ware Any hollow vessels, such as bowls and teapots.

Huguenot French Protestants who settled in England and the Netherlands following the revocation of the Edict of Nantes in 1685, which denied them religious freedom. Many were skilled silversmiths, weavers and furniture-makers, who introduced French styles into the decorative arts of England and Holland.

humpen Tall cylindrical German beer glass made from the mid-16th century to the 18th century.

husk Neoclassical decorative motif of formalized leaves.

hyalith glass Coloured glass, either sealing-wax red or jet-black, produced in Bohemia from 1819.

hybrid paste Formula that combines the ingredients of hard-paste and soft-paste porcelain in an attempt to produce a more malleable body.

Imari A type of Japanese porcelain with opulent decoration inspired by brocade designs, exported through the port of Imari.

impressed Term generally used to describe a mark or decoration that is stamped or indented into the surface of pottery.

incised Term generally used to describe a mark or decoration that is cut or scratched into the surface.

ingot Piece of cast metal obtained from a mould in a form suitable for storage

inlay A design most commonly cut from veneers, metal or mother-of-pearl and set into the surface of a piece of furniture to decorate it.

intaglio Incised gemstone or any incised decoration; the opposite of carving in relief.

iridescence A thin layer of metallic salts applied to glass to produce lustres.

ironstone Hard white earthenware popular from the early 19th century for dinner services and other ornamental and architectural pieces.

istoriato Narrative scenes painted on Italian *maiolica*.

Jacobethan 19th-century revival of motifs such as strapwork and grotesques found on 16th- and 17th-century decorative arts. The term is a combination of "Elizabethan" and "Jacobean".

japanning European imitation of Oriental lacquer.

jardinière Plant container made from a variety of materials, including glass, silver, or pottery.

jasper ware A hard, fine-grained stoneware decorated with high-relief medallions, developed by Wedgwood.

jewelled decoration Method of decoration created by drops of enamel over gilding, resembling jewels, popular in France in the 18th century and at Royal Worcester.

joined Term used to describe furniture made by a joiner.

kakeimon Sparsely decorated Japanese porcelain made by the Kakiemon family in the 17th century; much imitated by later potters.

kaolin A fine, white granite clay used in hard-paste porcelain, also called China clay.

kelim A flat-woven Persian rug (made with no pile).

kneehole desk A writing desk with drawers on either side and a central recess for the user's legs.

knop Decorative knob on a lid, or the bulbous moulding usually placed at the mid-point of the stem of a cup or candlestick.

lacquerwork Layers of varnish prepared from the sap of the Rhus vernicifera tree, used as a ground for Oriental decoration. European imitations are known as "japanning" and vernis Martin.

lacy glass Type of American pressed glass with a stipple-engraved background that gives a lacy effect.

ladderback A country chair with a back made from a series of horizontal bars between the two vertical uprights.

lambrequin Baroque border pattern of lacework, scrolls, and scalloped drapery.

lamination Method of gluing together sheets of wood with the grain in different directions to produce a material that is thinner and lighter than solid wood. Synonymous with the furniture-manufacturer John Henry Belter.

lampwork Glass that is blown or manipulated from clear or coloured glass rods over a blow lamp or torch.

lattimo From the Italian latte, meaning "milk"; an opaque-white glass made by adding bone ash or tin oxide to the glass batch. Also known as milk glass.

lead glass (crystal glass) Type of glass, discovered c.1676, containing a high proportion of lead oxide, from which it obtains a particularly clear brilliance.

library table A rectangular table with frieze drawers, end supports, and central stretcher.

linen chest A hybrid coffer/chest of drawers, which may have both drawers and a lift-up top.

liner Inner sleeve of a vessel, made of silver, plate or glass.

longcase clock A tall clock with a case containing weights and pendulum and hood housing dial and movement.

loper A pull-out support to hold up the fall front of a bureau.

lowboy A small dressing table, often a single frieze drawer flanked by a deeper one.

lunette Semi-circular decorative motif popular for carved friezes in the Jacobean and Victorian periods.

lustre ware Pottery decorated with metallic pigments, popular in the Middle East and Europe.

maiolica Tin-glazed earthenware produced in Italy from the 14th century.

majolica Corruption of the term *maiolica* that refers to a type of 19th-century earthenware in elaborate forms with thick, brightly coloured glazes.

malachite A marble-effect opaque pressed glass.

Mannerist style Decorative style of the late 16th century, employing twisted, exaggerated, and bizarre forms, often entrapped by strapwork and grotesques.

marquetry A refined form of inlay using veneers of variously coloured woods to decorate a surface.

millefiori Glass made by fusing differently coloured rods of glass, which resembles "a thousand flowers"; used especially for paperweights.

mitre-cutting Deep, V-shaped cuts.

monteith Cooler for wine glasses, resembling a punchbowl, but with a notched rim to suspend the glasses over iced water.

moons Air bubbles in porcelain paste that expand during firing, leaving translucent spots.

mortice and tenon Type of joint used in furniture; the mortice is a cavity, into which the shaped tenon fits and is held in place by dowels.

mote spoon Small spoon with a pierced bowl used to skim tea leaves, with a spike at the end of the stem to unblock the spout of the teapot.

mother-of-pearl Slices of shell often used for decorative inlay.

motif A decorative detail, often repeated to form a pattern.

moulded glass 19th-century glasswares manufactured in large quantities by forcing glass into a mould.

mould metal Expensive durable iron moulds, finely cut and chased.

mule chest Chest with drawers in the base; forerunner of the chest-of-drawers.

Neoclassicism Mid- to late-18th-century style of architecture and decoration based on the forms of Ancient Greece and Rome. Characteristic elements include Classical motifs such as garlands of flowers, palmettes, husks, vases, urns, key patterns, and mythical creatures.

nest of tables Set of graduated occasional tables that stack under each other when not in use.

nickel Any of various white alloys of copper, zinc and nickel used in electro-plating as a base for coating with silver.

nozzle On a candlestick, the detachable top in which the candle is placed.

occasional table Small, easily portable table.

ogee Shallow double-S-shape curve.

ojime Small, round, or oval beads for tightening cords holding small personal possessions in traditional Japanese dress.

onion pattern Popular decorative pattern in blue underglaze employed at Meissen and other Continental factories from the 18th century.

opaque twist A white or coloured twist of glass contained within the stem of a drinking glass.

openwork Pierced decoration.

ormolu Gilded bronze or brass; term also sometimes loosely used to describe any yellow-coloured metal.

overglaze A second glaze laid over a first and refired; also known as enamelling.

overlay glass (cased glass) A technique in which a glass body is covered by one or more differently coloured outer layers that may be carved in a relief design.

Palladian style Classical style of architecture as interpreted by the Italian architect Andrea Palladio (1508–80) in his seminal work *Quattro Libri*. Palladianism was introduced into England in the 1730s by Lord Burlington and William Kent.

palmette A stylized palm-leaf motif, often used to decorate Oriental carpets and furniture.

papier-mâché Paper pulp combined with glue, used to make small objects such as boxes and trays; also applied over a metal frame to make larger pieces of furniture, such as tables and chairs.

parcel gilt Wood that has been partly gilded.

parian Fine white biscuit porcelain resembling marble; popular from mid-19th century.

parquetry Decorative veneers of wood laid in a geometric pattern.

pâte sur pâte Decorative technique made by building up layers of slip on a contrasting ground to simulate the effect of a cameo.

patina The term used to describe the surface colour and sheen of furniture and silver which is built up from years of use and careful polishing.

pearlware Fine earthenware, similar to creamware but with a blueish glaze, introduced by the firm of Wedgwood *c.*1779.

pie-crust top Frilly carved decorative edge commonly seen on dish-top tripod tables.

piercing Intricate cut decoration, created by using a sharp chisel or fretsaw, and then punches.

pier table Small side table made to stand against the "pier" – the wall between two windows.

pietra dura Inlay used to decorate furniture, made from thin slivers of hard and semi-precious stones.

planish Initial stage in finishing the surface of plate before polishing, to remove the hammer marks which occur during raising, by using a special flat-headed hammer.

plate A generic term for gold and silver vessels, not to be confused with Sheffield Plate or plated wares.

plinth Square base at the bottom of a candlestick column.

porringer A two-handled dish sometimes with a lid, originally for holding porridge or broth. Made from silver and pewter.

potash glass Strong type of glass made from potash, lime and silica. Also called *verre de fougère* or *waldglas.*

pressed glass 19th-century glasswares formed by mechanical pressure applied to molten glass in a mould.

press moulding Method of producing ceramic objects by forcing clay into a mould.

prunts Blobs of glass applied to a glass surface as a decorative technique.

quadrant A quarter circle, marked with degrees of a circle and with a weighted line or pointer, used as a navigational aid.

quarter-veneered Four pieces of identical veneer, which are laid opposite each other to create a decorative effect.

quartetto tables A set of four graduating matching tables, that can be stored inside each other.

Queen Anne style Style characterized by plain surfaces and octagonal/hexagonal geometric shapes and faceting, popular during the 1710s and 1720s. It was revived during the second half of the 19th century.

Queen's ware Opaque, warm-cream vitro-porcelain glass that imitated later 18th-century creamware. Name borrowed from Wedgwood by Sowerby glassmakers.

rack The structure, comprising several shelves, at the top of some dressers.

rat's tail Short ridge of silver applied to the back of spoon bowls to reinforce the joint at the handle.

reeding Decorative moulding composed of narrow parallel convex threadlike forms, usually confined to borders.

re-entrant corner A corner that has been cut away with a decorative indentation, usually seen on the corners of table tops *c.*1720–40.

refectory table Term used to describe the long rectangular dining tables of the 17th century and later.

Régence The forerunner of the Rococo style in France, characterized by symmetrical, heavy forms typical of the Baroque but with elaborate scrollwork. It takes its name from the regency of Philippe, duc d'Orléans (1715–23).

Regency Style of British origin, named after the period during which George, Prince of Wales (later George IV) was Prince Regent (1811–20) and characterized by heavy, broadly Classical forms and ornament such as winged lions, masks, and palmettes. Stylistically the term covers the period *c.*1790–1830.

Renaissance Flowering of Classical scholarship, scientific, and geographical discovery at the end of the Middle Ages. In the decorative arts it was characterized by the use of elaborate grotesques, arabesques, flower swags, and scrollwork. This style was revived in the mid-19th century.

repoussé Term for embossing; relief decoration on metal is made by hammering from the reverse so that the decoration projects, then is finished from the front by chasing.

reproduction A piece that is a copy of an early design.

Restoration Re-establishment of the monarchy in 1660 in Britain; also the reign of Charles II (1660–85). Also the re-establishment of the monarchy in France under Louis XVIII (1814–24) and Charles X (1824–30).

"right" Dealers' term for something that is genuine and authentic, as opposed to "wrong", which means it is faked, altered, or restored.

Rococo Decorative style that evolved in the early 18th century partly as a reaction to the Baroque; it featured asymmetrical ornament and flamboyant scrollwork.

rolled edge Edges of Sheffield Plate or fused-plate articles were rolled to conceal the copper centre, which would otherwise be visible.

rubinglas German, "ruby glass": richly coloured red glass created by adding copper or gold oxide to the glass mix.

rummer 19th-century English drinking goblet, traditionally used for drinking rum and water.

sabre leg An elegant outward-curving leg, associated with Regency furniture.

salt A dish or cellar designed for holding salt.

salt glaze Glaze used on some stoneware made by throwing salt into the kiln during firing, first developed in the Rhineland.

salver Flat dish, sometimes footed, for serving food or drink; similar to a tray but with no handles and often with a moulded border and decorated with an engraved coat-of-arms.

sconce A plate or bracket on the wall to which lights or candle-holders could be attached. Also used to describe the wall lights themselves.

scratchweight Note made of the weight of a silver article at assay, usually hand-engraved lightly on the base or reverse; any change from the original weight may indicate that the piece has been altered or overly polished. With silver in sets, such as plates, the number of the individual piece was often also inscribed on the base, which may help with building up a complete set.

scroll Curved decoration, particularly used for handles.

seat-rail Framework that supports the seat of a chair and holds the legs together.

secretaire A writing cabinet with a flat front and a deep drawer that is hinged to open and form a writing surface.

serpentine Undulating shallow double "S" shape; this is the form often used on the fronts of quality furniture.

settle A long wooden seat with a back and arms, and possibly a box seat.

sextant Navigational instrument, formed from one-sixth of a circle.

sgraffito Decorative techinque whereby the surface has been scratched or incised to show a contrasting colour beneath; used mainly on ceramics and glass.

shagreen Untanned leather, originally the skin of the *shagri*, a Turkish wild ass; now used to refer to any granulated leather.

Sheffield Plate Silver substitute used from *c.*1740, made by binding and fusing together sterling silver and copper.

shoe piece Piece of wood at the back of a chair joining the base of the splat to the seat.

silica Fine sand, the basic raw material for glass; melts at very high temperature and requires fluxes (like soda) to reduce melting temperature to a practical level.

silver gilt Solid silver covered with a thin layer of gold.

slip Clay mixed with water, often used to decorate pottery.

soda glass Light, malleable glass with a faint brown or greenish tinge. Made using sodium carbonate as a flux, it has no lead content and does not ring when struck.

soft-paste porcelain Type of body developed in Europe in the 16th century, made from various materials that may include kaolin, glass, soapstone, or bone ash, in an attempt to create true hard-paste porcelain.

spandrel Space between a corner and a central arch, often filled with decoration.

splat Central flat piece of wood in a chair back.

standard Required amount of pure silver in an alloy.

sterling silver Silver of at least 925 parts per 1000 purity – the minimum standard for English silver.

stirrup cup Cup used for drinking prior to making a journey or going hunting. Usually shaped as the head of an animal.

stoneware Non-porous ceramic body made from clay and sand or flint, fired at high temperature.

stretchers Horizontal bars joining and strengthening legs.

stringing Fine inlaid lines around a piece of furniture, which were very popular in the Edwardian era.

studio glass One-off pieces designed and produced by usually independent artist-craftsmen.

swag Suspended festoon of foliage, flowers, fruit, or drapery.

swan-neck handle A handle with sinuous curves at either end that was popular in the mid-18th century.

tankard Mug with a hinged cover, usually for beer.

taperstick Small candlestick for holding a taper (thin candle) for lighting pipes and melting wax.

tazza Wide shallow bowl on a stemmed foot.

terracotta Red-coloured earthenware pottery, usually unglazed.

tester The wooden canopy over a bed; it may cover only half the bed and be supported by two or four posts, hence full-tester or half-tester beds.

tin glaze Opaque white glaze made from tin oxide, used on *maiolica, faience,* and delftware pottery.

transfer printing Printed decoration made by transferring a design created on a copper plate via transfer paper onto a pottery or porcelain body.

transitional In French furniture-making the style created from the fusion of Neoclassical decoration with Rococo forms.

treen Small wooden domestic objects, sometimes in the shape of fruit.

trefoil Three-lobed Gothic decorative motif - like a stylized clover leaf.

tripod table Popular small table with a tray top supported by a central pillar on a three-legged base.

tumbler cup Round-bottomed drinking vessel.

Tunbridge ware Objects decorated with pictures or designs made from bundles of differently coloured wood cut in sections.

tureen A large bowl on a foot used for serving soup.

turned furniture Pieces made by turning on a lathe.

underglaze Decoration applied to a body before glazing and final firing.

uprights The vertical pillars of a chair back.

vaseline glass Acidically coloured green or yellow glass.

veneer A thin sheet of wood applied to furniture for decorative effect.

verre de soie French for "satin glass"; a type of glass with a satin finish.

vetro a fili Italian "thread glass"; a type of filigrana. Other types include *vetro a reticello* (glass with a small network), *vetro a retortoli* (glass with a twist), and *vetro di trino* (lace glass).

waiter Small salver, less than 15cm (6in) in diameter.

whatnot Tall stand of four or five display shelves and sometimes a drawer in the base.

white metal Hard alloy of copper and zinc used as a base in electro-plating.

Windsor chair Country chair, usually with a saddle seat, hoop back, and simple turned legs.

wine funnel Cone with a spout and often a matching fish, for filtering and decanting wine.

wing chair Upholstered chair with a high back and wing-like side projections.

X-frame The X-shaped construction of some chairs and stools.

BIBLIOGRAPHY

GENERAL

Baudot, Francois and Demanchy, J., *A Passion for Collecting: Decorating with Art and Antiques* (New York, 2004)

Bly, John, *Is it Genuine? How to Collect Antiques with Confidence* (London, 1986)

Fleming, John and Honour, Hugh, *The Penguin Dictionary of Decorative Arts* (London, 1989)

Garner, Philippe (ed.), *Phaidon Encyclopedia of Decorative Arts 1890–1940* (Oxford, 1978)

Halbertsma, Hidde, *Complete Encyclopedia Of Antiques* (New York, 2004)

Haslam, M., *Marks and Monograms of the Modern Movement: 1875–1930* (Guildford, 1977)

Hughes, Therle, *The Country Life Antiques Handbook* (1986)

Jervis, Simon (ed.), *The Penguin Dictionary of Design and Designers* (London, 1984)

Knowles, Eric, *Miller's 100 Years of the Decorative Arts* (London, 1998, first published 1993 as *Miller's Victoriana to Art Deco*)

Miller, Judith, *How to Make Money out of Antiques* (London, 1995)

Miller, Judith and Martin, *Miller's Antiques and Collectables: The Facts at Your Fingertips* (London, 1993)

Miller, Judith and Martin (eds.), *Miller's Pocket Antiques Fact File* (1988)

Miller, Judith and Martin (eds.), *Miller's Understanding Antiques* (London, 1997)

Miller's Antiques Price Guide (annual)

Miller's Antiques Shops, Fairs, and Auctions in the UK and Eire (London, annual)

Miller's Antiques Under £1,000 (London, annual)

Miller's Buying Affordable Antiques Price Guide (London, annual)

Murray, Peter and Linda, *Dictionary of Art and Artists* (London, 1997)

Osborne, Harold, *Oxford Companion to the Decorative Arts* (1985)

Savage, George (ed.), *Dictionary of Antiques* (London, 1978)

Turner, Jane (ed.), *Dictionary of Art* (London, 1996)

ART NOUVEAU

Amaya, Mario, *Art Nouveau* (London and New York, 1966)

Aslin, Elizabeth, *The Aesthetic Movement: Prelude to Art Nouveau* (London, 1969)

Bayer, Patricia and Waller, Mark, *The Art of René Lalique* (London, 1988)

Becker, Vivienne, *Art Nouveau Jewellery* (London, 1985)

Cooke, Frederick, *Glass* (London, 1986)

Dawes, Nicholas M., *Lalique Glass* (New York, 1986)

Duncan, Alastair, *Art Nouveau* (London, 1994)

Duncan, Alastair, *Fin de Siècle Masterpieces from the Silverman Collection* (New York, 1989)

Feinblatt, Ebria, *Toulouse-Lautrec and his Contemporaries: Posters of the Belle Epoque from the Wagner Collection* (Los Angeles, 1985)

Hanks, D.A., *The Decorative Designs of Frank Lloyd Wright* (New York, 1979)

Johnson, Diane Chalmers, *American Art Nouveau* (New York, 1979)

Knowles, Eric, *Miller's Antiques Checklist: Art Nouveau* (London, 1992)

Knowles, Eric, *Miller's Art Nouveau and Art Deco Buyer's Guide* (London, 1995)

Koch, Robert, *Louis C. Tiffany's Glass-Bronzes-Lamps* (New York, 1971)

Revi, Albert Christian, *American Art Nouveau Glass* (Camden, NJ, 1968)

Sembach, K.J., *Henri Van De Velde* (London, 1989)

Timmers, Margaret, *The Power of the Poster* (London, 1998)

Vergo, P., *Art in Vienna, 1898–1918* (London, 1975)

Waissenberger, Robert, (ed.) *Vienna 1890–1920* (New York, 1984)

Weisberg, Gabriel P., *Art Nouveau Bing: Paris Style 1900* (New York, 1986)

Zapata, Janet, *The Jewelry and Enamels of Louis Comfort Tiffany* (London, 1993)

ARTS and CRAFTS

Anscombe, I. and Gere, C., *Arts and Crafts in Britain and America* (London, 1978)

Bowman, Leslie Green, *American Arts and Crafts* (Los Angeles, 1990)

Cathers, David M., *Furniture of the American Arts and Crafts Movement* (Philmont, 1996)

Gere, Charlotte and Munn, Geoffrey, *Artists' Jeweller: From the Pre-Raphaelites to the Arts and Crafts Movement* (Woodbridge, 1989)

Kaplan, W., *Charles Rennie Mackintosh* (Glasgow, 1996)

Naylor, Gillian, *The Arts and Crafts Movement: A Study of its Sources, Ideals and Influence on Design Theory* (London, 1990)

Tracey, Berry B., *19th-Century America: Furniture & Other Decorative Arts* (New York, 1970)

CERAMICS

Adams, Elizabeth, *Chelsea Porcelain* (London, 1987)

Atterbury, Paul and Batkin, Maureen, *Dictionary of Minton* (Woodbridge, 1990)

Atterbury, Paul, *History of Porcelain* (1982)

Bailey, Betty and Twitchett, John, *Royal Crown Derby* (London, 1976)

Barber, Edwin Atlee, *The Pottery and Porcelain of the United States* (New York, 1976)

Battie, David (ed.), *Sotheby's Concise Encyclopedia of Porcelain* (London, 1990)

Branyan, Lawrence, French, Neal, and Sandon, John, *Worcester Blue-and-White Porcelain* (London, 1989)

Carswell, John, *Chinese Blue-and-White and its Impact on the Western World* (Chicago, 1985)

Charleston, Robert, J., (ed.), *World Ceramics* (London, 1982)

Coysh, A.W. and Henrywood, R.K., *Dictionary of Blue-and-White Printed Earthenware* (Woodbridge, 1989–90)

Cushion, J.P., *Handbook of Pottery and Porcelain Marks* (London, 1996)

Cushion, John and Margaret, *A Collector's History of British Porcelain* (Woodbridge, 1992)

Danckert, Ludwig, *Directory of European Porcelain* (1981)

Dawes, Nicholas M., *Majolica* (New York, 1990)

Fay-Halle, Antoinette and Mundt, Barbara, *Nineteenth-Century European Porcelain* (London, 1983)

Frelinghuysen, Alice Cooney, *American Porcelain* (New York, 1989)

Gabszewicz, Anton and Freeman, Geoffrey, *Bow Porcelain* (London, 1982)

Garner, Harry, *Oriental Blue-and-White* (London, 1970)

Gaston, Mary Frank, *American Belleek* (Paducah, 1984)

Godden, Geoffrey, *An Illustrated Encyclopaedia of British Pottery and Porcelain* (Leicester, 1992)

Godden, Geoffrey, *Caughley and Worcester Porcelain* (Woodbridge, 1981)

Godden, Geoffrey, *Miller's Godden's New Guide to English Porcelain* (London, 2004)

Godden, Geoffrey, *Lowestoft Porcelain* (Woodbridge, 1985)

Godden, Geoffrey, *Mason's China and Ironstone Wares* (Woodbridge, 1980)

Godden, Geoffrey, *Minton Pottery and Porcelain of the First Period, 1793–1850* (London, 1968)

Godden, Geoffrey, *Ridgway Porcelain* (Woodbridge, 1985)

Godden, Geoffrey, *Staffordshire Porcelain* (London, 1983)

Halfpenny, Pat, *English Earthenware Figures 1740–1840* (1992)

Hillier, Bevis, *Pottery and Porcelain 1700–1914* (1968)

Holgate, David, *New Hall* (London, 1987)

Honey, W.B., *French Porcelain of the 18th Century* (1950)

Howard, David, *Chinese Armorial Porcelain* (London, 1974)

Ivanova, Elena (ed.), *Porcelain In Russia: 18th–19th Centuries, The Gardner Factory* (St Petersburg, 2005)

Jenyns, Soame, *Japanese Porcelain* (1985)

Kovel, Ralph and Terry, *Kovel's New Dictionary of Marks: Pottery and Porcelain 1850 to the Present* (New York, 1986)

Lang, Gordon, *Miller's Antiques Checklist: Porcelain* (London, 1996)

Lang, Gordon, *Miller's Antiques Checklist: Pottery* (London, 1996)

Lang, Gordon, *Miller's Pottery and Porcelain Marks* (London, 1992)

Langham, Marion, *Belleek* (London, 1993)

Lawrence, Louis, *Satsuma* (London, 1991)

Lockett, Terence and Godden, Geoffrey, *Davenport: China, Earthenware, and Glass* (London, 1989)

Macintosh, Duncan, *Chinese Blue-and-White Porcelain* (Woodbridge, 1994)

Medley, Margaret, *The Chinese Potter* (Oxford, 1976)

Menzhausen, Ingelore, *Early Meissen Porcelain in Dresden* (London, 1990)

Messenger, Michael, *Coalport* (Woodbridge, 1996)

Miller's Ceramics Buyer's Guide (London, annual)

Miller's Collecting Pottery & Porcelain: The Facts at Your Fingertips (London, 1997)

Neale, Gillian, *Miller's Blue-and-White Pottery: A Collector's Guide* (London, 2004)

Neale, Gillian, *Miller's Encyclopedia of British Transfer-printed Pottery Patterns 1790–1930* (London, 2005)

Oliver, Anthony, *Staffordshire Pottery: The Tribal Art of England* (1981)

Pugh, P.D., *Staffordshire Portrait Figures* (London, 1990)

Reilly, Robin, *Wedgwood* (London, 1989)

Ruckert, Rainer, *Meissener Porzellan 1710–1810* (Munich, 1966)

Sandon, Henry, *Royal Worcester Porcelain* (London, 1995)

Sandon, John, *Dictionary of Worcester Porcelain* (Woodbridge, 1993)

Sandon, John, *Miller's Collecting Porcelain* (London, 2002)

Sandon, John, *Starting to Collect Antique Porcelain* (Woodbridge, 1997)

Sato, M., *Chinese Ceramics, A Short History* (1981)

Savage, George and Newman, Harold, *An Illustrated Dictionary of Ceramics* (London, 1992)

Savill, Rosalind, *The Wallace Collection Catalogue of Sèvres Porcelain* (London, 1988)

Schiffer, Nancy, *Japanese Porcelain, 1800–1950* (West Chester, 1986)

Sotheby's Concise Encyclopedia of Porcelain (1990)

Twitchett, John, *Derby Porcelain* (London, 1980)

Van Lemmen, Hans, *Tiles: A Collector's Guide* (London, 1979)

Watney, Bernard, *English Blue-and-White Porcelain* (London, 1973)

Watney, Bernard, *Liverpool Porcelain of the Eighteenth Century* (Shepton Beauchamp, 1997)

Whiter, Leonard, *Spode* (London, 1978)

Wilson, Timothy, *Italian Maiolica* (Oxford, 1989)

Wojciechowski, Kathy, *Nippon Porcelain* (West Chester, 1992)

CLOCKS

Allix, Charles and Bonnert, Peter, *Carriage Clocks: Their History and Development* (London, 1974)

Britten, F.J., *Britten's Watch and Clockmaker's Handbook, Dictionary and Guide* (London, 1982)

Britten, F.J., *Old Clocks and Watches and their Makers* (London, 1975)

Cescinsky, Herbert and Webster, Malcolm R., *English Domestic Clocks* (London, 1976)

Dawson, P.G., Drover, C.B., and Parkes, D.W., *Early English Clocks* (Woodbridge, 1982)

Gould, Rupert T., *The Marine Chronometer, Its History and Development* (Woodbridge, 1989)

Hawkins, J.B., *Thomas Cole and Victorian Clockmaking* (Sydney, 1975)

Jagger, Cedric, *Clocks* (London, 1975)

Loomes, Brian, *Early Clockmakers of Great Britain* (London, 1981)

Loomes, Brian, *Painted Dial Clocks* (Woodbridge, 1994)

Loomes, Brian, *Watchmakers and Clockmakers of the World: Volume Two* (London, 1989)

Mercer, Tony, *Chronometer Makers of the World* (Colchester, 1991)

Mighell, John, *Miller's Antique Checklist: Clocks* (London, 1992)

Miller, Judith and Martin, *Miller's Clocks and Barometers Buyer's Guide* (London, 1997)

Roberts, Deryck, *British Skeleton Clocks* (Woodbridge, 1987)

Roberts, Deryck, *The Bracket Clock* (London, 1982)

Roberts, Deryck, *The English Longcase Clock* (London, 1989)

Robinson, Tom, *The Longcase Clock* (Woodbridge, 1981)

Rose, Ronald E., *English Dial Clocks* (Woodbridge, 1978)

Sellink, Dr J.L., *Dutch Antique Domestic Clocks* (Leiden, 1973)

Swedberg, Robert and Harriet, *Encyclopedia of Antique American Clocks* (Wisconsin, 2004)

Tardy, *The French Clocks* (Paris, 1982)

White, George, *English Lantern Clocks* (Woodbridge, 1989)

FURNITURE

Agius, Pauline, *British Furniture, 1880–1915* (Woodbridge, 1978)

Agius, Pauline and Jones, Stephen, *Ackermann's Regency Furniture and Interiors* (Ramsbury, 1984)

Alcouffe, D., *Le Mobilier du Musée du Louvre* (Dijon, 1993)

Aslin, Elizabeth, *Nineteenth-Century English Furniture* (1962)

Bahns, J., *Zwischen Biedermeier und Jugendstil* (Munich, 1987)

Barquist, David I., *American Tables and Looking Glasses* (New Haven, Connecticut, 1992)

Bazin, Germain, *Baroque & Rococo* (1964)

Beckerdite, Luke ed., *American Furniture* (New England, 1997)

Bennett Oates, Phyllis, *The Story of Western Furniture* (1981)

Bly, John, *Discovering English Furniture* (1976)

Chinnery, Victor, *Oak Furniture* (Woodbridge, 1986)

Collard, Frances, *Regency Furniture* (Woodbridge, 1983)

Comstock, Helen, *American Furniture* (New York, 1962)

Cooper, Jeremy, *Victorian & Edwardian Furniture* (1987)

Cooper, Wendy, *The Classical Taste in America 1800 to 1840* (New York, 1994)

Davidson, Richard, *Miller's Antiques Checklist: Furniture* (London, 1991)

Dell, T., *Furniture in the Frick Collection* (New York, 1992)

Edwards, Ralph, *The Shorter Dictionary of English Furniture: From the Middle Ages to the Late Georgian Period* (London, 1964)

Edwards, R., and Jourdain, M., *Georgian Cabinet-Makers* (1955)

Fastnedge, Ralph, *Sheraton Furniture* (London, 1962)

Fitzgerald, Oscar, *Three Centuries of American Furniture* (New York, 1982)

Forman, Benno M. and Norton, W.W., *American Seating Furniture, 1630–1840* (New York, 1988)

Garvan, Beatrice B., *The Pennsylvania German Collection* (Philadelphia, 1982)

Gilbert, Christopher, *Furniture at Temple Newsam House and Lotherton Hall* (London, 1978)

Gillham, Leslie ed., *Miller's Furniture Buyer's Guide: Late Georgian to Edwardian* (London, 1998)

Goyne Evans, Nancy, *American Windsor Chairs* (Winterthur, 1996)

Granjean, S., *Empire Furniture, 1800–1825* (London, 1996)

Groth, H. and von de Schulenburg, F., *Neoclassicism in the North: Swedish Furniture and Interiors, 1770–1850* (London, 1990)

Hayward, Helena, (ed.), *World Furniture* (London, 1990)

Hearnden, Jonty, *Miller's Late Georgian to Edwardian Furniture Buyer's Guide* (London, 1998)

Hechsher, Morrison H., *American Furniture at the Metropolitan Museum of Art: Late Colonial Period, Queen Anne, and Chippendale* (New York, 1985)

Janneau, G., *Le Mobilier Français* (Paris, 1967–74)

Jervis, Simon, *Victorian Furniture* (London, 1968)

Joy, Edward Thomas, *English Furniture* (London, 1977)

Kane, Patricia, *Three Hundred Years of American Seating Furniture* (New York, 1976)

Kenny, Peter, *Honoré Lannuier: Cabinetmaker from Paris* (New York, 1998)

Kirk, John, *The Shaker World* (New York, 1997)

Kjellberg, Pierre, *Le Mobilier Français du XVIIIe Siècle* (Paris, 1989)

Miller, Judith and Martin, *Miller's Pine and Country Furniture Buyer's Guide* (London, 1995)

Musgrave, Clifford, *Regency Furniture: 1800 to 1830* (London, 1970)

Payne, Christopher, *Miller's Collecting Furniture: The Facts at Your Fingertips* (London, 1995)

Payne, Christopher, *19th-Century European Furniture* (1985)

Paz Aguiló, M., *El mueble clásico español* (Madrid, 1987)

Pradère, A., *Die Kunst des französischen Möbels: Ebenisten von Ludwig XIV. bis zur Revolution* (Munich, 1990)

Richards, Nancy E. and Goyne Evans, Nancy, *New England Furniture at Winterthur: Queen Anne and Chippendale Periods* (Winterthur, 1997)

Schwarz, Martin D., Stanck, Edward J., and True, Douglas K., *The Furniture of John Henry Belter and the Rococo Revival* (New York, 1981)

Sotheby's Concise Encyclopedia of Furniture (1989)

Stevens, Christopher Claxton and Whittington, Stewart, *18th-Century English Furniture: The Norman Adams Collection* (Woodbridge, 1983)

Symonds, R.W. and Whinneray, B.B., *Victorian Furniture* (London, 1987)

Thornton, Peter, *Seventeenth-Century Interior Decoration in England, France, and Holland* (London, 1978)

Walkling, Gillian, *Bamboo: Antique Bamboo Furniture* (London, 1979)

Ward-Jackson, Peter, *English Furniture Designs of the 18th Century* (London, 1984)

Watson, Francis, *The History of Furniture* (London, 1976)

GLASS

Battie, D. and Cottle, S. (eds.), *Sotheby's Concise Encyclopedia of Glass* (London, 1991)

Bickerton, L.M., *Eighteenth-Century English Drinking Glasses: An Illustrated Guide* (Woodbridge, 1986)

Boggess, Bill and Louise, *Identifying American Brilliant-Cut Glass* (West Chester, 1991)

Bray, Charles, *Dictionary of Glass: Materials and Techniques* (London, 1995)

Broizova, Jarmila, *Bohemian Crystal* (Prague, 1984)

Charleston, R.J., *English Glass and the Glass Used in England c.400–1940* (London, 1984)

Curtis, Jean-Louis, *Baccarat* (London, 1992)

Davis, Derek C., *Glass for Collectors* (1971)

Dodsworth, Roger, *Glass and Glass-Making* (Buckinghamshire, 1982)

Frothingham, Alice Wilson, *Spanish Glass* (New York, 1964)

Grover, Ray and Lee, *Art Nouveau Glass* (1967)

Haanstra, Ivo, *Miller's Pocket Fact File: Glass A–Z* (London, 1994)

Hajdamach, Charles, *British Glass, 1800–1914* (Woodbridge, 1991)

Hayhurst, Jeanette, *Miller's Glass Buyer's Guide* (London, 2001)

Haynes, E. Barrington, *Glass Through the Ages* (Harmondsworth, 1970)

Husfloen, Kyle, *Collector's Guide to American Pressed Glass 1825–1915* (Radnor, 1992)

Janneau, Guillaume, *Modern Glass* (1931)

Klein, Dan and Lloyd, Ward, *The History of Glass* (London, 1984)

Lattimore, Colin R., *English 19th-Century Press-Moulded Glass* (London, 1979)

Mackay, James, *Glass Paperweights* (1973)

Melvin, Jean S., *American Glass Paperweights and their Makers* (New York, 1970)

Norman, Barbara, *Glass Engraving* (Rutland, 1987)

Notley, Raymond, *Miller's Collector's Guide: Popular Glass* (London, 2000)

O'Looney, Betty, *Victorian Glass* (1972)

Olivié, Jean-Luc and Petrova, Sylvia, *Bohemian Glass* (Paris, 1990)

Pfaender, Heinz G., *Schott Guide to Glass* (1996)

Philippe, Joseph, *Le Val-Saint-Lambert: Ses cristalleries et l'art du verre en Belgique* (Liège, 1980)

Slack, Raymond, *English Pressed Glass, 1830–1900* (London, 1987)

Spillman, Jane Shadel, *American and European Pressed Glass in The Corning Museum of Glass* (Corning, 1982)

Spillman, Jane Shadel, *The American Cut-Glass Industry* (Woodbridge, 1996)

Spillman, Jane Shadel, and Frantz, Susanne K., *Masterpieces of American Glass: The Corning Museum of Glass, The Toledo Museum of Art, Lillian Nassau Ltd.* (New York, 1990)

Swan, Martha Louise, *American Cut and Engraved Glass: The Brilliant Period in Historical Perspective* (Radnor, 1994)

Tait, Hugh ed., *Five Thousand Years of Glass* (London, 1991)

Welker, John, *Pressed Glass in America: Encyclopedia of the First Hundred Years, 1825–1925* (Ivyland, 1985)

West, Mark, *Miller's Antiques Checklist: Glass* (London, 1994)

Wilson, Kenneth M., *American Glass, 1760–1930* (New York, 1994)

Yates, Sarah, West, Mark, and McCarron, David, *Miller's Glass: The Facts at Your Fingertips* (London, 2000)

JEWELLERY

Becker, Vivienne, *Antique and Twentieth-Century Jewellery* (Colchester, 1980)

Bennett, David and Mascetti, Daniela, *Understanding Jewellery* (Woodbridge, 1989)

Bury, Shirley, *Jewellery 1789–1910: The International Era* (Woodbridge, 1991)

Bury, Shirley, *Sentimental Jewellery* (London, 1985)

Flower, Margaret, *Victorian Jewellery* (London, 1967)

Gere, Charlotte, *European and American Jewellery, 1830–1914* (London, 1975)

Gere, Charlotte, *Victorian Jewellery Design* (London, 1982)

Giles, Stephen, *Miller's Antiques Checklist: Jewellery* (London, 1997)

Hinks, Peter, *Nineteenth-Century Jewellery* (London, 1975)

Kaplan, Arthur Guy, *The Official Identification and Price Guide to Antique Jewelry* (New York, 2005)

Mary, Peter, *Collecting Victorian Jewellery* (London, 1970)

Munn, Geoffrey, *The Triumph of Love: Jewellery 1530–1930* (London, 1993)

Newman, Harold, *An Illustrated Dictionary of Jewelry* (London, 1981)

Phillips, Clare, *Jewelry: From Antiquity to the Present* (London, 1996)

Shields, Jody, *All that Glitters* (New York, 1987)

MISCELLANEOUS

Bennion, Elisabeth, *Antique Medical Instruments* (London, 1980)

Brett, Vanessa, *Guide to Pewter* (London, 1981)

Crompton, Dennis, *Servants of Light: the Book of the Lantern* (Ripon, 1997)

FitzMaurice Mills, John, *Encyclopedia of Antique Scientific Instruments* (London, 1983)

Fresco-Corbu, Roger, *Vesta Boxes* (Cambridge, 1983)

Gentle, Rupert and Feild, Rachael, *Domestic Metalwork, 1640–1820* (London, 1994)

Herbert, Peter and Schiffer, Nancy, *Antique Iron* (Exton, 1979)

Hornsby, Peter R.G., *Pewter of the Western World, 1600–1850* (Exton, 1983)

Husfloen, Kyle, *Antique Trader Teapots Price Guide* (Wisconsin, 2005)

Knowles, Eric, *Miller's 100 Years of the Decorative Arts* (London, 1993)

Launert, Edmund, *Perfume and Pommanders* (London, 1985)

Miller's Picture Price Guide (London, annual)

Olman, John M. and Morton W., *The Encyclopedia of Gold Collectibles* (Alabama, 1985)

Peal, Christopher, *Pewter of Great Britain* (London, 1983)

Ricketts, Howard, *Objects of Vertu* (London, 1971)

Sanders, Eugene and Christine, *Pocket Matchsafes* (Atglen, 1997)

Stirling, Lindsay and Glastris, George (ed.), *Miller's Collecting Science & Technology* (London, 2001)

Tinniswood, Adrian, *The Arts and Crafts House* (London, 2005)

Turner, Eric, *Brass* (London, 1982)

Turner, Gerard L.E., *Antique Scientific Instruments* (Poole, 1980)

Turner, Gerard L.E., *Collecting Microscopes* (London and New York, 1981)

Van Der Werff, Rupert and Rees, Jackie, *Miller's Garden Antiques: How to Source and Identify* (London, 2003)

ORIENTAL WORKS OF ART

Garner, H., *Chinese and Japanese Cloisonné Enamels* (London, 1970)

Hutt, Julia, *Understanding Far Eastern Art* (New York, 1987)

Kerr, Rose, *Later Chinese Bronzes* (London, 1990)

Peterson, Harold (ed.), *Chinese Jades: Archaic and Modern* (London, 1977)

Rawson, Jessica (ed.), *British Museum Book of Chinese Art* (London, 1992)

Seton, Alistair, *Collecting Japanese Antiques* (Boston, 2004)

Smith, Lawrence and Harris, Victor, *Japanese Decorative Arts from the 17th to the 19th Centuries* (London, 1982)

Watson, William ed., *The Great Japan Exhibition: Art of the Edo Period, 1600–1868* (London, 1981)

Whitfield, Roderick (ed.), *Treasures from Korea: Art Through 5000 Years* (London, 1984)

SILVER

Bace, Jill, Butcher, Alexis, and Nusser, Juliet, *Miller's Collecting Silver: The Facts at Your Fingertips* (London, 2000)

Bexfield, Daniel, *Miller's Silver and Plate Buyer's Guide* (London 2002)

Blair, Claude (ed.), *The History of Silver* (1987)

Bly, John, *Miller's Silver and Sheffield Plate Marks* (London, 1993)

Bradbury, Frederick, *Bradbury's Book of Hallmarks* (1975)

Bradbury, Frederick, *History of Old Sheffield Plate* (1968)

Brett, Vanessa, *The Sotheby's Directory of Silver* (London, 1986)

Bury, Shirley, *Victorian Electroplate* (1971)

Clayton, Michael, *The Collector's Dictionary of Silver and Gold of Great Britain and North America* (Woodbridge, 1985)

Davis, Frank, *French Silver, 1450–1825* (London, 1970)

Delieb, Eric, *Investing In Silver* (London, 1970)

Delieb, Eric, *Silver Boxes* (London, 1979)

Glanville, P., *Silver in Tudor and Early Stuart England* (London, 1991)

Grimwade, Arthur, *London Goldsmiths 1697–1837:Their Marks and Lives* (London, 1976)

Grimwade, Arthur, *Rococo Silver, 1727–1765* (London, 1974)

Hartop, Christopher, *The Huguenot Legacy* (London, 1996)

Hayward, J.F., *Huguenot Silver in England 1688–1727* (London, 1959)

Helliwell, Stephen, *Collecting Small Silverware* (London, 1988)

Helliwell, Stephen, *Understanding Silver Plate* (1996)

Hernmarck, C., *The Art of the European Silversmith 1430–1830* (1977)

Hughes, G. Bernard, *Small Antique Silverware (Including Flatware)* (1971)

Langford, Joel, *Silver: A Practical Guide to Collecting Silverware and Identifying Hallmarks* (London; 1991)

Marquardt, Klaus, *Eight Centuries of European Cutlery* (Stuttgart, 1997)

Newman, Harold, *An Illustrated Dictionary of Silverware* (London, 1987)

Oman, Charles, *English Domestic Silver* (London, 1967)

Oman, Charles, *English Engraved Silver 1150–1900* (1978)

Pickford, I. (ed.), *Jackson's Silver and Gold Marks of England, Scotland and Ireland* (Woodbridge, 1989)

Rowe, Robert, *Adam Silver (1765–1795)* (London, 1965)

Schroder, Timothy, *English Domestic Silver 1500–1900* (1988)

Truman, Charles (ed.), *Sotheby's Concise Encyclopedia of Silver* (London, 1993)

Wilson, John, *Miller's Antiques Checklist: Silver and Plate* (London, 1994)

TEXTILES

Bath, Virginia, *Churchill: Needlework in America: History, Designs, and Techniques* (London, 1979)

Beck, Thomasina, *The Embroiderer's Story: Needlework from the Renaissance to the Present Day* (Newton Abbot, 1995)

Blum, Dilys E., *The Fine Art of Textiles* (Philadelphia, 1997)

Blum, Dilys E. and Haugland, H. Kristina, *Best Dressed: Fashion from the Birth of Couture to Today* (Philadelphia, 1998)

Brett, Gerard, *English Samplers* (London, 1951)

Bridgeman, H. and Drury, E., *Needlework: An Illustrated History* (London, 1978)

Bryson, Agnes F., *Ayrshire Needlework* (London, 1989)

Earnshaw, Pat, *Needlelace* (London and New York, 1991)

Eddy, Celia, *Quilted Planet: A Sourcebook of Quilts from Around the World* (London, 2005)

Edwards, Joan, *Sampler Making 1540–1940* (Dorking, 1983)

Farrell, Jeremy, *Umbrellas and Parasols* (London, 1985)

Granick, Eve, *The Amish Quilt* (Intercourse, 1989)

Hughes, Robert, *Amish: The Art of the Quilt* (London, 1994)

Humphrey, Carol, *Samplers* (Cambridge, 1997)

Inder, P.M., *Honiton Lace* (Exeter, 1971)

King, Donald, *Samplers* (London, 1960)

Kiracofe, Rod, *The American Quilts* (New York, 1993)

Laval, June K, *Antique French Textiles For Designers* (Pennsylvania, 2004)

Laver, James, *Costume and Fashion: A Concise History* (London, 1995)

Leszner, Eva Maria, *Stickmustertücher* (Rosenheim, 1985)

Levey, Santina M., *Lace: A History* (London, 1983)

Orlofsky, Myron and Patsy, *Quilts in America* (New York and London, 1974)

Reigate, Emily, *An Illustrated Guide to Lace* (Woodbridge, 1986)

Ring, Betty, *Girlhood Embroidery: American Samplers & Pictorial Needlework, 1650–1850* (New York, 1993)

Ring, Betty ed., *Needlework: An Historical Survey* (Pittstown, 1984)

Rothstein, Natalie, ed., *Four Hundred Years of Fashion* (London, 1984)

Rubin, Stella, *How to Compare and Appraise American Quilts* (London, 2003)

Sichel, Marion, *History of Men's Costume* (London, 1984)

Sichel, Marion, *History of Women's Costume* (London, 1984)

Soltow, Willow Ann, *Quilting the World Over* (Radnor, 1991)

Tarrant, Naomi E.A., *The Development of Costume* (London, 1994)

DIRECTORY OF USEFUL ADDRESSES

AUCTION HOUSES

UK

Bonhams
101 New Bond Street
London W1S 1SR
Tel: +44 (0)20 7447 7447
www.bonhams.com

Christie's
8 King Street
St James's
London SW1Y 6QT
Tel: +44 (0)20 7839 9060
www.christies.com

Christie's South Kensington
85 Old Brompton Road
London SW7 3LD
Tel: +44 (0)20 7930 6074
www.christies.com

Dreweatt Neate
Donnington Priory
Donnington
Newbury
Berkshire RG14 2JE
Tel: +44 (0)1635 553553
www.dnfa.com

Gorringes
15 North Street
Lewes
East Sussex BN7 2PD
Tel: +44 (0)1273 472503
www.gorringes.co.uk

Lots Road Auctions
71–73 Lots Road,
London SW10 0RN
Tel: +44 (0)20 7376 6800
www.lotsroad.com

Lyon & Turnbull
33 Broughton Place
Edinburgh EH1 3RR
Scotland
Tel: +44 (0)131 557 8844
www.lyonandturnbull.com

Mallams
Bocardo House
St Michael's Street
Oxford OX1 2EB
Tel: +44 (0)1865 241358
www.mallams.co.uk

Outhwaite & Litherland
Kingsway Galleries
Fontenoy Street
Liverpool L3 2BE
Tel: +44 (0)151 236 6561
www.lots.uk.com

Sotheby's
34–35 New Bond Street
London W1A 2AA
Tel: +44 (0)20 7293 5000
www.sothebys.com

Sotheby's Sussex
Summers Place
Billingshurst
West Sussex RH14 9AD
Tel: +44 (0)1403 833500
www.sothebys.com

Wallis & Wallis
West Street Auction Galleries
Lewes
East Sussex BN7 2NJ
Tel: +44 (0)1273 480208
www.wallisandwallis.co.uk

USA

Bonhams & Butterfields
595 Madison Avenue
6th Floor
New York
NY 10022
Tel: +1 212 717 9007
www.butterfields.com

Bonhams & Butterfields
220 San Bruno Avenue
San Francisco
CA 94103
Tel: +1 415 861 7500
www.butterfields.com

Christie's
20 Rockefeller Plaza
New York
NY 10020
Tel: +1 212 636 2000
www.christies.com

Christie's
360 North Camden Drive
Beverly Hills
Los Angeles
CA 90210
Tel: +1 310 385 2600
www.christies.com

Doyle New York
175 East 87th Street
New York
NY 10128
Tel: +1 212 427 2730
www.doylenewyork.com

Freeman's
1808 Chestnut Street
Philadelphia
PA 19103
Tel: +1 215 563 9275
www.freemansauction.com

Garth's Auctions Inc.
2690 Stratford Road
PO Box 369
Delaware
OH 43015
Tel: +1 740 362 4771
www.garths.com

James D. Julia Inc
PO Box 830
Fairfield
MA 04937
Tel: +1 207 453 7125
www.juliaauctions.com

**Ken Farmer Auctions
and Appraisals**
105 Harrison Street
Radford
VA 24141
Tel: +1 540 639 0939
www.kenfarmer.com

Northeast Auctions
93 Pleasant Street
Portsmouth
NH 03801
Tel: +1 603 433 8400
www.northeastauctions.com

Rago Arts and Auction Center
333 North Main Street
Lambertville
NJ 08530
Tel: +1 609 397 9374
www.ragoarts.com

Skinner, Inc.
357 Main Street
Bolton
MA 01740
Tel: +1 978 779 6241
www.skinnerinc.com

Skinner, Inc.
63 Park Plaza
Boston
MA 02116
Tel: +1 617 350 5400
www.skinnerinc.com

Sanford Alderfer Auction Company
501 Fairgrounds Road
Hatfield
PA 19440
Tel: +1 215 393 3000
www.alderferauction.com

Sotheby's
1334 York Avenue at 72nd Street
New York
NY 10021
Tel: +1 212 606 7000
www.sothebys.com

Sotheby's
9 Hazleton Avenue
Toronto
Ontario M5R 2E1
Canada
Tel: +1 416 926 1774

ANTIQUES FAIRS

Please check with each
fair venue for details of dates

UK

Adams Antique Fair
Royal Horticultural Society Halls
Vincent Square
London SW1P 2PE

Antique & Collectors Fair
Alexandra Palace
Wood Green
London N22 7AY
Tel: +44 (0)20 8883 7061

**Ardingly International
Antiques & Collectors Fair**
South of England Showground
Ardingly
West Sussex
Tel: +44 (0)1636 702326

BADA Antiques & Fine Art Fair
Duke of York's Headquarters
Chelsea
London SW3
Tel: +44 (0)20 7589 6108

**The Bath & Bradford-on-Avon
Decorative & Antiques Fair**
The Pavilion
Bath BA2 4EU
Tel: +44 (0)1225 851466

British International Antiques Fair
National Exhibition Centre
Birmingham B40 1NT

Buxton Antiques Fair
The Octagon
The Pavilion Gardens
Buxton
Derbyshire SK17 6XN
Tel: +44 (0)1298 23114

Chelsea Antiques Fair
Chelsea Old Town Hall
King's Road
London SW3 5EE
Tel: +44 (0)20 7727 5045

Chester Antiques & Fine Art Show
County Grandstand
Chester Racecourse
Cheshire CH1

City Antiques & Fine Art Fair
The Business Design Centre
52 Upper Street
Islington
London N1 0QH

Decorative Antiques & Textiles Fair
King's College London
Manresa Road
London SW3 6LX

Dorchester Antiques Fair
Dorchester Hotel
Park Lane
Mayfair
London W1A 2HJ

Fine Art & Antiques Fair
Olympia
Hammersmith Road
London W14 8UX
Tel: +44 (0)20 7370 8211

Great Northern International Antiques Fair
Great Yorkshire Showground
Harrogate
North Yorkshire HG2 8PW
Tel: +44 (0)1775 767400

The Grosvenor House Art & Antiques Fair
Grosvenor House Hotel
Park Lane
London W1

Harrogate Pavilions Antiques & Fine Art Fair
Yorkshire Event Centre
Pavilions of Harrogate
Harrogate
North Yorkshire
Tel: +44 (0)1277 214677

Kenilworth Antiques Dealers' Fair
Chesford Grange
Kenilworth
Warwickshire CV8 2LD

LAPADA Antiques & Fine Art Fair
National Exhibition Centre
Birmingham B40 1NT
Tel: +44 (0)121 767 2760

National Exhibition Centre August Fair
National Exhibition Centre
Birmingham B40 1NT

West London Antiques Fair
Kensington Town Hall
Hornton Street
Kensington
London W8

USA
The American Antiques Show
The Metropolitan Pavilion
125 West 18th Street
New York
NY 10011

Baltimore Museum Antiques Show
Baltimore Museum of Art
10 Art Museum Drive
Baltimore
MD 21218

Connecticut Spring Antiques Show
State Armory
Hartford
CT 06105

Ellis Memorial Hospital Show
The Cyclorama
539 Tremont Street
Boston
MA 02116

Fall Show at the Armory
Seventh Regiment Armory
67th Street and Park Avenue
New York
NY 10021

Heart of Country Antiques Show
Opryland Hotel
2800 Opryland Drive
Nashville
TN 37214

International Fine Art and Antique Dealers Show
Seventh Regiment Armory
67th Street and Park Avenue
New York
NY 10021

Mid-Week Manchester Antiques Show
Sheraton Tara Wayfarer Inn
Bedford
NH 03110

New Hampshire Antique Dealers Association Show
Center of New Hampshire
Holiday Inn
700 Elm Street
Manchester
NH 03101

New York Winter Antiques Show
Seventh Regiment Armory
67th Street and Park Avenue
New York
NY 10021

Palm Beach Connoisseur
www.historicalsocietypbc.org/
specialevents.asp

Palm Beach International Art and Antiques Fair
www.palmbeachfair.com

Palm Beach Jewlery and Antiques Fair
Contact Robert Samuels:
Tel: + 1 561 833 7755

Philadelphia Antiques Show
103rd Engineers Armory
33rd and Market Streets
Philadelphia PA 19104

Riverside Antiques Show
New Hampshire
State Armory
Canal Street
Manchester
NH 03101

San Francisco Fall Antiques Show
Fort Mason Center
Festival Pavilion
San Francisco
CA 94123

Washington Antiques Show
Omni Shorham Hotel
2500 Calvert Street NW
Washington
DC 20008

ANTIQUES MARKETS & CENTRES

UK
Alfie's Antiques Market
13–25 Church Street
Marylebone
London NW8 8DT
Tel: +44 (0)20 7723 6066
www.alfiesantiques.com

Antiquarius
131–141 Kings Road
Chelsea
London SW3
Tel: +44 (0)20 7351 5353
www.antiquarius.co.uk

Bartlett Street Antiques Centre
5–10 Bartlett Street
Bath BA1 2QZ
Tel: +44 (0)1225 466689

Camden Passage Antiques Market
Camden Passage
London N1 8EG
Tel: +44 (0)20 7359 0190
www.camdenpassageantiques.com

Chappells Antiques Centre
King Street
Bakewell
Derbyshire DE45 1DZ
Tel: +44 (0)1629 812496
www.chappellsantiquescentre.com

Grays Antiques Market
58 Davies Street
London W1K 5LP
Tel: +44 (0)20 7629 7034
www.graysantiques.com

Hemswell Antiques Centres
Caenby Corner Estate
Hemswell Cliff
Gainsborough
Lincolnshire DN21 5TJ
Tel: +44 (0)1427 668389
www.hemswell-antiques.com

Herts & Essex Antiques Centre
The Maltings, Station Road
Sawbridgeworth
Herts CM21 9JX
Tel: +44 (0)1279 722044
www.antiques-of-britain.co.uk/
hertsandessexantiquescentre.htm

Holliday Wharf Antiques Market
164 Holliday Street,
Birmingham,
West Midlands B1 1TJ
Tel: +44 (0)121 643 7700

Portland Street Antiques Centre
27 Portland Street,
Newark
Nottinghamshire NG24 4XF
Tel: +44 (0)115 989 2925

Portobello Road Market
Portobello Road
London W11 1LU
Tel: +44 (0)20 7229 8354
www.portobelloroad.co.uk

The Swan At Tetsworth
Antiques Centre and Restaurant
High Street
Tetsworth
Oxon OX9 7AB
Tel: +44 (0)1844 281777
www.theswan.co.uk

PLACES TO VISIT

Arlington Court
Arlington
Nr Barnstaple
Devon EX31 4LP
Tel: +44 (0)1271 850296
www.nationaltrust.org.uk

Ascott House Wing
Leighton Buzzard
Bedfordshire LU7 0PS
Tel: +44 (0)1296 688242
www.ascottestate.co.uk

Ashdown House
Lambourn
Newbury
Berkshire RG17 8RE
Tel: +44 (0)1793 762209
www.nationaltrust.org.uk

Aston Hall
Trinity Road
Aston
Birmingham B6 6JD
Tel: +44 (0)121 327 0062
www.bmag.org.uk/aston_hall

Attingham Park
Shrewsbury
Shropshire SY4 4TP
Tel: +44 (0)1743 708162
www.nationaltrust.org.uk

Audley End House and Gardens
Saffron Walden
Essex CB11 4JF
Tel: +44 (0)1799 522399
www.english-heritage.org.uk

Bantry House
Bantry
Co. Cork
Ireland
Tel +353 (0)27 50047
www.bantryhouse.com

Basildon Park
Lower Basildon
Reading
Berkshire RG8 9NR
Tel: +44 (0)118 984 3040
www.nationaltrust.org.uk

Belton House
Grantham
Lincolnshire NG32 2LS
Tel: +44 (0)1476 566116
www.nationaltrust.org.uk

Berrington Hall
Nr Leominster
Herfordshire HR6 0DW
Tel: +44 (0)1568 615721
www.nationaltrust.org.uk

Blenheim Palace
Woodstock
Oxon OX20 1PX
Tel: +44 (0)8700 602080
www.blenheimpalace.com

Blickling Hall
Blickling
Norwich
Norfolk NR11 6NF
Tel: +44 (0)1263 738030
www.nationaltrust.org.uk

Braemar Castle
Braemar
Aberdeenshire
Scotland
Tel: +44 (0)1339 741219
www.braemarcastle.co.uk

Burghley House
Stamford
Northants
Tel: +44 (0)1780 752451
www.burghley.co.uk

Calke Abbey
Ticknall
Derby DE73 1LE
Tel: +44 (0)1332 863822
www.nationaltrust.org.uk

Castle Howard
York
North Yorkshire YO60 7DA
Tel: +44 (0)1653 648444
www.castlehoward.co.uk

Chatsworth
Bakewell
Derbyshire DE45 1PP
Tel: +44 (0)1246 565300
www.chatsworth-house.co.uk

Chiswick House
Burlington Lane
Chiswick
London W4 2RP
Tel: +44 (0)20 8995 0508
www.english-heritage.org.uk

Clandon Park
West Clandon
Guildford
Surrey GU4 7RQ
Tel: +44 (0)1483 222482
www.nationaltrust.org.uk

Claydon House
Middle Claydon
Nr Buckingham MK18 2EY
Tel: +44 (0)1296 730349
www.nationaltrust.org.uk

Cotehele
St Dominick
Nr Saltash
Cornwall PL12 6TA
Tel: +44 (0)1579 351346
www.nationaltrust.org.uk

Dunham Massey
Altrincham
Cheshire WA14 4SJ
Tel: +44 (0)161 941 1025
www.nationaltrust.org.uk

Felbrigg Hall
Felbrigg
Norwich
Norfolk NR11 8PR
Tel: +44 (0)1263 837444
www.nationaltrust.org.uk

Fenton House
Windmill Hill
Hampstead,
London NW3 6RT
Tel: +44 (0)20 7435 3471
www.nationaltrust.org.uk

Grantham House
Castlegate
Grantham,
Lincolnshire NG31 6SS
www.nationaltrust.org.uk

Greyfriars
Friar Street
Worcester WR1 2LZ
Tel: +44 (0)1905 23571
www.nationaltrust.org.uk

Gunby Hall
Gunby
Nr Spilsby
Lincolnshire PE23 5SS

Haddon Hall
Bakewell
Derbyshire DE45 1LA
Tel: +44 (0)1629 812855
www.haddonhall.co.uk

Ham House
Ham
Richmond-upon-Thames
Surrey TW10 7RS
Tel: +44 (0)20 8940 1950
www.nationaltrust.org.uk

Hampton Court Palace
Surrey KT8 9AU
Tel: +44 (0)870 752 7777
www.hrp.org.uk/webcode/
hampton_home.asp

Hardwick Hall
Doe Lea
Chesterfield
Derbyshire S44 5QJ
Tel: +44 (0)1246 850430
www.nationaltrust.org.uk

Harewood House
Harewood Estate, Harewood
Leeds LS17 9LQ
Tel: +44 (0)113 218 1010
www.harewood.org

Hatfield House
Hatfield
Hertfordshire AL9 5NQ
Tel: +44 (0)1707 287010
www.hatfield-house.co.uk

Heveningham Hall
Heveningham
Halesworth
Suffolk IP19 0PN

Holkham Hall
Wells-next-the-Sea
Norfolk NR23 1AB
Tel: +44 (0)1328 710227
www.holkham.co.uk

Holyroodhouse (Palace of)
Abbey Strand
Edinburgh EH1
Tel: +44 (0)131 556 5100
www.royal.gov.uk/output/page559.asp

Houghton Hall
King's Lynn
Norfolk PE31 6UE
Tel: +44 (0)1485 528569
www.houghtonhall.com

Houses of Parliament
London SW1A 0AA
Tel: +44 (0)20 7219 3000
www.parliament.uk

Hughendon Manor
High Wycombe
Hertfordshire HP14 4LA
Tel: +44 (0)1494 755573
www.nationaltrust.org.uk

Ickworth House
Ickworth
The Rotunda, Horringer
Bury St Edmunds
Suffolk IP29 5QE
Tel: +44 (0)1284 735270
www.nationaltrust.org.uk

Ightham Mote
Ivy Hatch
Sevenoaks
Kent TN15 0NT
Tel: +44 (0)1732 810378
www.nationaltrust.org.uk

Kedleston Hall
Derby DE22 5JH
Tel: +44 (0)1332 842191
www.nationaltrust.org.uk

Kelmscott Manor
Kelmscott
Lechlade
Gloucestershire GL7 3HJ
Tel: +44 (0)1367 252486
www.kelmscottmanor.co.uk

Kensington Palace
Kensington
London W8 4PX
Tel: +44 (0)870 751 5170
www.hrp.org.uk/webcode/
kensington_home.asp

Knebworth House
Knebworth
Hertfordshire SG3 6PY
Tel: +44 (0)1438 812661
www.knebworthhouse.com

Knightshayes Court
Bolham
Tiverton
Devon EX16 7RQ
Tel: +44 (0)1884 254665
www.nationaltrust.org.uk

Knole
Sevenoaks
Kent TN15 0RP
Tel: +44 (0)1732 462100
www.nationaltrust.org.uk

Longleat House
Longleat, Warminster
Wiltshire BA12 7NW
Tel: +44 (0)1985 844400
www.longleat.co.uk/attractions/
longleat-house.html

Malahide Castle
Malahide, Co. Dublin
Ireland
Tel: +353 1 846 2184
www.malahidecastle.com/malahide castle

Montacute House
Montacute
Somerset TA15 6XP
Tel: +44 (0)1935 823289
www.nationaltrust.org.uk

Moseley Old Hall
Moseley Old Hall Lane, Fordhouses
Wolverhampton WV10 7HY
Tel: +44 (0)1902 782808
www.nationaltrust.org.uk

Ormesby Hall
Ormesby
Middlesbrough
Cleveland TS7 9AS
Tel: +44 (0)1642 324188
www.nationaltrust.org.uk

Osbourne House
East Cowes
Isle of Wight P)32 6JY
Tel: +44 (0)1983 200022
www.english-heritage.co.uk

Osterley Park
Jersey Road
Isleworth
Middlesex TW7 4RB
Tel: +44 (0)20 8232 5050
www.nationaltrust.org.uk

Oxburgh Hall
Oxborough
Nr Kings's Lynn
Norfolk PE33 9PS
Tel: +44 (0)1366 328258
www.nationaltrust.org.uk

Parham House
Storrington
Nr Pulborough
West Sussex RH20 4HS
Tel: +44 (0)1903 742021
www.parhaminsussex.co.uk

Petworth House
Petworth
West Sussex GU28 0AE
Tel: +44 (0)1798 342207
www.nationaltrust.org.uk

Polesden Lacey
Great Bookham
Nr Dorking
Surrey RH5 6BD
Tel: +44 (0)1372 452048
www.nationaltrust.org.uk

Royal Pavilion
The Old Steine
Brighton
East Sussex BN1 1EE
Tel: +44 (0)1273 290900
www.royalpavilion.org.uk

Rufford Old Hall
Rufford, Nr Ormskirk
Lancashire L40 1SG
Tel: +44 (0)1704 821254
www.nationaltrust.org.uk

Saltram
Plympton, Plymouth
Devon PL7 1UH
Tel: +44 (0)1752 333500
www.nationaltrust.org.uk

Shugborough
Milford
Nr Stafford
Staffordshire ST17 0XB
Tel: +44 (0)1889 881388
www.nationaltrust.org.uk

Sizergh Castle
Sizergh
Nr Kendal
Cumbria LA8 8AE
Tel: +44 (0)15395 60951
www.nationaltrust.org.uk

Southside House
Wimbledon Common
Woodhayes Road
London SW19
Tel: +44 (0)20 8946 7643
www.southsidehouse.com

Standen
West Hoathly Road
East Grinstead
East Sussex RH19 4NE
Tel: +44 (0)1342 323029
www.nationaltrust.org.uk

Sutton House
2 & 4 Homerton High Street
Hackney
London E9 6JQ
Tel: +44 (0)20 8986 2264
www.nationaltrust.org.uk

Syon House
Brentford
Middlesex TW8 8JF
Tel: +44 (0)20 8560 0881
www.syonpark.co.uk

Tatton Park
Knutsford
Cheshire WA16 6QN
Tel: +44 (0)1625 534400
www.nationaltrust.org.uk

Tattershall Castle
Tattershall
Lincoln LN4 4LR
Tel: +44 (0)1526 342543
www.nationaltrust.org.uk

Temple Newsam House
Leeds
West Yorkshire LS15 0AD
Tel: +44 (0)113 264 7321
www.leeds.gov.uk/templenewsam

Trerice
Kestle Mill
Nr Newquay
Cornwall TR8 4PG
Tel: +44 (0)1637 875404
www.nationaltrust.org.uk

Uppark
South Harting, Petersfield
Hampshire GU31 5QR
Tel: +44 (0)1730 825415
www.nationaltrust.org.uk

The Vyne
Sherbourne St John
Basingstoke
Hampshire RG24 9HL
Tel: +44 (0)1256 883858
www.nationaltrust.org.uk

Waddesdon Manor
Waddesdon
Nr Aylesbury
Buckinghamshire HP18 0JH
Tel: +44 (0)1296 653203
www.nationaltrust.org.uk

Wallington
Cambo, Morpeth
Northumberland NE61 4AR
Tel: +44 (0)1670 773600
www.nationaltrust.org.uk

Wilton House
Wilton
Nr Salisbury
Wiltshire SP2 0BJ
Tel: +44 (0)1722 746720
www.wiltonhouse.co.uk

Wimpole Hall
Arrington
Royston
Cambridgeshire SG8 0BW
Tel: +44 (0)1223 206000
www.nationaltrust.org.uk

Windsor Castle
High Street
Windsor
Berkshire SL4 1LH
Tel: +44 (0)1753 743900
www.windsor.gov.uk

Woburn Abbey
Woburn
Bedfordshire MK17 9WA
Tel: +44 (0)1525 290666
www.woburnabbey.co.uk

MUSEUMS

UK
The American Museum in Britain
Claverton Manor
Bath BA2 7BD
Tel: +44 (0)1225 460503
www.americanmuseum.org
Ceramics, clocks, furniture, silver

Apsley House, The Wellington Museum
149 Piccadilly
Hyde Park Corner
London W1J 7NT
Tel: +44 (0)20 7499 5676
Ceramics, militaria

Ashmolean Museum
Beaumont Street
Oxford OX1 2PH
Tel: (0)1865 278000
www.ashmol.ox.ac.uk
Antiquities, ceramics, clocks, glass, silver

Birmingham Museum & Art Gallery,
Chamberlain Square
Birmingham B3 3DH
Tel: +44 (0)121 303 2834
www.bmag.org.uk
Glass, paintings

Bristol City Museum & Art Gallery
Queen's Road
Bristol BS8 1RL
Tel: +44 (0)117 922 3571
www.bristol-city.gov.uk/museums
Glass, ceramics, silver, paintings

The British Museum
Great Russell Street
London WC1B 3DG
Tel: +44 (0)20 7323 8299
www.thebritishmuseum.ac.uk
Antiquities, ceramics, clocks, glass, silver

The Burrel Collection
Pollock Country Park,
Glasgow
www.glasgowmuseums.com/
venue/index.cfm?venueid=1
Antiquities, decorative arts, Oriental arts

Castle Museum and Nottingham Art Gallery
Nottingham Castle
Friar Lane
Nottingham NG1 6EL
Tel: +44 (0)115 915 3700
www.nottinghamcity.gov.uk/sitemap
/leisure_and_culture/museums_and_
galleries/nottingham_castle
Silver, glass, armour, paintings

Derby Museum & Art Gallery
The Strand
Derby DE1 1BS
Tel: +44 (0)1332 716659
Porcelain

The Fitzwilliam Museum
Trumpington Street
Cambridge CB2 1RB
Tel: +44 (0)1223 332900
www.fitzmuseum.cam.ac.uk
Ceramics, clocks, glass

Geffrye Museum
Kingsland Road
Hackney
London E2 8EA
Tel: +44 (0)20 7739 9893
www.geffrye-museum.org.uk
Furniture, textiles, paintings

Glasgow Art Gallery & Museum
Kelvingrove
Glasgow G3 8AG
Tel: +44 (0)141 287 2699
www.g3web.co.uk/glasgow_museums/
art_gallery/
Ceramics, silver, textiles

Jewel House
Tower of London
Tower Hill
London EC3N 4AB
Tel: +44 (0)870 756 6060
www.hrp.org.uk/webcode/
tower_home.asp
Silver, metalware

Imperial War Museum
Lambeth Road
London SE1 6HZ
Tel: +44 (0)20 7416 5320
www.iwm.org
Armour, arms

Lady Lever Art Gallery
Port Sunlight Village
Wirral CH62 5EQ
Tel: +44 (0)151 478 4136
www.liverpoolmuseums.org.uk/
ladyLever
Furniture

National Maritime Museum
Park Row
Greenwich
London SE10 9NF
www.nmm.ac.uk/
Navigational and scientific
instruments

National Museum of Ireland,
Collins Barracks
Benburb Street
Dublin 7
Ireland
Tel: +353 1 677 7444
www.museum.ie

National Museum of Scotland
Chambers Street
Edinburgh EH1 1JF
Tel: +44 (0)131 247 4219
www.nms.ac.uk/

The Science Museum
Exhibition Road
South Kensington
London SW7 2DD
Tel: +44 (0)870 870 4868
Barometers, scientific instruments

**Stoke-on-Trent City Museum
and Art Gallery**
Bethesda Street
Hanley
Stoke-on-Trent ST1 3DE
Tel: +44 (0)1782 232323
Ceramics

Victoria and Albert Museum
Cromwell Road
London SW7 2RL
www.vam.ac.uk
Tel: +44 (0)20 7942 2000
Art Nouveau, Ceramics, Clocks,
Furniture, Glass, Rugs and Carpets,
Silver, Textiles

Wallace Collection
Hertford House
Manchester Square
London W1U 3BN
Tel: +44 (0)20 7563 9500
www.wallacecollection.org
Ceramics, furniture, silver

William Morris Society (UK)
Kelmscott House
26 Upper Mall
Hammersmith
London W6 9TA
Tel: +44 (0)20 8741 3735
www.morrissociety.org

Worcester Porcelain Museum
Severn Street
Worcester WR1 2NE
Tel: +44 (0)1905 746000
www.worcesterporcelainmuseum.org.uk
Ceramics

York Castle Museum
Eye of York
York Y01 9RY
Tel: +44 (0) 1904 687687
www.yorkcastlemuseum.org.uk
Ceramics, silver, Sheffield Plate

USA
American Clock and Watch Museum
100 Maple Street
Bristol
CT 06010
Tel: +1 (860) 583 6070
www.clockmuseum.org

The Art Institute of Chicago
111 South Michigan Avenue
Chicago
IL 60603-6110
Tel: +1 312 443 3600
www.artic.edu/
Ceramics, silver

Birmingham Museum of Art
2000 Eighth Avenue North
Birmingham
AL 35203-2278
Tel: +1 205 254 2566
www.artsbma.org
Ceramics

Brooklyn Museum
200 Eastern Parkway
Brooklyn
New York
NY 11238-6052
Tel: +1 718 638 5000
www.brooklynmuseum.org
Ceramics

Cincinnati Art Museum
953 Eden Park Drive,
Cincinnati
OH 45202
Tel: +1 513 721 2787
www.cincinnatiartmuseum.org
Art Nouveau

Corning Museum of Glass
One Museum Way
Corning
NY 14830-2253
Tel: +1 800 732 6845
www.cmog.org

Fogg Art Museum
Harvard University
32 Quincy Street
Cambridge
MA 02138
Tel: +1 617 495 9400
www.artmuseums.harvard.edu
Ceramics, silver

Fort Morris
2559 Fort Morris Road
Midway
GA 31320
Tel: +1 912 884 5999
www.gastateparks.org/info/ftmorris
Arms, armour

John Paul Getty Museum
The Getty Center
1200 Getty Center Drive
Los Angeles
CA 90049
Tel: +1 310 440 7300
www.getty.edu
Furniture

The Metropolitan Museum of Art
1000 Fifth Avenue
New York
NY 10028-0198
Tel: +1 212 535 7710
www.metmuseum.org
Art Nouveau, furniture, glass,
rugs and carpets, silver

The Minneapolis Institute of Arts
2400 Third Avenue South
Minneapolis
Minnesota 55404
Tel: +1 612 870 3200
www.artsmia.org
Silver

National Gallery of Arts
Constitution Avenue, NW
Washington
DC 20565
Tel: +1 202 737 4215
www.nga.gov

Otis House
141 Cambridge Street
Boston
MA 02114
Tel: +1 617 227 3956
www.historicnewengland.org/
visit/homes/otis.htm
Furniture, carpets, etc

The Textile Museum
2320 S Street, NW
Washington
DC 20008-4088
Tel: +1 202 667 0441
www.textilemuseum.org

Toledo Museum of Art
2445 Monroe Street
at Scottwood Avenue
Toledo
OH 43620
Tel: +1 419 255 8000
www.toledomuseum.org
Glass, paintings

Willard House and Clock Museum
11 Willard Street
North Grafton
MA 01536
Tel: +1 508 839 3500
www.willardhouse.org

William Morris Society (USA)
PO Box 53263
Washington
DC 20009
www.morrissociety.org

Wistariahurst Museum
238 Cabot Street
Holyoke
MA 01040
Tel: +1 413 322 5660
www.wistariahurst.org
Furniture, textiles

INDEX

Page numbers in *italics* refer to
picture captions or feature boxes

ACKNOWLEDGEMENTS

My grateful thanks to friends in the antiques trade, auction houses, and museum departments who have helped with this book.
John Bly

Mitchell Beazley would also like to thank the following for their editorial assistance: Kathy Rubenstein, Sue Farr, and Lara Maiklem.

Mitchell Beazley would like to acknowledge and thank the following for providing images for publication, or allowing their pieces to be photographed. Special thanks also to Jon Culverhouse at Burghley House and Anne Trodella at Skinner, Inc.

Key: t top b bottom l left r right c centre

Jacket:
Front: tl V&A Images, The Victoria & Albert Museum; tr www.bridgeman.co.uk/Coram Foundation, Foundling Museum, London, UK; br www.bridgeman.co.uk/National Gallery, London, UK. Back: l akg-images/Museum Boymans-van Beuningen; c V&A Images, The Victoria & Albert Museum/by permission of The Calthorpe Family.

akg-images: 91 b, 119 l, Sotheby's 115 b; The Art Archive: 46 l, Joseph Martin 53, Museo di Palazzo Venezia, Rome/Dagli Orti (A) 45 tl; Aston Hall/Birmingham Museums & Art Gallery: 18 tl; Barometer World Ltd, Merton, Devon: 167; BBC *Homes and Antiques Magazine*: 186; Courtesy of John Bly: 1, 22 l, 25 b, 26 b, 39 r, 42 tl, 50, 52 br, 56 br, 62 br, 64 l, 72, 73 l, 74, 78, 79 b, 80 r, 83, 85 b, 88 r, 96 tl, 100, 108 tl, 116, 119 r, 122 l, 123 br, 125 t, 126 b, 127, 129, 137-139, 145, 149, 150, 151, 152 t, 154, 157, 158 r, 159, 160-161, 177, 180, 182, 183, 184 t, 185, 191 bl, 194-197, 199, 200 l, 204, 206, 207 b, 209, 236, The Burghley House Collection 73 r, 77 b, 79 t, Collection Lord Lloyd-Webber 105 t; Bonhams: 40 r; www.bridgeman.co.uk: Bargello, Florence, Italy 45 tr & bl, Château de Laarne, Belgium, Giraudon 57 tr, Christopher Wood Gallery, London, UK 156, The Crown Estate 173, Heveningham Hall, Suffolk, UK, John Bethell 97 r, Holburne Museum, Bath, UK 90 l, Houses of Parliament, Westminster, London, UK 148, Louvre, Paris, France, Giraudon 65, Mallett & Son Antiques Ltd, London, UK 58, Museo Correr, Venice, Italy 57 b, National Gallery, London, UK 105 b, Normanby Hall, Lincolnshire, UK 98 b, Private Collection 20 r, 46 r, 64 r, Private Collection/Paul Freeman 43 l, Private Collection/Giraudon 8, Private Collection/The Stapleton Collection 9, Staatliche Museen, Berlin, Germany 32 r, The Victoria & Albert Museum, London, UK 38 l, 43 r, 45 br, 61, 76, 96 b, Victorian Society, Linley Sambourne House, London, UK 170-171, Walker Art Gallery, Liverpool, Merseyside, UK, National Museums Liverpool 13; The Burghley House Collection: 14, 18 tr, 22, 30-31, 40 l, 67, 84 l, 85 l & r; Ceredigion Museum, Aberystwyth: 146 r; VisitCheltenham/David Sellman: 110 t; © The Chippendale Society: 84 c & r, 99; Christie's Images: 18 br, 23, 27 b, 29, 33, 38 r, 39 l, 41 t, 42 r, 44, 47, 48 l, 49 l, 52 t, 55 l, 57 tl, 59, 75 b, 86, 88 l, 89 b, 101, 103 l, 104 l, 106 l, 110 b, 113 l, 114 br, 117-118, 122 r, 128, 132 t, 136, 147 b, 162, 165 b, 166, 179 t, 181 t, 187, 191 t & br, 211 b, 212, 214 tl, 216, 226, 228, 229, 230, 231 b, 233 b, 237 b; Corbis: Michael Boys 18 bl, Kim Sayer 56 l; Image supplied by the Earl of Leicester (Holkham): 68-69; Courtesy of The Geffrye Museum (Photo: Chris Ridley): 24; Ann Grossman of Porcelain Parlor on Ruby Lane, www.rubylane.com/shops/irishantiques: 3, 213; Halcyon Days, 14 Brook Street, London, W15 1BD, 020 7629 8811, Halcyondays.co.uk: 107 b; Courtesy of Historic New England/SPNEA/ Parlor, Harrison Gray Otis House, Boston, MA. Photograph by David Bohl: 114 t; Hotspur Ltd: 48 r, 51 r, 62 bl, 87, 109; Hulton Archive/Getty Images: 95; Interior Archive/Simon Upton: 34-35; A. F. Kersting: 111; Mallett & Son (Antiques) Ltd: 112, 124, 133 b, 146 l, 232, 233 t; Marks Antiques, London: 126 t; The Minneapolis Institute of Arts, The Putnam Dana McMillan Fund: 5; National Trust Photo Library: Ian Shaw 10-11, Andreas von Einsiedel 19, 77 t; National Museum of Fine Arts, Stockholm: 115 t; Octopus Publishing Group: 188 b, 205 r, Ken Adlard 132 b, A J Photographics/Christie's South Kensington 217 b, 224, 225 t, 121 r, Ian Booth 2, 141, 143 bl & br, Ian Booth/ Nigel O'Gorman 158 l, Ian Booth/Mark J West 207 t, 222, 223, Ian Booth/Sotheby's 214 tr, 220, 235 t, Lennox Cato, Edenbridge, Kent, 01732 865988, www.lenoxcato.com 227 b, Chevertons of Edenbridge Ltd, Kent, 01732 863196 144, Christie's, South Kensington 234, Gorringes inc Julian Dawson, Lewes, East Sussex, 01273 472503, www.gorringes.co.uk 217 t, 231 t, Hampton Antiques, London, 01604 863979, www.hamptonantiques.co.uk 214 br, 221 t, John Howard at Heritage, Woodstock, Oxfordshire, 0870 4440678 155 br, Pastorale Antiques, East Sussex, 01273 473259, pastorale@btinternet.com 219 b, Penny Fair Antiques, 07860 825456 221 b, Phelps Antiques, Twickenham, Middlesex, 020 8892 1778, www.phelps.co.uk 218, 219 t, John Read, Ipswich, Suffolk, 01473 624897 106r, Tim Ridley/ Bonhams 98 l, Courtesy of John Sandon/Chris Halton 133 t, Corrine Soffe 01295 730317, soffe@btinternet.co.uk 214 bl, 235 b, Swan Antiques, Cranbrook, Kent, 01580 712720 155 bl, Steve Tanner/courtesy of Alan Blakeman/BBR Auctions 165 t, Steve Tanner/ Broadfield House 89 t, Steve Tanner/C. Sykes 107 t, Steve Tanner/Mark J. West 153; Pepys Library, Magdalene College, Cambridge: 54; Rago Arts & Auction Center: 104 r, 200 r, 201, 203, 208 l; Images courtesy of M.S. Rau Antiques, New Orleans: 163; Private Collection: 179 b, Fritz Curzon 37; © The Royal Pavilion, Libraries and Museums, Brighton & Hove: 134; Paul Rocheleau: 125 b; Science Museum/Science & Society Picture Library: 152 b; Skinner, Inc: 28, 51 l, 80 l, 91 t, 98 tr, 102, 103 r, 108 r, 121 l, 130 l, 135, 143 t, 155 t, 164, 168, 169, 188 t, 189, 192, 202, 205 l, 208 r; Courtesy of Sotheby's Picture Library: 7, 16 r, 21, 32 l, 41 b, 49 r, 55 r, 56 tr, 62 t, 63, 81, 85 c, 90 r, 108 b, 113 r, 114 bl, 120, 174, 176, 181 b, 184 b, 190 r, 193, 210, 211 t, 225 b, 227 t, 237 t; Sothebys, New York: 16 c; Reproduced by kind permission of the Spode Museum Trust; © Spode: 147 t; Strike One: 130 r, 190 l; V&A Images, The Victoria & Albert Museum: 15, 16 l, 17, 20 l, 25 t, 26 t, 27 t, 96 r, By Permission of The Calthorpe Family 66, The Chapel of Trinity College, Oxford 60, Network Modelmakers 92-93; By courtesy of the Wedgwood Museum Trust, Staffordshire (England): 82, 97 l.